CONSERVATIVE THOUGHT IN TWENTIETH CENTURY

LATIN AMERICA

CONSERVATIVE THOUGHT IN TWENTIETH CENTURY

LATIN AMERICA

The Ideas of Laureano Gómez

by

James D. Henderson

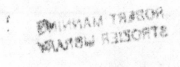

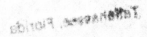

Ohio University Center for International Studies
Center for Latin American Studies

Monographs in International Studies
Latin America Series Number 13

Athens, Ohio 1988

LIBRARY OF CONGRESS
Library of Congress Cataloging-in-Publication Data

Henderson, James D., 1942-
    Conservative thought in twentieth century Latin America: the ideas of Lau-
reano Gómez/by James D. Henderson.
    p. cm. — (Monographs in international studies. Latin America series; no. 13)
    Bibliography: p.
    Includes index.
    ISBN 0-89680-148-9
    1. Gómez, Laureano, 1889-1965—Political and social views. 2. Latin
America—History-20th century. 3. Conservatism—Latin America—History—
20th century. 4. Liberalism—Latin America—History—20th century. 5. Colombia—
Politics and government—20th century. I. Title. II. Series.
F1414.G58H46 1988
320.5′2′09861—dc19   87-33957
                                                       CIP

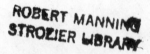

For my parents

CONTENTS

vii

Chapter page

ACKNOWLEDGMENTS

This work was made possible, in part, through financial support provided by Grambling State University and by the American Philosophical Society. The author extends his thanks to those institutions.

The two principal depositories of information on twentieth century Colombia, the Biblioteca Nacional and the Biblioteca Luis Angel Arango, were integral to the preparation of this volume. Personnel of the Sala de Investigadores of the Biblioteca Nacional deserve special mention for their assistance during the year the author labored in their pleasant domain.

The counsel provided by friend and colleague Eddy Torres merits special mention. Eddy extended his help during the research phase of this project, first as a fellow researcher and later as Director of the Biblioteca Nacional. His sudden death in late 1982 was lamented by this writer, and by other researchers of the Sala de Investigadores, all of whom appreciated his dynamic leadership of the library.

Many people were supportive of this effort. Among them were Fernando Cepeda, Enrique Santos Molano, Jaime Zárate, Eduardo Rueda, and Julio Tobon Páramo. Donald E. Worcester, David Bushnell, Fredrick B. Pike, Charles Hale, Robert H. Dix, and Francine Cronshaw all offered valuable suggestions on improving the manuscript. To all of them, and to my family--especially to my wife Linda--I express my deepest appreciation.

INTRODUCTION

Conservative thought in twentieth century Latin America is a subject of considerable interest and importance, yet curiously it has not received much attention from academic writers. A few scholars have investigated aspects of nineteenth century Latin American conservatism.[1] Others have examined the theme in works embracing both the nineteenth and twentieth centuries.[2] Numerous others have offered valuable insights on conservatism in the course of writing on other matters.[3] Given its magnitude and importance, however, Latin American conservatism has been relatively neglected by the scholarly community.

This work presents a detailed analysis of the ideas of Colombia's most significant conservative of the present century, and it locates his thought in the greater context of late nineteenth and twentieth century Latin American conservatism.

At least two things complicate the effort at ordering a subject matter as diverse as the one at hand. The first has to do with the length and turbulence of the chronological period delimiting it. By any standard, this century has been the most eventful in recorded history--one of change so rapid and so replete with human drama that no historian comes to terms with it easily. Add to this the necessity of taking into account nineteenth century origins of Latin American conservatism, and the complexity of the task can be appreciated. In speaking of the history of conservative thought in a single nation--Colombia, for example--it is necessary to relate men seemingly as dissimilar as conservative traditionalist Laureano Gómez and conservative populist Belisario Betancur, to a common intellectual heritage.[4] It is also necessary to link the two with earlier copartisans such as Mariano Ospina Rodríguez and Miguel Antonio Caro.[5] To understand the evolution of Chilean conservatism, Eduardo Frei must be considered along with Alberto Edwards Vives, and both of them with a notable countryman a hundred years their senior, Diego Portales.[6] It must be

1

demonstrated that though they were of two very different worlds, Manuel Gómez Morín, founder of Mexico's conservative Partido de Acción Nacional, and Lucas Alamán, a century removed from him, shared a common intellectual heritage.[7]

The second analytic stumbling block involves definition. What is Latin American conservatism? Conservatives themselves have answered the question in innumerable statements of principle and party platforms, in philosophic essays and books, in newspaper articles and handbills. They have done so in each of the nations lying between the Rio Bravo and the Straights of Magellan over nearly 150 years. The sheer bulk of those materials and their chronological and thematic breadth creates for the student an embarrassment of archival riches, an overwhelming mass of material with which to contend. The fact that the conservative parties of many Latin American nations have been metamorphosing, fragmenting, and in many cases changing their names, further complicates the problem.

Nonconservatives contribute to the problem of coming to grips with the subject. They muddy the water through their use of an assortment of terms, most of them unflattering, in describing conservatives and their philosophy. The term "the right" is widely used, as are "conservadurismo," "the reaction," and "partisans of 'strong man' rule." Those less friendly to conservatism frequently use the denominations "Fascist," "Nazi," and "Falangist," as well as terms that must be omitted in the interest of civility.

There are also literary, philosophic, and religious ways of describing conservatives. Early in the twentieth century, young conservatives were sometimes called arielistas for their adherence to ideas contained in José Enrique Rodó's essay titled Ariel and were seen as peopling a "generación de novecientos" in Peru and forming an intellectual circle called the Ateneo de Juventud in Mexico. The critics of positivism and materialism in Brazil were sometimes labeled "spiritualists." In Spanish-speaking parts of Latin America, defenders of traditional ways who denounced their erosion by modern "mechanistic civilization" sometimes adopted the name "Hispanist." Throughout Latin America, those stressing the efficacy of church doctrines as antidotes to the mal de siècle were often called neo-Thomists.

Given this welter of terms, it is no wonder that Latin American conservatism is not an easy

2

subject to discuss. We sympathize with non-Latin Americans trying to make sense of what at times seems a confused, even spurious philosophy. Their relative lack of success is suggested by Russell Kirk, the dean of North American conservative theoreticians, who lamented the "feebleness of conservative elements" there, concluding that "one cannot look to Latin America for signs of conservative imagination and hope."[8]

This book dispels the misconceptions surrounding Latin American conservative thought by analyzing the ideas of Gómez of Colombia (1889-1965), one of twentieth century Latin America's leading conservative politicians. As well as exploring the nature and sources of Gómez's ideas, it compares them with the ideas of other Latin American conservatives who were his contemporaries.

Gómez professed to be oriented by a conservative philosophy that he believed gave mankind the best, indeed the only entirely satisfying approach to the truth. He claimed to be the voice of conservative orthodoxy in Colombia over a lifetime spanning the first two-thirds of the twentieth century; hence, this inquiry into Gómez's ideas offers an excellent opportunity to study a major Western sociopolitical philosophy as expounded and acted upon by one significant individual. It is an intellectual biography, a study of ideology in an age dominated by ideologies. Young Gómez rode into the twentieth century on the crest of a conservative reaction against nineteenth century liberalism in its varied forms. As a twentieth century Hispanic conservative, it was his lot to confront vigorous liberalism, as well as militant socialism and fascism. Here then is a new attempt to perceive the principal social philosophies of our day and the manner of their interaction. Through comparison of Gómez and his ideas with those of other Latin American conservatives, we have a way of gauging the subject of the study in hemispheric context and of demonstrating how his ideas related to the broader scene. By perceiving the Colombian drama as part of a larger one of major twentieth century sociopolitical doctrines in conflict, we free Gómez and his Latin American contemporaries from the confines of regional history, allowing them to take the stage as actors in an ideological debate of global dimensions.

3

Chapter I

THE NINETEENTH CENTURY BACKGROUND
OF LATIN AMERICAN CONSERVATISM

Origins of Political Conservatism
in Latin America

The wars of independence were not long over
when the trials of nationhood began, causing grief
throughout mid-nineteenth century Latin America
(Brazil, and perhaps Chile, being exceptions).
Caudillo-led armies repeatedly threatened the
integrity of the young nation states, many of which
appeared ever on the brink of dissolution. As the
post-independence years passed and the problems of
nationhood persisted, increasing numbers of Latin
Americans came to believe that the source of their
troubles lay in attitudes and institutions dating
from colonial times. They were critical of the
traditional privileges enjoyed by special interests
and of infringements on personal liberties that they
deemed harmful to the spirit of democratic republicanism. Consequently they strove to free their
citizenries from traditional restrictions of all
sorts. Their efforts typically resulted in the
abolition of slavery, in the adoption of free trade
policies, and in reducing the role of the church in
civil society.

At mid-century, the drive to increase national
well-being through liberal social reform reached its
greatest intensity. Inspired by ever more liberal,
even radical, and utopian formulae for achieving
human happiness, national leaders stepped up their
campaigns to rid their societies of elements they
deemed impediments to progress. Because it was
perceived as the mainstay of the old order, the
church bore the brunt of reforming vigor. Throughout Latin America, there were attempts to weaken the
church and to separate church and state. In most
cases those actions were undertaken in an anticlerical spirit and with a heavy hand.

The attempt to reform Latin American society

at the expense of the church sparked formulation of national conservative parties. Political parties bearing the name "Conservative" appeared in Ecuador in 1830, in Colombia in 1848, in Mexico in 1849, and in Chile during the 1850s. In some countries the opposition to liberalism was expressed through support of authoritarian figures. Among them were Antonio López de Santa Anna in Mexico, Juan Manuel Rosas in Argentina, and Dr. Francia in Paraguay.[1]

Latin America's nineteenth century experiments with social reform and the ensuing reaction against them were but one aspect of a phenomenon generalized throughout the Western world in the eighteenth and nineteenth centuries. As such they illustrate both the unity of Western history and the element of lag in the spread and acceptance of new ideas. Ideological lag can be observed in the fact that ideas of the Enlightenment began to make their impact in Latin America a half-century or more after they gained currency in Europe. The books so avidly read by liberal romantics during the 1840s, 1850s, and 1860s were frequently translations of works first published in Europe a generation earlier. Lag also is evident in the timing of conservative party formation in Latin America. The Latin American movements paralleled a much earlier development among tradition-minded Europeans.

Shortly after the French Revolution, the term "conservative" began to appear in the writings of European intellectuals such as Edmund Burke and Madame de Staël. In 1799, for example, Napoleon Bonaparte remarked that "conservative, tutelary, and liberal ideas" were coming into their own in France.[2] F.R. de Chateaubriand's newspaper Le Conservateur appeared in the year 1818, and during the 1820s the British began to speak of the "conservative party when referring to those opposing radical demands in the interest of maintaining traditional privilege."

Conservative party formation in Latin America differed from the European movement in that its chief catalyst was the liberal attack on clerical privilege. Retention of the traditional union of church and state was an irrevocable plank in the platforms of all mid-nineteenth century Latin American Conservative parties. But there was far more at stake than the question of vested interest. At the heart of the liberal-conservative issue lay a fundamental disagreement about the nature of man. For liberals, men were autonomous, rational creatures whose power of analysis made them "the

6

measure of all things." For conservatives, men were imperfect beings who, with proper guidance and with divine help, could perhaps be taught to live good and productive lives. In the great scheme of things, men were small indeed--nothing more than "blades of grass in the hands of God."

At its most elemental level, the difference between liberals and conservatives was one of clashing world views. Against liberal notions of individualism and social contract, conservatives posited a society governed by natural law. The conservative version of the "good society" was one of harmony and organic wholeness, governed by the ethical imperatives contained in divine law. It was a unity of natural social forms, hierarchical, and governed by the principle of distributive justice. Within it the individual was guaranteed certain autonomy before the state through the principle known as "subsidiarity," and his right to private property was protected, for only through the ownership of property could the individual achieve true liberty and reach his full potential.

The church played an integral, indeed transcendent, role in the conservative vision of man and state. As well as serving as the interpreter of divine law, it was charged with monitoring the state's success in protecting the common good, that quality so necessary if social harmony was to be achieved. In the eyes of nineteenth century Latin American conservatives, the liberals' attempt to effect church-state separation was tantamount to freeing society from the restraints imposed by moral law. Such a program, if successful, held the potential of creating an anarchic society in which morality and virtue would be lost along with the common good.

Party formation in mid-nineteenth century Latin America was a complex process. Those who chose to align themselves with one group or the other did not do so for ideological reasons alone; yet it must not be forgotten that between thoughtful liberals and conservatives, there was an ideological chasm. Their mutually exclusive views of man, institutionalized in the political parties, could neither be dissolved nor reconciled. The convinced liberal's was a secular vision, one predicated on the notion that man can and must control his own destiny. The conservative perceived man as a member of a greater community divinely commissioned to promote the common good along lines prescribed for him in the philosophia perennis of the Roman Church.

Nineteenth Century Colombian Conservatism:
"Historicals" and "Nationalists"

Conservatism became institutionalized in Colombia in a particularly dynamic way. In the year 1849, Mariano Ospina Rodríguez and José Eusebio Caro founded the newspaper La Civilización to act as the political voice of their new Conservative party, one of the few bearing that name anywhere in the Western world.[3] Like their European counterparts, they felt a need to respond to the revolutionary political philosophies that were appearing in Colombia at that moment. In the first edition of La Civilización, Ospina Rodríguez defined the link between European and Colombian political thought. He criticized his nation's leaders for following French theoritical works full of anti-Christian, materialist doctrines. They were fomenting "Jacobinism," which threatened to throw the nation into anarchy by leading the masses away from their traditional religious beliefs. Such tracing of national and global social problems to the forces unleashed in France in 1789 is common to modern Colombian conservatism of the traditional sort. Laureano Gómez would lay modern man's troubles at the threshold of the French Revolution nearly a century after Ospina denounced the Jacobin clubs in Nueva Granada for threatening to "corrupt the ignorant masses and hurl them against the more civilized element. . . ."[4]

Laureano Gómez and his contemporaries counted a number of major nineteenth century formulators of party doctrine among their ideological progenitors. Throughout his lifetime, Gómez insisted that his political inspiration came from Caro, Ospina Rodríguez, Sergio Arboleda, and José Manuel Groot, to name the most frequently cited.[5] The beliefs of Gómez's ideological mentors can be categorized into three broad areas: first, their conception of the ideal social system; second, their critique of liberal social philosophy; and finally, their view of history.

Colombia is a Catholic nation, argued Ospina, Caro, Arboleda, and the others; therefore, since Catholics believe that God's law is superior to man's, society must follow the philosophy of the state posited by the church. By divine plan, national society is properly conceived as an organic entity in which each citizen gives to society and receives from it as befits his position in the social hierarchy. Justice is thus distributive in nature and is predicated on an appreciation of human inequalities. Systems founded on absolute social equality under the law abandon those individuals who are less capable of defending their interests to the mercy of the rest and lead to social discord and ultimately anarchy; thus, all social acts must be carried out with sensitivity to the common good. This is particularly important in the area of economics. To avoid the socially destructive exploitation of one man by another, economic activity must be controlled in the interests of society at large, determined not by the lifeless schemes of rationalist natural law, but rather by first principles emanating from God.

Colombia's first Conservatives approached their Liberal antagonists both defensively and offensively.[6] First, they answered the Liberal critique of their theological, metaphysical vision of society with morally indignant restatements of the virtues of Catholicism while berating Liberals as lacking a coherent philosophy and as spiritually impoverished materialists. Second, they launched an attack on the various schools of thought embraced by Colombian Liberals. Both José Eusebio Caro and his son Miguel Antonio devoted much effort to demonstrating that Bentham's utilitarianism opened the door to dangerous relativism and socially destructive egotism-that its sensualism was pernicious because in addition to belittling man's reason and devaluing the spiritual side of life, it negated his ability to achieve personal perfection through the exercise of free will. The younger Caro and religious leaders like Rafael María Carrasquilla attacked Comtian positivism for placing unrealistic faith in the promise of science and technology, for its rejection of theology and metaphysics, and for positing deterministic "laws" governing the stages of human development.[7]

Conservative rejection of positivist determinism and Liberal visions of unilinear human development, coupled with their stress on free will in a context of divine omnipresence, led them to develop a pluralist, somewhat historicist view of history. As their Liberal contemporaries were writing national history as a process of inevitable movement toward an ever more perfect society cast along liberal lines, Conservatives like Sergio Arboleda were arguing that all social phenomena must be studied to discover the role they played in Colombian history. Arboleda's theological yet pluralist approach led him to examine Colombian history with a degree of openness denied the

Liberals by their more ideological approach to the past.[8]

The ideas and attitudes summarized above hardened into intractable beliefs over some three decades during which the Radical Liberals tried to impose their doctrines upon New Granada. At length, by the 1880s, the Radicals were unseated by conservative Liberal Rafael Núñez who, with supporters like Miguel Antonio Caro, set about recasting Colombian politics along conservative lines.[9]

Rafael Núñez came to power, thanks to the support of his own dissident Liberal faction and a substantial number of Conservatives. Out of their collaboration grew the ephemeral Nationalist party that dominated Colombian politics for as long as Núñez lived. Conservative Nationalists, led by Caro, joined Núñez in strengthening the government through the Constitution of 1886. In doing so, they adopted the positivist attitude that a centralizing regime could more effectively deal with the emerging "social problem" by speeding industrialization. The Nationalists accepted the notion that human progress is inevitable, though the laconic and skeptical Núñez could never bring himself to embrace the universalistic notion of progress posited by Herbert Spencer. The Núñez-led Nationalists were a historical anomaly in Colombia. Where most Liberals and Conservatives were uncompromising in their beliefs, the Nationalists' party was founded in the spirit of compromise. Núñez, whose political style is summed up in his remark that the shortest distance between two points isn't always a straight line, possessed a political eclecticism and an ability to transcend ideological narrowness unique in the Colombia of his day.

The Nationalist party disintegrated following the death of Rafael Núñez in 1894. From its inception, it was a delicate and exotic flower in the jungle of Colombian politics. Without the charismatic Núñez to hold the new party together, the powerful Liberal-Conservative polarity quickly reshaped national politics along the old, uncompromising lines. But reversion to the old dichotomy did not take place before a significant split developed in Conservative ranks. Men of conservative principles and an absolutist turn of mind were repulsed by the idea of trafficking with Liberals, no matter how moderate they had become. That smacked of a betrayal of principle, a dangerous weakening of religious conviction. Besides, the Liberals were infected by atheistic principles that

10

might become contagious to "liberalized" Conservatives. These feelings were shared by members of
the Conservative faction that came to be known as
the "Historical" wing of the party. Factors other
than like-mindedness intervened to precipitate
formation of the Historicals--dislike of the
Nationalists' policy of political centralization
(one of the few beliefs shared by the doctrinaire
Conservatives and laissez-faire Liberals), abhor-
rence of the Nationalist notion that Colombia's
"social problem" should be solved through modernization rather than perfection of its "organic"
nature, uneasiness over positivistic Nationalist
assertions of the "inevitability" of national
progress, a suspicion that the Nationalist Conservatives' flexibility and ability to compromise
indicated moral laxness. But it was a fundamental,
underlying difference in temperament that finally
separated the Historicals from the Nationalists.[10]
Many years after the party split occurred, Liberal
journalist Luis Eduardo Nieto Caballero pointed to
this difference in personality. In a perceptive and
humorous essay that he signed "Lenc," he held up the
Historicals as "bad humored, hirsute, austere
Conservatives," and the Nationalists as "better
friends, more companionable, and more human." For
good measure, he added Santiago Ospina's definition
of the factions, one that held special meaning for
Liberals after the Historicals' failure to join them
in their 1899 revolt that touched off Colombia's
disastrous War of the Thousands Days: "The Historical is a grim Conservative; the Nationalist is a
cheerful Conservative; and both are cannibals."[11]

The Turn-of-the-Century Division in
Conservative Ranks

     The split within Colombia's Conservative party
is described above in some detail because it illustrates the breach in conservative ranks occurring
everywhere in late nineteenth century Latin America.
That split, having a right-left character, would
become an important feature of twentieth century
conservative thought there. Conservatives on the
left were moderates, less wedded to tradition,
more open to change. In short, they were more
"liberal." Their copartisans to the right were more
ideological in the sense of seeing conservative
doctrine as organic and God-defined, not subject to
modification by mortal man.
     The philosophy of positivism lay at the heart

11

of the Conservative division, both in Colombia and elsewhere in Latin America. Positive philosophy was expounded by French thinker Auguste Comte in a series of volumes published between 1830 and 1842. Like many conservative-minded men, Comte was concerned that the Enlightenment had undermined the intellectual and social bases of Western civilization and had not replaced them with anything of lasting worth. But where he parted company with other conservatives--his contemporaries Joseph de Maistre and L.G.A. de Bonald, for example--and where he placed himself within the Enlightenment tradition was in his insistence that man had progressed beyond theological and metaphysical stages of development and had reached a culminating "positive," scientific stage. Through the use of rigorous scientific method, insisted Comte, man could discover truth.

In spite of its rejection of metaphysics and insistence that all knowledge must be based upon the facts of experience, there was much in Comte's philosophy to which conservatives could adhere. Indeed, at the heart of his positivism was the notion that, as Comte himself put it, "no great progress may be accomplished if it does not lead finally to the consolidation of order;"[12] and the order that would be established through close adherence to Comte's precepts was a hierarchical one. Conservatives took special note of positivism's claim that society progressed naturally though successive stages. They found it easy to gloss over deterministic aspects of the concept by couching it in the doctrinally acceptable idiom of organicism.

Two Colombian writers and politicians illustrate the positivist turn of early twentieth century Latin American conservative thought. They are Miguel Antonio Caro and Marco Fidel Suárez, leaders of the Nationalist faction of their nation's Conservative party. Both were obsessed with helping Colombia achieve the progress so long denied her by internecine civil wars.[13] "Those of us who have served the Nationalist party since its inception," wrote Caro in 1903, "have honorably believed that we've thus served the cause of civilization in this section of Latin America." He went on to point out that "liberty and order" were the watchwords of his conservative faction.[14]

The positivist cast of Nationalist thought is explicit in an 1896 letter of Marco Fidel Suárez: "Progress is the movement of peoples toward civilization, whether in the sense of acquiring it, as happens in savage or barbarous nations, or whether in increasing it, as happens in all societies, however advanced they may be. . . . Liberty is a prerequisite for progress . . . and disorder is the ruin of liberty."[15]

Neither man left doubt that his words of uplift were grounded in thoroughly conservative principles. Suárez assured his readers that progress without Christianity was nothing: "National morality is obtained through the diffusion of Christianity and popular education."[16] For Caro the philosophy of his Nationalist faction of conservatism "has been and always will be that proclaimed by . . . Jesus Christ himself, when, correcting the narrow jealousy and aggressiveness of several of his disciples, said 'he who is not against you is of your party.'"[17]

At the opposite extreme, two Brazilian contemporaries of Caro and Suárez occupied what is here described as the right wing of early twentieth century conservatism. Julio César de Morais Carneiro, a Catholic priest, and Jackson de Figueiredo, an orthodox Catholic, fulminated against positivism as destructive of values they cherished. "Without religious faith peoples are eunuchs [and] true progress will never germinate," Morais wrote in 1898, adding that "in nations as in men the generative vigor of spirit, that which produces the great work of civilization, draws inspiration from Christ."[18] His belief in hierarchy and natural social inequalities is clearly seen in an essay written in 1897 in which he asserted that "true human dignity does not come through teaching man to strive for power, wealth, and greatness at all costs. On the contrary, it comes through giving man the profound conviction that inequalities in class and status are a vital element in all constituted societies."[19]

Writing some two decades later, Jackson de Figueiredo was unequivocating in opposing the dominant spirit of the age and in cleaving to the philosophia perennis. "I believe that Catholicism remains capable of giving us better political and moral orientation [than] those ideas we see disorienting the Western spirit--that is, Positivism--which is simply Catholicism without God . . . called by Auguste Comte a synthesis of Catholicism."[20]

A group of influential essayists and novelists of early twentieth century Latin America can be called conservative if the word is broadly construed. Creative license placed its members at liberty to range widely in their effort to give literary form to their social analysis, which helps explain why they resist easy categorization as either "left" or "right" conservatives.

One of the best known of this group was Uruguayan essayist José Enrique Rodó. His Ariel, published in 1900, contained an antimaterialist, spiritual, and elitist message that was later echoed by arielistas like José Vasconcelos, Manoel Oliveira Lima, Victor Andrés Belaúnde, and Francisco García Calderón. Rodó wrote about the bourgeois mediocrity and moral laxness of the industrialized nations. Latin America and her people, he explained, possessed a superiority of spirit and a sensitivity to enduring moral and aesthetic values that would humanize the crude and destructive materialism of the Northerners (specifically, the North Americans). Rodó concluded his essay with a scenario in which the Latin Ariel would triumph over the Nordic Caliban:

> The work of North American positivism will serve Ariel's cause in the end. What that nation of cyclopses has conquered directly for material well-being, though its sense of the useful, and its admirable aptitude for mechanical invention, other peoples . . . will put to better use. The genius of superior peoples will transfigure it, converting it into its purest and most luminous essence."[21]

Rodó argued the need for an authoritarian democracy in the Latin American republics, one "directed by the ideas and emotions of truly superior human beings. . . . The idea of equality was born in the spirit of Christianity . . . while the sense of order, hierarchy, and respect for the religious side of man was part of the classical heritage, a heritage vitiated by a certain aristocratic disdain for the weak and the humble."[22]

Later writers bore the optimistic message of Ariel to all parts of Latin America. Twenty years after the publication of Rodó's slim volume, Argentine arielista Manuel Gálvez was advising his countrymen that

> we possess hidden energy. But ours will not be a barbarous and automatic energy,

14

like that which boils incessantly in the United States of North America. Ours is and will be a harmonious energy, a force tempered by Latin elegance, an intelligent impulse, the spiritual arm of a being in whom action has not destroyed the ability to dream.[23]

Three writers of marked deterministic bent complete this glance at articulators of early twentieth century conservative ideas. The first of them, Peruvian Francisco García Calderón, is often counted among the arielistas of Andean America; yet as one who spent much of his adult life in Paris, he was influenced by racist theories in vogue there and elsewhere in Europe prior to World War I. The social organicism and racial determinism of writers like Gobineau and Le Bon run through Calderón's best known work Les démocraties latines de l'Amérique, published in Paris in 1912. The following passage reveals the centrality of race in his thinking: "The race question is a very serious problem in American history: it explains the progress of some nations, the decadence of others; it is the key to the incurable malady which is lacerating America."[24]

The grave malady afflicting Latin America was fully diagnosed just three years earlier in Bolivian writer Alcides Argüedas' famous work Pueblo enfermo. Argüedas was unremittingly pessimistic throughout his analysis of his nation's ills. Mounting his argument of rigid racial and environmental determinism, he concluded bravely that "we must agree, frankly, vigorously, and directly that we are sick; or rather, that we have been born sick and that our total collapse may be certain."[25]

Perhaps least conservative of the writers discussed here, at least in an orthodox sense, is Laureano Vallenilla Lanz, a Venezuelan writer whose study Cesarismo democrático appeared in the year 1919. In attempting to explain Venezuela's traditional caudillo rule as part of a radically democratic process, Vallenilla had set himself a difficult task. He completed it with the help of an argument bolstered by ample doses of organic determinism: "The typical character of pastoral peoples, in Venezuela as in all countries where rangelands and cattle exist," he began, "is that of equality of condition and the complete absence of social hierarchy." But it is an "undisciplined, adventuresome, irreducible and heroic sort of

15

equality," one demanding the strong guiding hand of a Caesar; yet the Venezuelan Caesar is always one who has risen from the common people, thanks to his own skill and intelligence. In the words of Vallenilla, that leader "is democracy personified-- the nation incarnate. In him are synthesized two concepts that at a glance seem antagonistic: democracy and autocracy. Democratic Caesaring: equality under the chief, individual power sprung from the people through a great collective equality."[26]

Vallenilla goes on to say that his argument is based on the "definitive" theory of natural organicism that explodes the foolish idea that nations are made by the conscious act of man. Such concept, he said, did not accord with modern scientific knowledge. "All perfectly constituted states are the result of a long process that culminates with all forces in equilibrium and all men suffused with what can and must be called the national soul, with that which in individuals we call the human soul."[27]

The ideas of Latin American conservatism presented a broad spectrum around the turn of the twentieth century. From a positivistic left wing so temporizing as to seem almost apolitical, it extended rightward to include messages that smacked of old style militance. Between left and right was a muddy terrain difficult if not impossible to define. It was occupied by younger thinkers, some of whom recklessly commingled orthodox conservative and deterministic, positivist ideas. The same center ground was also peopled by men who resist categorization. They are included here in part because of their antiliberalism and their general dislike of positivist postulates. Some of them were akin to the European "Generation of 1890," described by H. Stuart Hughes as "loyal critics of the Enlightenment" who were not attacking the humane values of the West, but rather "its late nineteenth century reincarnation in travestied form as the cult of positivism."[28] Others among them were broadly eclectic.

It was into this complex world that the central figure of this study was born. A conservative educated at the turn of the century, he reflected the ideological complexity of his era.

Chapter II

LAUREANO GOMEZ OF COLOMBIA

Man of Polemic and Paradox

Conservative Laureano Gómez is one of the two most important figures of twentieth century Colombian history[1] and the least understood. Taken together, these facts represent a considerable misfortune for those who try to make sense of the historical process in that nation, or who try to locate Gómez in the history of twentieth century Latin American conservatism. During his lifetime, his fellow citizens, friends and enemies alike, referred to Gómez as "the Monster." It was a nickname suggesting his opponents' dread of the Conservative leader's devastating oratory and his admirers' awe of him. Today, however, a majority of Colombians accept the nickname in a literal sense. This is so, in large part, because the image of a monstrous Gómez has been the one presented to them in the pages of their most widely read newspapers and in most historical volumes.[2] Partisans of Gómez, a minority in Colombia, though an influential one, remember him as their peerless leader. Their writings are worshipful in tone and entirely uncritical. It is ironic, though perhaps appropriate, that the long-time leader of his nation's Conservative party is remembered in the same polemical idiom that he himself employed with consummate skill.

Polemic aside, Colombians agree that Gómez was a politician whose career was long, spanning nearly half a century; that through the 1920s, he delighted liberals by attacking members of his own party, notably Conservative President Marco Fidel Suárez; that from the early 1930s, Gómez was Conservative party chief and unstinting critic of Liberal presidents up to the year 1946; that Gómez was elected president in 1949 during the civil war called the Violencia; that he tried to recast the national constitution along organic, corporative

17

lines, but was overthrown and exiled by the coup of General Gustavo Rojas Pinilla in 1953; that he returned four years later, after the fall of Rojas, endorsing the bipartisan Frente Nacional crafted by himself and Liberal party notable Alberto Lleras Camargo; and that he died calling for an end to the Liberal-Conservative enmity underlying the Violencia. The foregoing sketch suggests both the pivotal role of Gómez and the difficulty many observers have in finding either logic or consistency in his actions.

The confused image of Gómez, "the Monster," takes on a quality of paradox upon closer inspection. The man who bent every fiber of his being to the political cause between 1909 and 1965, suffering three exiles and the destruction of home, possessions, and family business along the way, insisted throughout his lifetime that he was not a politician! He who made and unmade national presidents, who ruled the Conservative party with an authority that moved party members to cry out against his "discipline for dogs," insisted that he had little interest in party politics and that he was, in fact, an inept politician. That Gómez sincerely and consistently protested his political disinterest suggests a starting point for any study of him. That point of departure is his own comment on his beliefs and what he was about. Gómez's words are keys to understanding this most controversial of all twentieth century Colombians. Reflection upon what Gómez said during his lifetime dispels most of the confusion that surrounds him.

Gómez was not from a political family and consequently was not destined for public life from the first, as were others of his generation. On the contrary, his father prevailed on him to study engineering at Bogotá's National University. Engineer Gómez, university degree in hand, was on his way to the department of Antioquia to build railroads when events conspired to thrust him into the field for which he would so frequently profess disinterest and disdain, even as he mastered the Byzantine world of Colombian party politics as few had before him.[3] With his "accidental" entry into politics in mind, consider several revealing statements of his political beliefs, the first of which is contained in an interview granted to El Tiempo reporter Luis D. Peña in September 1940:

I am not a politician! It's a mistake to think that I am. My intellectual and

18

spiritual preparation was entirely non-political. Fascinated by mathematics, sincerely interested in scientific investigation, I was, in my early years, profoundly divorced from politics. I'm not a tactician; I know nothing of strategy. I don't have the foresight to gauge the impact of my words and actions upon my public life. I obey the impulse of limitless sincerity and don't seek predetermined results. For these reasons I am not a politician.[4]

The key phrase is "I obey the impulse of limitless sincerity." In other words, there was a driving force behind Gómez that moved him to the political feats in which he took less than full pleasure. Two years later, this time in a speech before the Colombian Senate, Gómez delivered another self-analysis: "I possess a conviction that is total, one rooted in the depths of my soul, in religious sentiment. It is a conviction that suffuses, and is reflected in all my actions."[5] He was, in his own words, a man pursuing a vision with religious overtones that transcended the petty world of elections, patronage, and political conquest. Twenty years later, in one of his last public pronouncements, Gómez reflected on his political career in the following manner: "You can't imagine the satisfaction this produces: to look back and to see that one's life has been devoted to a single thing, a thing eminently good for the nation."[6] The "single thing" to which Gómez referred obviously was not politics, for politics had not dealt gently with him. Rather, he spoke in the manner of countless others who readied themselves for death, convinced that all their suffering had been worthwhile. Regardless of their personal misfortunes, they believed they were never false to the sublime idea.

Ideas were, in short, significant motive forces in the life of Gómez. Logically, then, if one wishes to understand Gómez--and by extension his era and the nation upon which he had considerable impact--one must understand his ideas. One must understand what Gómez called that "conviction that is total . . . that suffuses all my actions."

The study of ideas in their historic context is not immune to criticism from several quarters. There is skepticism about the value of studying ideas as causal agents in and of themselves. This is owing to the conceptual vigor of two schools of

19

thought, the first of which interprets ideas sociologically, as instruments used to achieve specific social ends, and the second which views ideas psychologically, as a means for helping people adapt to the demands of greater society. In line with the former view, Marx called ideas a "super-structure" masking or justifying the economic base; Sorel dismissed them as myth. Talcott Parsons and Daniel Bell have interpreted ideas as functional devices used to achieve satisfactory integration of society. To Sigmund Freud, best known of the psychological theorists, ideas and ideologies aid individuals in handling stress and anxiety, whether sprung from personal sources or from social pressures.

It is the contention of the present writer that none of these theories is based on empirical evidence. Specifically, it cannot be demonstrated that Gómez was not moved, as he claimed to be, by his ideals, or that his followers did not share those ideas. On the contrary, the gradual dwindling of Conservative party strength in Colombia over the course of the twentieth century indicates that political ideas were other than static, and that there was, in fact, transaction and change at the level of political ideology. Unless we dismiss as absolutely meaningless propaganda the utterances of all public figures who claim, as Gómez did in his day and as others do today, to represent the "moral conscience of Colombia," then we must attribute a degree of transcendence over class interest to intellectuals and politicians who speak in moral terms. This writer assures the reader, furthermore, that he in no way maintains that Gómez was somehow able to transcend either his carnal state or his cultural conditioning to live as one with the revered Idea, as both Hegel and Marx claimed certain men are able to do at a given moment in the histori-cal process. It is therefore suggested that this study is justified, in the absence of proof that ideas are merely blunt instruments wielded by exploiters of their fellow men, and in the presence of evidence that the subject of this book acted on his ideals--conservative ideals--and led a significant number of like-minded Colombians during an important time in national history.

Gómez of Colombia and the Conservative Assault on Liberalism

Colombian history has, at certain junctures, seemed to be strangely out of step with developments on the larger global stage. One such moment in the country's past was during the presidency of Gómez. Thanks to his own personal qualities and to the nature of Colombian politics, the conservative was able to keep his political ideas in the forefront of national life at a time when many of his key beliefs had been elsewhere consigned to the ash heap of outmoded philosophies. In 1950, the first year of the Gómez presidency, most of the world was preoccupied with the global struggle between liberalism and Marxism-Leninism. Conservatism, particularly conservatism of the neo-Thomist variety professed by Gómez, was decidedly not part of the Cold War political equation; yet there Colombia was, at the height of the struggle between East and West, led by a regime intent on uniting social classes and setting all citizens in harmonious pursuit of the "common good." In late 1952, an optimistic Gómez reminded his people that "the myth of universal suffrage" and facile acceptance of positive law had led them away from true morality. In Gómez's words, moral law was that founded on "the thought of Christian philosophers (that) makes up the doctrine of the common good, which is itself chiseled from the inexhaustible mine of the philosophia perennis. . . ."[7] He concluded with the prediction that reform of the national constitution along corporative lines would earn Colombia the admiration of other nations in the hemisphere.

The story of Gómez's rise to the presidency is told in Colombian political history and need not detain us here. But it must be pointed out that Gómez was not so much out of step with global political currents as his words and deeds suggested. Throughout his life, he was part of that group of thinkers who, convinced that Western liberalism had failed, acted on their conviction. However improbable it may seem, Gómez shared at least one belief with Lenin, Trotsky, and all others of the left: liberalism had ill served mankind; its pernicious ideas must be replaced by those better suited to human society.

Gómez was born at a pivotal moment in history. To paraphrase Virginia Woolf, we may say that on or about the year 1889,* world history changed. The liberal world view that dominated men's minds throughout the nineteenth century had reached its point of greatest vigor--a point at which it first became the target of a critique from which it would never fully recover. The liberal vision, shaped over the preceding two centuries by men like Newton and Descartes, Rousseau and Voltaire, and modified in more recent times by Bentham, Comte, Mill, and Spencer, was a confident one characterized by a belief in man's essential goodness and in the inevitability of his achieving a good and humane society if allowed the proper measure of personal freedom. Europeans, specifically Northern Europeans, led the march of progress, a fact obvious to all, given their intellectual domination of the world. In the 1880s, only the most perceptive could see that the apogee of nineteenth century liberalism also marked the beginning of its decline. The industrialization upon which European might rested brought a kind of misery to the lower classes not known before, that made the gap between rich and poor more palpable than at any other time in history. European colonialism, made possible by consolidation of European nation states and invigorated by industrialization and the search for ever greater markets, would soon produce a Pandora's box of problems. Nationalism, at first limited to the Western world, would become a global phenomenon taking on an undreamed of intensity. Demographic realities were changing the image of the European, rendering him no larger than other mortals. Technological developments would presently introduce an element of unpredictability unknown to the self-assured nineteenth century liberal. All of this, along with two wars that devastated Europe, ended the long era of European dominance over the world. It also gave rise to the attack on that complex of ideas known as liberalism.

The heaviest criticism came from Europe itself. The assault from the left was led by Marxist socialists in their Bolshevik-Leninist, social-democratic, existential, and other variants. From the right came strident voices running the gamut from Burke and Maistre to Carlyle and Novalis, from Pius IX and Leo XIII to Maurras and Barres. There were also eclectic critics. Sorel, Neitzsche, and Spengler were one in damning the liberal myth as

---

* Laureano Gómez was born on February 20, 1889.

puerile and absurd. Even thinkers not ostensibly part of the anti-liberal juggernaut contributed heavy artillery to the attack. Freud and Einstein, to name but two, brought old certainties crashing to the ground in particularly telling ways.

In Latin America, the assault on liberalism was initially less devastating. The leftist critique was virtually nonexistent in the nineteenth century. It would be well into the twentieth century before levels of industrialization and urbanization, the formation of labor unions, and increased foreign investment lent resonance to Marxist arguments. Nor was conservative criticism strident in the nineteenth century, due to the rightward drift of liberalism itself. The popularity of certain determinist notions, notably racism and geographic determinism, and the example of the errors and excesses of radical liberals earlier in the century, all contributed to a conservatization of liberalism by the late 1880s. In fact, the neologism "conservative liberal" had to be coined to describe the sort of leader disposed to sacrifice the restraints imposed by constitutions and representative bodies to achieve social qualities that were by then more highly valued: order and progress. The Mexican conservative liberal was personified by Porfirio Díaz, the iron-fisted ruler whose notion of progress was spelled out in the writings of Francisco Cosmes, Justo Sierra, and the rest of his positivist "científico" advisers. Carlos Pellegrini headed the movement toward "scientific" politics in Argentina, Benjamim Constant and Teixeira Mendes assured that Brazil would continue to pursue positivist goals after it became a republic in 1889, and in that same year Chile's Valentín Letelier lectured his Partido Radical on the virtues of responsible authoritarianism, citing Bismarck as a model.

The "conservatizing" of Latin American liberalism was nowhere more overt than in Colombia, where former Radical Liberal Rafael Núñez carried out his celebrated "Regeneración" of national politics. Núñez pointed out, as he formulated his plan to reorder national political structures, that his actions were not so much personalist as they were "in the logic of Spanish-American history."[8] That logic, as perceived by Núñez, dictated that he install a presidential regime in Colombia, weaken representative bodies, restrict suffrage, and restore the church to a position of pre-eminence. While skeptical of doctrinaire positivism, he did

endorse Spencer's notion that wise public administration dictated the shaping of political institutions to the "body politic" rather than attempting
the impossible task of forcing the social organism
into a strait jacket shaped around an ill-fitting
alien ideology; thus, by rewriting the national
constitution in 1886 and bringing the church back
into national governance through the Concordat of
1887, Núñez kept Colombia politically in step with
her sister republics.

This was the world into which Gómez was born
and came to political maturity. Part of a unique
national culture, he also belonged to the intellectual movement against the dominant sociopolitical
philosophy of the day. Gómez was but one of a vast
group of thinkers and activists whose collective
critique would effectively challenge the assumptions
of twentieth century liberalism.

His Philosophy Summarized

It is a common mistake for those familiar with
the career of Gómez to judge him as a man out of
step with his time, to call him medieval or
unenlightened in his approach to the world's
problems. In short, there is a tendency to label
him a human anachronism. Such perception could not
be more mistaken, for the Conservative party leader
was much a man of the twentieth century. He was
conversant with the great debates of the day and
their literature, and he commented on them in a
steady stream of essays and editorials published in
the Colombian press between the first and sixth
decades of the century. This is not to say that
Gómez liked the age in which he lived. Because he
feared and detested the growing secularization of
global society, he was one with his greatly admired
contemporary, the Russian thinker Nicholas Berdiaev,
who in 1914 wrote a line that captures Gómez's own
belief: "Human culture is, in its most profound
religious sense, an immense failure."[9]

Gómez possessed a rare combination of
idealism, tenacity, combativeness, and energy--
qualities that he employed from an early age in
attempting to repair the damage that he saw the
modern age inflicting upon his nation. One can but
marvel at the success with which he conducted his
Sisyphean struggle. At great expense to himself--
critics would say to his country--Gómez expounded
his philosophy of man and society and alerted
Colombians to the dangers that the modern era held

for both.

What was the philosophy that Gómez transmitted with impassioned insistence? It can be synthesized in the following summaries of what he said over his career in thousands of essays, editorials, speeches, and interviews. (Although the sixth and last of the beliefs listed below was voiced publicly only between 1956 and Gómez's death in 1965, he insisted that his endorsement of the Frente Nacional in no way implied renunciation of the convictions enumerated in items one through five.)

(1) Western society is in crisis. That crisis is the logical, inevitable result of the process of social decay set in motion by the destruction of Christian unity in the sixteenth century and by the growth of destructive individualism and materialism in the seventeenth and eighteenth centuries and afterward.

(2) Modern man's salvation lies in the philosophia perennis of the Roman Catholic church. In that universal, inclusive, and irrefutable body of thought are found eternal truths, as well as the only proven method of harmonizing human society.

(3) Colombia and her people are profoundly Roman Catholic. Any attempt to deal with national problems must be guided by that fact. Contrarily, any action not in strictest accord with church teachings is by definition unacceptable, counterproductive, and, ultimately, evil.

(4) Colombia possesses a splendid cultural heritage transmitted to her by imperial Hapsburg Spain. Following independence, the nation developed a unique cultural personality. That personality was nurtured by beneméritos (founding fathers) who were wise enough to escape the influence of foreign ideologies that subverted the universal values enshrined in Christian doctrine. Since independence, Colombia has suffered at the hands of her own sons who have misguidedly sought to address national problems through the application of damaging alien solutions, who in doing so merely served foreign

25

enemies bent on exploiting Colombia for their own purposes.

(5) Citizens holding views contrary to those expressed above are not only wrong, they are dangerous to the nation. They are infected with the same virus that has weakened the Western world and plunged it into crisis.

(6) Colombia has been grievously injured by its tradition of polemical political debate. It is time for the nation's leaders to set aside sterile partisanship and support the Frente Nacional. Bipartisan government will allow the Violencia to be ended and will permit Colombia to resume national progress.

These ideas were obviously not original with Gómez. He was not a philosopher, but rather an engineer turned politician. His duty as he conceived it was to become his nation's chief articulator of conservatism, a pattern of thought that in twentieth century Colombia included strong elements of nationalism, romanticism, and the sense of social crisis. Gómez was one with other conservative theorists in his emphasis on the organic and hierarchical characteristics of society and in his tracing of the contemporary crisis back to the Enlightenment. These were pivotal elements in the analyses of Edmund Burke and Joseph de Maistre in the nineteenth century, of Hugo van Hofmannsthal and Adam Müller in the late nineteenth and early twentieth centuries. They were also important in the critiques of twentieth century conservatives like Hilaire Belloc, Charles Maurras, and Jacques Maritain. Like them, Gómez drew inspiration for his indictments of bourgeois capitalism and socialist progress, and his sense that the world was in a period of crisis, from the influential writings of Renan, Taine, Michelet, Dostoevski, Spengler, and many others who found fault with twentieth century society.

Throughout his lifetime, Gómez did his best to stay abreast of contemporary social thought, taking from it views doing no violence to his own and attacking others that he felt to be socially destructive. In this way he transcends the parochial confines of Colombian history. The large body of critical work left by Gómez provides us with a highly subjective but nevertheless structured and profound commentary on the principal themes of world history during the first two-thirds of the twentieth century.

Gómez was never unfaithful to his ideas, nor did he accept philosophic views contrary to his own. But it does appear that at the end of his life he became reconciled to the fact that Colombia was changing in ways he deplored, but that the better part of patriotism was to accept that reality. His endorsement of the Frente Nacional suggests as much. If this assessment is correct, then, that final and least controversial of the intellectually inspired actions of Gómez may be the most notable of his personal achievements.

Chapter III

ROMAN CATHOLIC UNDERPINNINGS OF GOMEZ'S THOUGHT

The Early Years, His Jesuit Mentors

It has been said, and truthfully so, that Colombia's foremost conservative of the twentieth century was most comfortable when on the attack. He may have come by his disposition genetically, for his family was from Norte de Santander, a part of Colombia famous for producing men of an uncompromising and warlike disposition. But it was the supercharged political atmosphere of the Bogotá of Gómez's youth that stimulated his natural combativeness, and it was the people around him who taught him to relish ideological warfare undertaken with religious zeal.

Two battles raged in the Colombia of the 1890s. The first was a civil war, actually two civil wars, one beginning in 1895 and ending the same year, and the other, the atrocious Guerra de los Mil Días, beginning in 1899 and ending in 1902. The second battle, waged not with rifle and machete but with ideas, was philosophical in nature, pitting Roman Catholic social and political thought against modern secular philosophies. No Colombian, least of all young Gómez, could avoid being touched by the two civil conflicts that were in significant ways one and the same. Both the military and the intellectual struggles were rooted in conflicting views of man and society that had been at odds in the Western world since the Enlightenment. The Liberals and Conservatives who fell in windrows at Peralonso and Palonegro and a thousand other places during Colombia's endless civil wars of the latter nineteenth century were in fact fighting for principle even as they fought for more mundane things. That is precisely what gave the fighting its peculiar savagery and caused the violent debate to continue past the era of the civil wars and through half the twentieth century. Youngsters of Gómez's generation would see to that, for their elders taught them that ideological struggle was a moral imperative.

Laureano Gómez began his formal education at the Jesuit-run Colegio San Bartolomé when the intellectual movement known as the Counter Enlightenment was in full flower. The Counter Enlightenment was diverse, having conservative and reactionary components as well as liberal and revolutionary ones. It was unified only in its attack on the central belief of the Enlightenment--that rational men are, through the objective application of universal principles accessible to the human mind, able to achieve permanent solutions to life's problems. Since the seventeenth century, leaders of the Roman Catholic church had attacked the individualism and secularism implicit in Enlightenment thought; but only in the nineteenth century did social realities support their contentions. Creation of the modern proletariat in European nations, and its suffering at the hands of rational men acting under the tenets of liberal individualism, provided ample and objective support for their attacks. These developments and their criticism by two strong-willed and vocal popes, Pius IX and Leo XIII, made the church the greatest voice in the conservative wing of the nineteenth century Counter Enlightenment. These men and countless others down through the church hierarchy led millions of the faithful in meditation on the old verities found in natural and divine law, as expounded in the teachings of St. Thomas Aquinas. In rural, nonindustrialized Colombia, the conservative counterattack on liberal philosophy acquired political overtones rarely seen elsewhere in the Western world. Formation of the Liberal and Conservative parties institutionalized and politicized what in most other places was a dispute carried out only at the level of ideas. With the government of "Regenerator" Rafael Núñez and his successor, pro-clerical Miguel Antonio Caro, a key goal of the conservative Counter Enlightenment was achieved in Colombia. The church regained its old status and its rights were formalized in both the Constitution of 1886 and the Concordat of 1887. In accord with the constitutional provision specifying that "public education will be organized and directed in accord with Catholic religion," the Jesuit order, only recently readmitted to Colombia, was placed in charge of Colegio San Bartolomé. When Gómez enrolled there in 1897, Colombian anti-liberalism, as articulated by the church and as taught in schools like San Bartolomé, had assumed the character of revealed truth.

30

The eight years that Gómez spent at San
Bartolomé armed him spiritually and provided him the
ideological foundation upon which he would build for
the rest of his life. The philosophy he learned at
his beloved school--"lighthouse of the purest
wisdom,"[1] as he called it--may be reduced to a
single proposition and its corollary: the Christian
philosophy of man and society is correct; all
others, especially the one(s) posited by liberals,
are incorrect. Drawing from the works of Thomas
Aquinas, Suárez, Balmes, Mariana, Soto, and Vitoria,
the Jesuit fathers systematically schooled their
young charges in the belief that freedom comes from
God, not from the social contract; that the state is
organic in nature, with its obligations spelled out
in organic and divine law; and that within the
Christian state, man's freedoms and liberties are
limited in order to protect the common good. This
was the Christian philosophia perennis. All ideas
in conflict with it, Gómez was taught, were
"heterodox" and socially harmful. Liberalism and
socialism were held up as particularly dangerous
beliefs for the materialism that undergirded them.
Materialist propositions such as the assertion that
all knowledge is experiential were countered with
disquisitions on the fallibility of man and science
and with assertions that God is the source of all
knowledge. Metaphysics was seen as the antidote to
materialism. Bartolinos were taught that the ultimate reality found in God can only be approached
subjectively, through mind and imagination.

In the San Bartolomé of Gómez's youth, religious education was seen as the counterbalance to
the materialism that corrupted and destroyed men.
Through religion young men would gain the spiritual
and moral strength to resist destructive social
philosophies. Such teaching would strengthen their
characters. In fact, character formation was
considered the principal goal of education, a view
stated by no less a personage that Colombia's
leading educator, Archbishop Bernardo Herrera
Restrepo: "We often worry about how much knowledge
our students will acquire, but we should remember
that above all else, it is essential to produce men
of character."[2] The students at San Bartolomé
attended classes in catechism and religion, partici-
pated in daily masses and rosaries, celebrated feast
days and holy days, and periodically attended
spiritual retreats. It is no wonder that in this
intensely spiritual setting, the bartolino developed
a close relationship with his priestly mentors.

31

Years after graduation, Gómez recalled that aspect of his education: "At that austere school we were taught a manly concept of life . . . the Jesuit fathers taught us more than did our books. The example of their lives enriched our youthful souls."[3]

The curriculum at San Bartolomé was heavily oriented toward classical education in the years when Gómez was in attendance. Latin and Greek were given equal status with the pure and social sciences and other modern subjects. This is explained in part by the fact that, as one of Bogotá's most exclusive schools, its students were not thought to need training to equip them for any but the most prestigious occupations. Only two hundred students attended the school in Gómez's day, and his graduating class was made up of just five persons. It was a very exclusive group indeed, and the proud bartolinos knew it. The educational philosophy of that day was precisely stated by Colombia's Apostolic Nuncio when, in 1905, he wrote, "We must see that the doors of higher education do not open to just any type of individual, but only those privileged few with talent."[4]

For all its exclusiveness and the other worldly character of much of its curriculum, San Bartolomé and its students were caught up in the issues and events moving turn-of-the-century Colombia. At one point early in the year 1899, the Liberal and Conservative press of Bogotá engaged in debate on the merits of traditional education, with its emphasis on philosophy, religion, and the classics, as opposed to the modern liberal education taught at other schools in the city. The debate grew heated, with terms such as "priest-ridden," "medieval," and "troglodytic" hurled by one side, and "atheistic," "Benthamite," and "rationalist revolutionaries" used injudiciously by the other. High school students took up the cry, and in mid-March Bogotá witnessed several street fights between students from San Bartolomé and the Liberal-run Liceo Mercantil and Colegio Araujo.

By far the most serious incidents of 1899 were those touching off the War of the Thousand Days. The war left a profound impact on Gómez, for, as he put it, the conflict "opened his eyes for the first time to public issues" and to the true nature of his homeland.[5] Gómez recalled that war bulletins posted in the streets of Bogotá provided him his earliest readings in political literature. Those accounts of battles and campaigns, and the lists of dead, made an indelible mark on the schoolboy: "It was a crushing experience--those three long years of hopeless and futile war, of pure barbarism, of public displays of dead and wounded, some of whom I had occasion to see!"[6]

By 1902 the war was well into its third year. The nation was prostrate, yet the fighting grew more savage. Secretary of War for the government was Aristides Fernández, an intransigent Conservative who owed his position in large part to the vow that he would show no quarter to the Liberal rebels, and why should he? Fernández was fond of reminding the nation that the government's was "the cause of God," leaving no doubt as to the cause of the Liberals. In March of that last, most terrible year of the war, news reached Bogotá that Liberal General MacAllister had captured three Conservative officers and was proposing to use them to bargain with the government. War Minister Fernández responded by selecting three Liberal prisoners of comparable rank and promising to execute them forthwith if the Conservatives were not released. His arbitrary act threw the capital into tumult and was debated even in the halls of San Bartolomé. Ultimately, a group of bartolinos sent Aristides Fernández a petition in which they pledged their "enthusiastic support" for his action.[7] It is not known whether Gómez signed the petition, but there can be no doubt that the incident brought home the lesson that strongly held beliefs and actions are intimately connected-- sometimes mortally so.

Another bitter lesson not learned in books followed hard on the heels of the war. Gómez, by then in his last year of high school, followed closely the Panama Canal debate in the national Senate. From his place in the spectators' gallery, he listened raptly as Senators Miguel Antonia Caro, Pérez y Soto, and Oscar Terán argued eloquently and successfully against the insulting treaty proposed by the North Americans. It was nevertheless, as Gómez recalled, obvious to all that the government, "stupid and blind, implacable in its policy," was going to lose Panama. When the news of Panama's loss reached the capital, fourteen-year-old Gómez ran through the streets crying and shouting. He attended a meeting called by General Enrique Arboleda where, as he remembered, "all we could do was shout against the Americans." Later that day, Gómez tried to offer his services to President Manuel Marroquín, who he hoped would lead the schoolboys of Bogotá on a campaign of reconquest.[8]

Gómez was learning a great deal. The time was drawing near when Colombia would learn the conclusions he had drawn from it all.

Gómez's four years at the National University coincided with the "Quinquenio" of President Rafael Reyes. The Reyes regime was one of dictatorial rule carried out amidst national recovery from the bitter experiences of the preceding decade. Among those suffering most from Reyes's arbitrary acts were a number of Conservative parliamentarians who refused to go along with his plan to extend his term in office and suffered internal exile for their obstinance. One of them, Manuel Dávila Flórez, would later become the political mentor of Gómez. It was Dávila who encouraged Conservative university students to work for the overthrow of Reyes, promising "if you decide to join the revolt let me know so I can die with you in the streets!"[9] Those words hastened Gómez's first political act, an angry speech denouncing "the cruel, sordid, tropical dictatorship of General Reyes," delivered to fellow students in the patio of the College of Engineering at the National University.[10] The speech earned Gómez a brief stay in jail, an episode he no doubt recalled as he characterized the "Quinquenio" as a time when "all constitutional protection of individual rights was erased with a flourish, and the ax of the tremendous and unappealable sanctions hung over the heads of the citizens."[11] After the fall of Reyes on March 13, 1909, events bore Gómez--now Doctor Gómez, engineering degree in hand--toward his political destiny. Selected by his former high school principal, Father Luis Jáuregui, to deliver a speech at the ceremony commemorating the twenty-fifth anniversary of the return of the Jesuits to Colombia, Gómez waxed so eloquent that one of the dignitaries in attendance, General Ramón González Valencia, came forward and embraced the orator. "You could say that it granted me a relative fame," was Gómez's laconic recollection of the event.[12] Shortly thereafter, Father Jáuregui summoned Gómez to his rooms. He said that plans were afoot to found a newspaper, one that would answer attacks of the anticlerical press, and that he, Jáuregui, wanted Gómez to edit it. The younger man protested that he knew nothing about newspapers and in fact had already accepted an engineering job in Antioquia. But the Jesuit persisted. He argued that the Gómez family was not in immediate need and that editing a proclerical newspaper would be "the noblest of tasks, the only one whose rewards were

34

certain and whose disillusionments were few." Then
sensing the engineer's resolve crumbling, Jáuregui
added: "Seek ye first the kingdom of God and his
righteousness, and these things shall be given unto
you."[13] With the scripture ringing in his ears, and
beneath Father Jáuregui's beatific gaze, Gómez took
charge of proclerical La Unidad. Thus began his
career as newspaperman and politician.

Roman Catholic Sources of Gómez's Ideas

Gómez never tired of pointing out that his
philosophy of life was rooted in strictest Roman
Catholic doctrine. His teachers at San Bartolomé
laid the foundation for his system of belief, and
Gómez later broadened and deepened it through study
of the sociopolitical thought of Plato and
Aristotle, early church fathers, medieval schoolmen,
and modern religious philosophers. That reading was
not of the questioning variety, but rather was aimed
at reinforcing what he knew to be true--that "we are
in the right," as he often said. "I speak in the
name of the principles of Catholic doctrine, expressed in the philosophic works of St. Thomas Aquinas,
that tell how a state must be organized in order
that the rights of the citizens are respected," he
explained to Liberal Minister of Government Darío
Echandía in 1942.[14] Such statements led many to
argue that the Conservative party leader wanted
Colombian society to conform to an anachronistic
medieval or "feudal" pattern. This is a misleading
generalization, as are most that have been made
about Gómez. As will be seen, he was a reconciler
of ideas who understood the forces that were
changing modern society--though it must be remembered that he understood them through the lens of
ideology--and tried to bring them into line with his
neo-scholastic ideal of Christian community.
Complicating his struggle was the fact that his own
thought was influenced by certain of the secular,
even anti-Catholic intellectual currents at large in
the twentieth century world.[15] Some of those ideas
fit clumsily into his overreaching philosophic
framework and sometimes stood out as overtly antithetical to it. But how could it have been
otherwise? The era was one of ideological ferment
and social change unequaled in human history, and
Gómez was trying to harmonize it with an idealized
vision of antique inspiration; yet for all that, it
is remarkable that he remained true to his essential
ideals in the face of adversities that made other

men question their beliefs or reject them altogether.

It is his consistency that invests the study of Gómez's though with special importance. Students of the twentieth century can thank him for providing a kind of standard against which social and ideological change may be gauged. From the year 1932 on, he formulated the ideology of a political party that commanded the allegiance of half the Colombian people. It is true that structural political peculiarities made Colombia's people "captives" of the Liberal and Conservative parties during that period, and that Gómez's leadership was constantly challenged during the two decades of his personal hegemony over the Conservative party; yet the fact remains that the Conservative masses endorsed his ideas, and a significant minority within his party continued to do so even after his four-year Spanish exile and subsequent conversion to bipartisanship.[16]

It is even more significant that a substantial majority of Colombians never accepted Gómez's notion that harmonious Christian community was appropriate to their nation. Even in the nineteenth century, half of all Colombians found liberal individualism more appealing than conservative community and expressed that predilection by affiliating with the Liberal party. Within the party of Mariano Ospina Rodríguez and José Eusebio Caro there were many liberal Conservatives who questioned the extreme ideological position propounded by their more doctrinaire partisans. Their story is told in the history of the Nationalist-Historical dispute in the nineteenth century and later, in the twentieth century, in that of Conservatives who found common ground with Liberals in the ephemeral, bipartisan, Unión Nacional regime of President Carlos E. Restrepo, 1909-1914, and later in the República Liberal of the 1930-1946 period. Most recently progressive Conservatism found its home in ospinismo and its personalist derivations.[17] At Gómez's death in 1965, a clear majority of Colombians were liberals in the sense that they believed in democracy and liberal economic developmentalism. Gómez himself had managed to reconcile developmentalism and his neo-scholastic belief that economic activity must be subordinated to the common good. From that time on in succeeding years, a growing number of Colombians deserted both the traditional political parties in favor of others promising populist or socialist solutions to

36

national problems, or they became alienated and apolitical.

Biography has been described as a metaphorical record of a people. Likewise, the study of a single person's ideas may be called an individualized portrait of the like-minded. That Gómez was for many years able to exercise great influence over millions of conservatives, this in considerable part through the persuasiveness of his ideas, tells us much about the people of Colombia. So too does the fact that while the Catholic political philosophy articulated by Gómez steadily lost popularity over his lifetime, that system of belief retained its validity for a significant minority of Colombians.

Roman Catholic political philosophy teaches that man is a rational, social being, born into society through the family. He is a free individual who forms and is formed by the several communities into which he is born or with which he voluntarily associates. "Community" is defined as the complex of occupational, educational and religious groups, marriage, the family, political associations, and all other collectivities with which the human being becomes involved during his lifetime. It is through his corporative communities that man unites to form the state. As a rational creature, man freely forms the state, but in doing so, he acts in accord with his social nature. He thus complies with natural law which is of divine origin. The Catholic reasons that while God is the state's ultimate authority, man creates the state and measures its effectiveness against eternal, natural laws. Man makes his laws, but he makes them in accord with standards provided in natural law.

The question of order is uppermost in Catholic thinking about man and the state. Much effort has been expended in reconciling the belief that man is born with an inalienable right to freedom with the opposing view that man's freedom must be restrained lest it threaten the greater community. Church philosophers achieved their goal of granting man freedom, and at the same time denying him full exercise of it, by stressing his rationality and the concept of natural law, according to which rational man voluntarily restrains himself by governing society in accord with unchanging standards of behavior of divine origin. Putting it another way, man's God-given freedom does not imply license. This method of reconciling two opposing principles places a great burden upon the individual, that imperfect creature who tends to do wrong even as he

37

has it within his power to perfect himself through reason. While this lends dynamism to Catholic social philosophy, it also posits a society characterized by eternal tension created in the unending struggle to grant citizens the maximum possible freedom while maintaining perfect social order. In final analysis, order is the more important social quality, for in Catholic thought the individual can achieve his full potential only in an atmosphere of order.

This conservative political philosophy, teaching that man is rational and able to create a more perfect society but also weak and inclined to error, left modern Catholic thinkers great leeway in formulating approaches to the ordering of human society. Some of them, moved by personal liberalism and the desire to move the church away from its ultramontane stance, formed the "modernist" movement within the church. During the nineteenth and early twentieth centuries, men like the Marquis de Montalembert, Lord Acton, and Father Hecker stressed the positive view of contemporary man and his ever-improving world in an attempt to bring the church into step with their optimistic age. At the same time, there were Catholics like Donoso Cortés, de Maistre, and Bonald who, with equal attention to orthodoxy and encyclical, posited a world imperiled by social decay brought on by willful human excesses. Their gloomy perception led them to propound the need for strict restraints over inherently sinful mankind.

The ambivalence in Catholic thought concerning man and society was reflected in the sociopolitical pronouncements of Gómez. The Colombian conservative was alternately optimistic about man's potential and pessimistic over the likelihood that he would ever realize it. His remarks to a largely Conservative audience in Medellín in the year 1933 are those of Gómez the Catholic optimist. He lectured that Catholic social theory, founded in "profound and ample wisdom," instructs that man can transcend selfish individualism and overcome his weakness and natural venality through identifying with the natural organic groups making up Christian community. "We are supported in the religious system that we have received and that we profess," Gómez explained. He portrayed the ideal society as "a harmonious edifice, free of all profanation and menace . . . a sacred temple, free of impurity and fraud, of violence, injustice, and tyranny."[18]

Gómez liked to say that human freedom and dignity did not exist prior to Christianity, and that

38

his own political party was the undisputed voice of man's better instincts. "The Conservative party is, before all else, the party of reason," he told a 1932 party convention held in Chía, Cundinamarca. "Beside the noble cause we defend, what are our personal aspirations and ambitions, our vanities and greed, but mud that sometimes splatters the altar of the doctrine that we venerate?"[19] His piety so impressed the Liberals of El Líbano, Tolima, that one of them composed a "novena" celebrating the Chía speech. Its title was "Novena to the Glorious Senator, St. Laureano of Chía."[20]

Countering his rationally founded optimism was a more fundamental, visceral pessimism. One of his earliest judgments of a political nature was "this nation cannot be governed . . . because we've never wanted to have true government."[21] One of his last, perhaps the most bitter of all his statements of a political nature, made during the third year of his exile imposed by General Rojas Pinilla, was that the Colombian people "have the government they deserve."[22] Like most philosophic conservatives, he dwelt more on man's inclination to do wrong than on his ability to live a moral life through self-discipline and rational attempts to follow moral law. Gómez, like Maistre, Bonald, and many others, believed that it was the rationally founded institutions that collapsed first, and that the irrational ones, particularly the family, were of greatest importance in stabilizing society. This helps explain the intense attack he unleashed in the 1930s and 1940s when he perceived Colombian society to be under attack by a myriad of forces intent on dissolving traditional institutions. On this conviction, he based his campaign against a Liberal proposal to grant illegitimate children increased civil rights. To Gómez the legislation was "frankly destructive of the family and of Christian morality. . . . Christianity raised the status of women, establishing the inviolability of the home, which is or should be a sanctuary. This project negates a thousand years of civilization. . . . It is immoral to destroy society by writing laws that are themselves immoral."[23] Even after he failed to convince Colombians of the correctness of his moral vision, suffering exile for his trouble, he continued to warn of the nation's social decay. A few years before his death, he delivered the following critique of national life:

Integrity in all its aspects is clearly

39

in ruin. There is no protection of
property, or of the honor and lives of
the citizenry. This is to say, civil
life is falling apart. Before this sad
phenomenon there is an increase in
moral laxness that heralds disaster.[24]

In spite of his pessimism, Gómez believed in
the Christian idea of progress. According to that
concept, as it is explained in Roman Catholic philosophy, it is man's divine vocation to improve his
society, making it ever more like the perfect city
of God. At the same time, it is accepted that as an
imperfect creature, ultimate perfection is beyond
the reach of man. Gómez was faithful to the injunc-
tion that moral man must be unflagging in his
attempts to improve his society. His was not an
abstract longing for a better society, but rather a
drive to improve it physically. It was a quest for
progress born of the feeling that social stagnation
would make inevitable the triumph of communist
revolution and the destruction of Christian
Colombia; thus, it was not with a sense of irony or
cynicism but with frankness and sincerity that Gómez
called on Colombians to accept an authoritarian
reform of the national constitution in 1953. The
semi-corporative system that he proposed was to
bring with it greater "efficiency and progress."
Just days before his overthrow in 1953, Gómez
published a long newspaper article that he introduced by recalling the days prior to 1930 when
Colombians believed that "the long awaited imperative to progress was finally being fulfilled.
Citizens were proud of having achieved a high degree
of civil culture, a notable respect for human life,
a remarkable level of probity in public administration, and a tolerance of opinions contrary to their
own." But those gains were thrown away after 1930
when a Liberal-induced process of decay set in.
Finally, inevitably, came the widespread rioting:
"In just a few hours Colombia's civil reputation,
acquired slowly, patiently, was ruined. . . . The
moral and material backwardness of our nation
reveals that there has been a squandering of the
vital forces of our race, a nearly total waste of
the creative and organizational talent of Colombians."[25] Pursuant to his political philosophy,
Gómez tried to address the fundamental problem of
government: guaranteeing the greatest possible
amount of individual liberty while curbing freedom
sufficiently to insure the maintenance of order. In

his authoritarian constitutional reform of 1953, Gómez found his solution to Colombia's problems, one that he saw as perfectly consistent with his Christian principles and belief in progress. Gómez's "First Message to Colombians," transmitted from New York two months after the military coup, argues that fact with eloquence. He explained that prior to his presidency there had been an incomplete integration of philosophic doctrine with public administration, and that upon entering office he had felt it his duty to demonstrate his ability to provide such leadership. He claimed that during his months as president he had undertaken a vigorous fight to structure the state in accord with "the only doctrinal system that harmonizes the elements of Colombian nationality and channels the nation toward progress."[26]

Catholic political philosophers teach that the state is an organic community in which men function as members of groups rather than as individuals. Care is taken to define the state as a moral organism as distinct from a biological one. The former is a human creation brought into existence by free men in accord with moral law. The latter is an irrational thing falling outside the intellectual-moral world. The Catholic organic state further contrasts with the individualist one posited by liberalism, in which man is an autonomous, self-sufficient individual who creates the state in order that he may more effectively pursue his particularist interests.

Gómez fully endorsed the Catholic concept of the organic state founded on "natural" groups and hierarchies. He drew on organic and corporative terminology to help him identify and describe the incorrect ideologies that were subverting Christian Colombia, and to explain what Colombians must do to reverse the decline of the body politic. In 1941, for example, he asserted that because the Liberals rejected natural, distributive law, the national legal system was in a state of "complete putrefaction."[27] After the assassination of Jorge Eliécer Gaitán and the riots attending it, organic terminology filled his speeches. In one short address of June 1949, he repeatedly employed organic metaphors to describe the state that Conservatives were morally bound to defend. He referred to the historic moment as one calling for "missionary activity" in the defense of the various "organisms of state and society."[28] He saw the movement of Western history since the Enlightenment as a

sustained attack on organic community. In the sixteenth century, Cartesian philosophy "incubated a
rationalism that denied the supernatural foundations
of Catholicism. This weakness was paid for with the
horror of the French Revolution and the contagion of
savage and rancorous naturalism that that movement
spread over the world."[29] French revolutionaries
set out methodically to destroy the coherent organic
community: "Their first task, . . . perhaps their
only one consisted of destroying and then impeding
the rebirth of all the organic social groups that
until then had sustained and defended mankind within
the recesses of human dignity."[30]

With corporate groups under attack and discordant individualistic pluralism the rule, Gómez
pointed out that liberal jurisprudence of positivist
savor was completing the destruction of traditional
Christian community. Following his lugubrious
analysis, he concluded that by failing to govern in
accord with the ethical precepts contained in
Christian philosophy, in substituting "positivist"
standards for the traditional religious ones,
Colombia's Liberal regimes had corrupted the social
organism.

Gómez's answer was to defend the key organisms
of the state. He argued the orthodox Catholic view
of the family in his memorable debates on the
Concordat, constantly stressing the need of
restoring "Christian solidarity" to Colombia in
order to turn back subversive forces. His was an
eminently hierarchical view predicated on the notion
that authority is the boundary of freedom, and
freedom the boundary of authority. From such logic
came the seeming incongruity of Gómez calling for
authoritarian government while disparaging those who
saw in such statements an appeal for dictatorship.
In 1949 and 1950, as he was moving to consolidate
his hold on national politics and to invigorate the
organic concept of the state, Gómez lamented that
some Colombians saw dictatorship as the only cure
for political chaos.

> It pains us to observe how the people
> assume the inefficiency of the demo-
> cratic systems they revere, to the point
> that when an intractable problem pre-
> sents itself they irresponsibly exclaim
> 'only a dictatorship can resolve
> it.' . . . The fact that the idea of
> dictatorship seems to some minds the
> hopeless remedy for a situation that has

42

become intolerable for a majority of
Colombians points up the gravity of the
situation in which the republic finds
itself.[31]

The solution that Gómez, the Colombian president, evolved to address the nation's political
problem harmonized perfectly with the metaphysical
Catholic view of the state as a cosmos of natural
groups and hierarchies. He spoke in terms of
"hierarchies of virtue" and "hierarchies of order"
through which harmony would be restored to a society
rent by the excesses of modern civilization and
brought near to collapse. It was his idealized
vision of social harmony founded in social hierarchy
that inspired Gómez's explanation of the change he
hoped to bring to violent, divided Colombia. It was
the duty of leaders of society--politicians,
teachers, artists, writers, and philosophers--to
repudiate

repugnant vulgarity and cultivation of
the ugly and monstrous, strident and
excessive fads that under the pretext of
novelty have been so influential in
giving contemporary life a disagreeable
roughness and tone of insolvency that is
destructive to the unchanging manners of
a refined civilization.[32]

Members of other social groups--industrialists,
businessmen, merchants, workers, and farmers,--all
had their parts to play in the work of cultural
restoration. If the members of all these social
groups worked with a healthy spirit of loyalty
and strived for perfection in their particular
endeavor, Gómez wondered if anyone then could
deny that Colombia would experience a marvelous
change.
     Catholic political theory embraced by Gómez is
based on natural law, a kind of eternal law to which
all others must conform and in reference to which
men must design their legal system. That notion,
accepted unreservedly during the Middle Ages, came
under attack during the Enlightenment, particularly
after rationalist philosophers created elaborate
theories of natural law using empirical rather than
metaphysical insights to guide them. In the nineteenth century, Western thinkers dismissed natural
law as scientifically unsound. Drawing on the
optimistic view that man is inherently good and is

capable of infinite perfectability, they reasoned
that purely positive law was the soundest basis for
government.

Conservative followers of natural law complained that under the impact of a secularism that
discounted the validity of metaphysical universals,
positivistic law was subject to dangerous relativism
that in turn might permit, even engender, philosophical and moral chaos. They recalled that God-
given natural law was a compass orienting man in
stormy times. Such was Gómez's argument when he
debated liberals on questions involving law. In one
of his earliest newspaper editorials, he accused a
Senate member of cruel Spencerian positivism for
proposing a cut in funds for Indian missions: "For
the Senator there are no souls, only bodies, there's
no spirit, only matter . . . for him the only law is
brute force."[33] In 1934, in Senate debate with
Minister of Education Luis López de Mesa, he blasted
the "Kantian spirit" at large in Germany, "the
scientistic tendency making possible the Hitlerian
massacres that would be exotic occurrences in a
nation constituted on a foundation of Roman law."[34]
In that statement, Gómez made clear his belief that
the moral imperatives forming part of natural and
Roman law doctrines were far superior to the
dangerous relativism that he saw as inherent in
liberal positivist jurisprudence. Sixteen years
later, in 1950, he was still arguing for the
superiority of legislation founded in natural law:

> The collection of positivistic laws that
> men have written for the government of
> nations have never made possible good
> government in and of themselves. We
> have abundant proof of this fact in the
> example of nations whose leaders have
> created aberrant and iniquitous laws.
> On the other hand, humanity knows no
> case of good government in which that
> government has not willingly obeyed
> moral law.[35]

Dislike of majoritarian democracy was a trait
in Gómez's political personality. Conservative
criticism of the Rousseauian idea of social contract
is based on the Catholic belief that the state
originates in man's nature and that it is part of
the divine order. The state is seen as an order of
communities and families and individuals in which
the needs of each component group must be equitably

44

addressed. This was the philosophic origin of
Gómez's constant disparagement of majority rule, the
"one-half plus one," through which he saw Liberals
imposing their will on Conservative minorities. For
Catholics, the state was the objective moral order,
an institution needed by man if he were to realize
his human nature and reap the fullest benefit of his
natural rights. As an institution of the objective
moral order, the state does not derive its authority
from free will. Neither is it created by transfer
of individual rights. Laureano Gómez could not have
been closer to the conservative, orthodox Catholic
view of society than when he wrote, in 1910, that
"public power isn't the sum of the rights transmitted by each citizen. It is something else
altogether. It is the uniting of rights transmitted
by God to the government. Political authority
doesn't come from man, but rather from God. This is
the truth clearly taught by St. Paul who, speaking
precisely of civil principles, said 'there is no
power that doesn't come from God.'"[36]
     On another occasion, he contrasted Liberal and
Conservative views of the state. In that analysis,
cited below, he also indicates his profoundly conservative, metaphysical belief that citizens freely
and rationally form the state and maintain it in
good order through the ongoing exercise of civic
virtue. Also evident in his analysis is the belief
that the state is organic, composed of groups having
unequal status, that are led and directed by elites
who are more virtuous than the ordinary citizen by
right of their more perfect understanding of moral
law. Finally, Gómez indirectly acknowledges his
Platonic view that there is eternal tension between
man's rational, right-seeking side and his evil,
willful one. Plato wrote in The Republic that man's
soul contains spiritual and appetitive parts, likening them to a lion and a dragon. The lion is ever
ready to help man do right; the dragon constantly
threatens social order. It was Plato's argument,
and that of Gómez, that mankind requires a social
order in which reason dominates emotion and with the
help of the lion keeps the dragon at bay. If a
people selects democracy as its political form, let
it be an elitist authoritarian one lest that democracy turn to license.
     Political ideas, argued Gómez, may be divided
into two great sections:

          In one are grouped the ideas of those
          who consider politics an art whose

45

precepts express the belief that it is based in private interest. Accordingly, politics is nothing more than a subtle game played between those who arrogate power and those who wield it. . . . In the other are grouped the ideas of those who locate political principles in the interests of society at large, attributing to governors and to the governed interrelated rights and duties. There, law and morality are commingled, and no limits are admitted other than those compatible with humanity and justice. As eternal as the morality that supports it, this view of politics doesn't have a clearly defined ancestry. But if one omits the utopianism in 'the divine colloquy of the Republic'--the division of society into castes, the abolition of private property and family, the equality of men and women, the elimination of law, simply replacing it with education, the turning of government exclusively over to philosophers, the proscription of poetry--one might well argue that Plato lighted an eternal beacon for philosophers through his luminous idea that justice is the end of society, that governments must engender concord among citizens, that virtue is the true underpinning of the state and of education that begets customs.[37]

Understanding that Gómez viewed the state as a moral organism makes it possible to search out the intellectual source of his attitude toward persons whom he considered subversive to the constituted order. In Catholic thought, the state requires a certain homogeneity if it is to remain strong and virtuous--but not so much as to render it dictatorial. This means that political leaders like Gómez were necessarily sensitive to individuals and groups who might corrupt the social organism and set it on the path to destruction. Such sensitivity to perceived subversion and the determination to combat it were obvious in all of Gómez's speeches in months prior to his election as president. In June 1949, he said, "Two courses are open to us: The recuperation of our nationality, or leftist subversion. . . . Public administration cannot continue to be menaced by demands that threaten

46

public order."[38]

In believing that Colombia and all Western society were under attack, Gómez was in good company. Since the time of Pope Pius IX, Catholic thinkers had deplored the growth of individualism and the concomitant weakening of the conservative ethic. That society was being subverted by liberal secularizers and nefarious Jewish-Communist-Masonic enemies of Catholic Christianity was a major theme of Gómez's fight against modification of the Concordat of 1887. He could see signs of weakening moral fiber even in his own political party. In 1938 he blasted the nonconformity of some Conservatives: "These acts of insubordination have an individualistic and utilitarian savor that makes them particularly hateful. Each time they occur they demonstrate a repugnant moral deformity."[39] He lamented the liberal attack on socially stabilizing corporate groups that had been going on in the West since the French Revolution and before. Once, he explained, the state guaranteed human liberty and natural rights. But the organic, Christian view of society was eclipsed following the French Revolution. In Gómez's view, that led to the rise and domination of social doctrines that did not posit man's natural dignity as primordial, but rather placed the individual at the mercy of "artificial formulae giving the state a dangerous autonomy over essential human rights." Mankind thus "lost its way" and was pushed to ominous extremes of left and right wing totalitarianisms:

> Those of us who hasten to proclaim our conservative doctrine aren't subject to buffetings by the winds of political innovation. Nor do we trod the dangerous shifting ground of theories of social experimentation that we know beforehand will lead to the spoiling and discrediting of human life and dignity.[40]

In the view of Gómez and other Catholic proponents of the state of virtue and order, once extreme individualism robbed the people of their self-imposed discipline, in part through dissolving intermediate corporative institutions, they became an undifferentiated mass, emotional and vague. They became a political mob, easy prey to any demagogue, "an immense mass of . . . men, nearly indifferent to the antagonistic principles of virtue

47

and vice . . . moved by chance to one extreme or the other."[41]   For Gómez, modern history clearly revealed the inescapable consequence of the destruction of public virtue.

> Thrown together in a confusion of preju-
> dices, self-interests, and animosities
> that are cleverly manipulated, the
> masses aren't able to transcend their
> immediate environment, They walk the
> rim of an abyss and don't even notice
> the moment when they fall. They haven't
> the ability to study the past, which in
> any event is artfully hidden from
> them. . . . Oxen aren't led to the
> slaughterhouse in a more servile way.[42]

Gómez's point of reference during his decades-long critique of liberalism was the concept of the "common good." Catholicism holds that rational men, in this case those directing the state, must exercise leadership always in accord with the needs of all society. When any distortion occurs in the balanced functioning of the state, political leaders have the right and duty to intervene; hence Catholic political leaders not only endorse the idea of the interventionist state, but they also condemn the liberal "watchman state" as allowing an unhealthy growth of individualism that permits conscienceless exploitation of one citizen by another. This breeds social strife and the formation of an antagonistic class society. Gómez preached the dangers of this philosophy to his Liberal colleagues, always holding up to them the superior virtues of a polity informed by the common good. He frequently went to the source of his belief, as when in a Senate debate of 1940, he cited the Spanish Catholic philosopher Jaime Balmes. Human society was not conceived for the benefit of an individual, or for a group, said Gómez, referring to Balmes's writings on the subject. The common good is a touchstone in judging the laws and acts of a government.[43]

The common good concept touches heavily on economic matters: private property, capitalism, and exploitation of one man by another. Gómez closely followed Pope Leo XIII's endorsement of private property as essential to personal fulfillment, and his criticism of liberalism as sacrificing the rights of the lower classes, especially labor, through its extreme individualism. Speaking to a

48

Conservative audience in 1933, Gómez said that while the cause of conservatism is not that of the wealthy, it still defends the existence of private property as necessary to the common good. Echoing the Pope, he referred to the ownership of property as the foundation of human civilization, and he denounced the communalization of property underway at that moment in the Soviet Union as both mistaken and immoral. The collectivization of property in communist Russia was, in Gómez's words, "perverse, cruel . . . and destructive of human life and dignity."[44]

In addressing the plight of workers in capitalist societies, Gómez cited papal authority: "Leo XIII astutely pointed to a 'voracious usury' that recreates the worst kind of tyranny, subjecting workers to all manner of economic abuse." The word "fraternity," he added, "has never been more bereft of meaning than under the regime of capitalism . . . under the dominion of the proud, cold, and implacable captains of industry."[45] Gómez was consistent with Catholic doctrine, too, when shortly before his election as president in 1949, he declared his intention to deal firmly with Liberals whose acts he interpreted as destructive to the common good. Their individualistic philosophy, he explained, represented substitution of "upright and austere rule in the common interest" with "the use of state power for the cover-up of lies, fraud, and deceit."[46] In that same speech, he promised to intervene in economic matters on behalf of the lower classes "because we know that economic forces must be directed in order that popular needs be attended and that the weak be protected from the insufferable domination of the strong." A sound economy cannot exist, he said, "except where there is organic integration that renders impossible the excess of options for some and misery and penury for others." Two weeks before the election, he again announced his intention to "secure the common good" for all citizens.

The phrase "common good" appeared prominently in the proposed constitutional reform of 1953. Even in the time of the Liberal-Conservative coalition government known as the Frente Nacional (1958-1974), Gómez explained his actions in terms of that ideal rooted in Catholic political theory: "I challenged the most doctrinaire Conservatives to present programs that would best contribute to the common good," he told a party convention in October of 1958.[47]

The most difficult of Gómez's political tasks, and probably the most controversial, was to state his case against majoritarianism convincingly and to posit a kind of "authoritarian democracy" for Colombia. It can be argued that his caloric campaign against majoritarianism was self-serving in the sense that Gómez's party formed a national minority by the 1940s. His detractors outside the Conservative party and inside it accused him of tailoring his political and even his religious philosophy to changing conditions in the temporal world of Colombian party politics. To what extent Gómez the politician adjusted his ideological message to meet political exigencies is a question separate from that concerning the sources of his views. His attack on the "one-half plus one" was, after all, firmly rooted in Roman Catholic thought.

The starting point in coming to grips with Gómez's concepts of democracy is the theory of political authority. According to Catholic thought, the object of political authority is not so much the individual as it is the people as an organic whole. It is the common good. Political authority manifested in the apparatus of the state commands the individual's obedience not as an aggregation of individual wills, but as a power of a higher kind that is fundamentally different from the individual will or the sum of those wills. The political authority vested in the state is thus a divinely inspired institution existing in accord with natural law. In this sense it stands apart from and is superior to the individual wills that called it into existence. This is the reasoning employed by Gómez and other Colombian Conservatives who felt the need to counter Liberal assertions that the state is called into existence by the people through the social contract, and that the will of the majority is the will of the state. Gómez's refusal to accept democratic majoritarianism echoes the response that Leo XIII gave when asked if he was opposed to democracy. The Pope answered that he did not intend to reject the opinion of Catholics, "but only those doctrines that taught authority in no way originates in God but exclusively in the arbitrary will of men."[48]

The Conservative Catholic position on majoritarian democracy, highly qualified when not waffling and ambivalent, helps explain the absolute disagreement among persons who have tried to gauge Gómez's democratic sensibilities. Like many Catholic conservatives, he endorsed democratic rule only

50

when it functioned on the basis of inegalitarian principles. That is why he could praise the concept unreservedly when it was based on discipline and elite rule as in 1912, when he wrote, "peoples of democratic customs and inclinations, such as those in Colombia, are very watchful of political authority; the congressional session is an escape valve for political antagonisms."[49] On other occasions, particularly in his later years, he employed an antidemocratic argument in condemning a national majority that "wishes to vanquish reason with numbers"--that wants "to pervert the natural and obvious order of things with vacuous, poorly conceived and labored formulae."[50] Speaking to Congress on October 31, 1951, he pointed out that Colombia's problems began years earlier when "out of intellectual arrogance or improper submission to the reigning myths, our legal institutions were placed at the mercy of majoritarianism." Politics, he continued, corrupted national life: "Today politics is oriented not by the common good, but rather by a numerical majority of artificial, capricious wills."[51]

Gómez's critics, convinced of his totalitarian proclivities, greeted his oft-expressed scorn of dictatorship with frank disbelief; yet there is no denying that from his early denunciations of Rafael Reyes through his prediction that Mussolini and Hitler would fail because they violated the natural rights of their peoples, to his blasts at the regime of Rojas Pinilla, Gómez was consistent with Roman Catholicism's contempt for tyranny. Gómez explained in his "Second Message to Colombians" in 1953 that he was on solid ground in attacking the legality of the Rojas Pinilla government. He cited the Old and New Testaments, Jaime Balmes, Thomas Aquinas, Gregory XVI, Pius IX, Leo XIII, and Francisco Suárez in arguing that Rojas was in violation of God's laws. He affirmed his faith in democracy and asserted that while president of Colombia, he was never unfaithful to his Catholic political ethic: "This is the doctrine in which I was educated. . . . No one can deny it. Now that there is no liberty in Colombia, but rather adulation of the despot and calumination of me, I lift my voice before slanderers and opportunists, challenging them to prove otherwise."[52]

A key to understanding Gómez's constitutional reform of 1953 lies in Roman Catholic indifference to the form of government employed by citizens of a nation state. As long as they act in the common good and in keeping with natural and divine law, they are at liberty to adopt any political system that will achieve a society more like the perfect city of God. When the social organism is threatened and the common good is violated, furthermore, it is the moral duty of the governing power to address those ills. This is the standpoint from which one must interpret Gómez's relativism in regard to political institutions. He frequently delivered the opinion "political science is eminently relative. No political system created by human beings is optimal, infallible, and universally applicable."[53] That is the spirit in which his abortive restructuring of Colombian political institutions must be understood.

Gómez believed with unshakeable conviction that Roman Catholic philosophy showed mankind the way to perfection, both in the personal and political spheres. Over the course of his life, he acted on that belief as completely and in as orthodox a manner as he was able. This is not to say that he was unremittingly clerical and purely idealistic in his approach to politics; nor is it to say that Gómez was untouched by many intellectual currents outside the religious sphere. To call Gómez a man inspired by a sublime vision of a moral political order is far from implying that he even came close to bringing political Colombia into conformity with his ideal. Just the opposite is true. History judges the Gómez presidency a failure, a fact that Gómez himself acknowledged in 1956 when he said, "Mine was a faultless presidency and I made myself unpopular because in my country it seems that people don't like things to be correct. You might say that I'd rather be unpopular than incorrect."[54] Had anyone pressed the issue, Gómez would have been forced to admit that in keeping with his neo-scholastic, Suárezian philosophy, constituent power rests with the people, and Colombians therefore had the legal right to overthrow him. The military coup that unseated him spared Gómez the need to admit that his government was unacceptable to Colombians; yet in all fairness, it must be admitted that the Colombian political system was dysfunctional fully nine months before he took his oath of office. His was an impossible task from the outset. In August 1950, Colombia's bipartisan democracy had long since collapsed under the weight of violence and civil war. One can but pity the upright idealist who set out to govern in 1950, convinced that "in a society organized in accord with Catholic doctrine, conflict will be eliminated, injustice mastered, passions subdued, and crime quelled; perfect peace will reign in a land that is ordered by reason, presided over by justice, and blessed by God."[55]

Chapter IV

LIBERAL AND POSITIVIST ELEMENTS

Liberalism in the Thought of Laureano Gómez

From the first, Gómez never hid his conservatism. For more than half a decade, 1909-1916, he proclaimed it in his proclerical newspaper, La Unidad, as he did during the 1920s from his seat in the Colombian Chamber of Representatives, and later as a cabinet minister of Conservative President Pedro Nel Ospina; yet for all that, Colombian Liberals found elements in Gómez's thought that were to their liking. Some of them were so intrigued with the progressive, reformist side of Gómez that they supported him politically and vowed to help him should he ever run for the national presidency. By the mid-1920s, Gómez was as popular with liberal-minded Colombians as he was disliked and feared by members of the entrenched old guard of the Conservative party. This apparent paradox is explained by the fact that Gómez came to maturity at the moment Latin American elites became imbued with positivistic faith and zeal. Like his contemporaries, Gómez believed that there is a "law that presides over human societies," that it is possible to "discuss with exactitude the concept of progress," to "analyze completely the effect of natural phenomena upon the human being."[1]

In time Gómez would move away from the naive determinism of early twentieth century positivism, for it could not be reconciled with the anti-determinism of orthodox Catholicism; yet an idealistic, perhaps liberal faith that Colombia could be made to progress remained. The liberal content of Gómez's inherently conservative thought is particularly clear in his earliest writing, even in the polemical editorials written for his first newspaper. The hundreds of editorials written during his nearly seven years as director of La Unidad fall into six broad categories that may be described, in order of frequency of appearance, as follows:

55

anti-schismatic, nationalistic, anti-liberal, conservative, pro-clerical, and liberal.

Gómez's most frequently exploited theme combined the need for ideological purity within the Conservative party with criticism of bad party members, defined initially as those who collaborated with the coalition Unión Republicana government of Carlos E. Restrepo (1910-1914) and later as Suarista "Nationalist" Conservatives. It is the most political and therefore least important theme for purposes of the present study. Editorials falling within that category are better analyzed in the context of national politics during the period 1909 to 1916, and as an indication of Gómez's desire to become a major force within the Conservative party. Still, we can see in his railings against "collaborationists" and against Conservatives who deviated from strict partisanship and otherwise revealed less than total adherence to party doctrine, the inflexibility and the tendency to view human actions in terms of absolutes for which Gómez became famous.

With slightly less frequency, the editor of La Unidad wrote about his country. Those editorials were almost never of the flag-waving variety, but rather consisted of warnings against foreign threats and indictments of unpatriotic acts. Colombia's recent loss of territory through diplomatic negotiations and machinations of the predatory "Colossus of the North" are obvious reasons for Gómez's fear of threats from without. The United States and Great Britain were most frequently seen as dangerous to Colombian interests. Gómez explained his newspaper's support of Germany during World War I in the following words: "The triumph of that power would favor . . . the autonomy . . . of the South American nations, menaced by Yankee imperialism,"[2] although neighboring countries, notably Peru, were also objects of suspicion. But Gómez reserved his harshest words for his own countrymen, upon whose venality, apathy, weakness, and incompetence he placed major blame for the nation's predicaments. "Colombia's problem is that of getting rid of crooks," he explained in his La Unidad editorial of September 14, 1912. Though generally opposed to capital punishment, Gómez endorsed it when the crime committed was treason.[3] His celebrated phrase "Colombia is an ungovernable country par excellence,"[4] among his earliest public statements, is found in one of his accusatory, nationalistic editorials.

Another theme frequently and hotly exploited

by Gómez was antiliberalism. Within that category,
his editorials were fairly evenly divided between
condemnations of the Liberal party and its members,
and criticism of the liberal philosophy. A good
example of the former is the sarcastic June 1, 1911,
La Unidad editorial in which Gómez suggested that a
new ministry, complete with patronage and perqui-
sites, be constituted for Liberal leader General
Rafael Uribe Uribe and his friends; thus, "the
innumerable Uribe Uribes, the eternal and incor-
rigible directors of slaughter and havoc, would stop
being anarchists," having as they would "a practical
way of enriching themselves far from the horror of
the battlefield, far from the assault, far from
their bandit gangs." Another example of anti-
Liberal party editorials is found in La Unidad of
February 28, 1912. There Gómez repeats a refrain
from the poem "Advice from the Enemy": "Listen
well, Liberals! You're being addressed by a
Conservative spirit who detests your corrupting and
unpatriotic doctrines, and who knows that if you
declare civil war, you'll be defeated for the last
time . . . !"
      At the philosophical level, editorials adopted
the tone of the La Unidad piece of February 16,
1912. There Gómez defended Christian morality as
providing the soundest prescription for social
well-being and attacked liberal doctrines as nothing
more than "pseudo-conviction" through which their
proponents "want to erase the idea of God from the
minds of the people, wiping from the soul of nations
the doctrine of Calvary, replacing it with a rationalist morality, a . . . worship of sensualism and of
physical pleasure." Colombian history reveals, he
continued, that the two parties have, at various
times, implemented their ideological programs:

> Liberals, with Santander and the
> Azueros,[5] imbuing the people with the
> perverse and immoral doctrines of Tracy
> and Bentham; Conservatives, with Herrán
> Mallarino, and Ospina, rescuing truth
> with Tocqueville, Leibnitz, and, later,
> most decidedly with Aristotle, Aquinas
> and Francisco Suárez.[6]

      Perhaps once each month, the young editor of
La Unidad published a statement of his Conservative
principles, usually couched in terms of praise for
notables of the party with whose views Gómez concur-
red. These personages were identified with the

"Historical" faction of the party, among whose outstanding figures Gómez counted Mariano Ospina Rodríguez, José Eusebio Caro, Julio Arboleda, Pedro Justo Berrío, Manuel Briceño, and José Vincente Concha. In his editorials devoted to praise of conservatism as a social and political philosophy were occasional references to syndicalism, mass movements, women's liberation, Masonry, and revolution. In all cases Gómez denounced them as harmful to society and proposed that if Conservatives were faithful to the principle of authority, then all these movements could be held in check.

Given the origin of La Unidad—founded to defend interests of the church—it is noteworthy that proclerical editorials appeared regularly only in the first years of the newspaper's existence. Several factors explain this. As the paper's director was increasingly drawn into the political battles of his day, he had less editorial space to devote to proclerical pieces. Besides, the theme of Conservative religious orthodoxy ran consistently through most of the editorials on Conservative principles and on Liberalism. As one firm in his religious convictions and certain that no one doubted that fact, Gómez felt little inclination to belabor the obvious. Finally, there was the matter of Gómez's difficulties with the church hierarchy. In 1912 he attacked the Archbishop Primate of Colombia, Bernardo Herrera Restrepo, for showing moral laxity in a matter related to the Muzo emerald mines. The indictment stood his friends' hair on end, shocked and angered his devout elders, and resulted in the temporary suspension of La Unidad.

Least frequent in the pages of La Unidad, but nonetheless surprising, were editorials that can be described as liberal in tone. These were condemnations of dictatorship, endorsements of progressive taxation and government spending for social programs, assertions of belief in the idea of progress, and praise of republicanism and representative government. While it is true that none of these concepts is incompatible with Catholic political philosophy, they were editorial themes usually developed in the Liberal, not the Conservative, press. Their inclusion in Gómez's first newspaper indicates a certain openness in his approach to national problems that sounded a note of incongruity in the ears of Colombian Liberals.

Gómez was an enigmatic figure to Liberals during his early years. Even as they raged over his slashing attacks on their leaders and their beliefs, they admired his bravado in attacking leaders of his own party and their ecclesiastical supporters. His seemingly liberal ideas gave some of them cause to wonder if he were not at heart a liberal progressive. When Gómez left the directorship of La Unidad, temporarily beaten but unbowed, in 1916, vowing never to rest until Marco Fidel Suárez was no longer party chief, he was in the unusual position of counting a number of Liberals among his friends and supporters.

The years between 1916 and 1928 are uninformative on the intellectual development of Gómez, though they were eventful ones in personal and political ways. During that period, he married and worked to provide for his family, all the while staying close to the political struggle against the entrenched Conservative party machine. In 1918 he was prominent in the joint Liberal-Conservative dissident effort on behalf of presidential candidate Guillermo Valencia and against Conservative candidate Marco Fidel Suárez. The dissidents were beaten badly, but Gómez emerged with his reputation for eloquence and energy enhanced, and with a new nickname--"the Human Storm"--bestowed on him by Valencia; in addition he had a number of new Liberal friends, the most notable of whom was party leader and War of the Thousand Days hero General Benjamín Herrera. Less than three years later, while serving in the House of Representatives, he had the immense satisfaction of seeing Suárez resign his presidency in the face of a furious Liberal-Conservative dissident attack that Gómez himself headed. General Pedro Nel Ospina, elected president in 1922, brought Gómez into his government first in a diplomatic capacity and then as Minister of Public Works, a position from which Gómez directed the largest public works program seen in Colombia to that time. The public works minister's lavish expenditures left his enemies remarking bitterly that the person who most assiduously fought the treaty with the United States, bearing a twenty-five million dollar indemnity, was the same one who later spent most of the money. Following Ospina's presidency, Gómez briefly retired to private life and contented himself with criticizing the tired, unimaginative Conservative regime, at the time wonderfully personified by Miguel Abadía Méndez, a do-nothing president depicted by political cartoonists as sleeping while the nation fell into ruin.

More than a year after Gómez left the public works ministry, he was elected to the representative

assembly of Santander, a Colombian department lying
several hundred kilometers north of Bogotá. In
early 1927 he traveled to take his seat in
Bucaramanga, the departmental capital.

Gómez's arrival in Santander was one of the
most exciting things to happen there since the
Battle of Palonegro more than a quarter-century
before.[7] That appearance, replete with near riots,
assassination threats, polemical speeches, disrup-
tion of departmental government, and even a eulogy
to Marco Fidel Suárez pronounced by none other than
Gómez, is not properly part of this study.[8] What is
germane are the things Gómez said during his brief
stay in Santander during the months of March and
April 1927. He went there with the express intention of concerning himself with the department's
economic affairs. Gómez was not many months past
his stint as Minister of Public Works in the administration of Pedro Nel Ospina, and he considered
himself eminently qualified to advise the people of
Santander on economic matters. Upon his arrival in
the capital of Santander, he announced that he would
deliver a public lecture on foreign loans and their
implications for the department. While not a
subject to excite the masses, the lecture drew a
large and expectant audience. Among them was young
Milton Puentes, at that time a reporter for the
local newspaper Vanguardia Liberal. Later he would
become a leading historian of the Liberal party with
little good to say of Gómez; yet that evening he
left the lecture filled with admiration for the
speaker, and what he termed his "magistral conference." He heaped praise on Gómez, describing him as
"one of the most revolutionary spirits the nation
has seen in recent years, one destined to lead the
great transformation that Colombia needs."[9] Elsewhere in his report, he wrote that the public was
left "astonished by the multifaceted spirit and the
limpid intelligence" of the speaker.

Clearly something does not ring true here, at
least from the perspective of Gómez's antipathy to
liberal ideas. How could this admirer of Aquinas
and Caro come into the Liberal heartland of
Santander and be so persuasive that, in the words of
Puentes, "the fire of the most lively emotion con-
sumed the souls of the listeners, and they punctu-
ated each phrase with enthusiastic and prolonged
applause"--all this from a largely Liberal audience
listening to a Conservative lecture on economics.

The Liberals of Bucaramanga were responding
to a Gómez other than the one of intractable

conservatism and metaphysical bent. They were applauding Gómez the social critic and man of action, the "doer" who was at the peak of his popularity in 1927, the man many Colombians thought was soon to become the nation's first progressive president of the twentieth century. That Gómez should project such an image at the midpoint in his life is explained first by the fact that he was not a one-dimensional man. There were conflicting elements in his thought that occasionally led to inconsistencies in his actions and created the mistaken impression that he was fundamentally mercurial. That in turn helps account for the controversy constantly surrounding him, and the difficulty his countrymen had in assessing his character.

Gómez and the Liberals shared a faith in progress and the belief that Colombia was destined to move ever forward through thoughtful application of scientific principles. That he should think thus was quite consistent with his background in engineering, and with the fact that he was, after all, a man of the twentieth century living on a continent greatly influenced by positivist thought. Nor was it incompatible with his training by the Jesuits who taught him to view the world in absolute terms, nor with his dogmatic temperament that led him always to speak with great vigor and conviction. Add to these qualities his unquenchable thirst for the current European thinking on a wide range of subjects that gave him an impressive number of names and concepts to cite at will, and a splendid speaking ability, and one is left with a Conservative capable of mesmerizing even Liberals and filling auditoriums with audiences eager to hear him expound on ostensibly boring subjects. A few examples will suffice to reveal this progressive, "liberal" side of Gómez, the doctrinaire Conservative.

Early in his career and before he began devoting all of his time to Conservative party politics, when Liberals like Milton Puentes could still refer to him as a standard bearer in the march toward national transformation, Gómez was frequently called upon to speak on subjects related to national economic development. One such speech was delivered in Bogotá on July 20, 1917, when Gómez, acting in his capacity as Engineer of the Department of Cundinamarca, inaugurated the Sabana Railroad Station. Because it is an excellent example of his oratory during this phase of his career, and since it reveals more clearly than any other the faith in progress that he shared with others of his generation, a significant portion of it is cited below:

Ladies and gentlemen: This ceremony, in which we celebrate a vast and fecund labor marking one of the principal phases in the progress of our beloved capital city, is not merely the celebration of a mutely eloquent collection of stone and metal, as future generations might believe. Still less is it a frenzy of rejoicing, soon forgotten by those who witness it and meaningless in the long run. With indisputable wisdom, we celebrate the completion of an important work of material progress, at the same time initiating another work of moral progress no less great. The corporation for which I so clumsily speak . . . isn't content with having taken this monumental step that so delights Colombians. Rather, it continues vigorously, showing the way and awakening patriotic hopes for progress toward new horizons. . . .
What better, stronger, more worthy apprenticeship is there than the one that puts the fury of fire, the strength of steel, the power of steam, and the subtle marvel of electricity at the discretion of youthful humanity? What is nobler than using our power of analysis to study the movement of living creatures and natural laws in order to produce ingenious machines that surpass the legendary inhabitants of the air, the land, and even undersea domains? Nothing in the universe seems beyond man's reach. Eagles that until now have been the absolute rulers of blue space have seen their realm invaded by faster, more agile birds, enormous and tireless. Neptune's fearful domain, that tragic kingdom from which no living human had ever escaped, is today the highway of prodigious ships that steal from the fish secrets of the seabed. As with philosophy in ancient Greece, oratory in Imperial Rome, art in Renaissance Europe, and the Encyclopedia

in the most recent era, chemistry and
engineering predominate in modern
times. Today nothing is more important
than steeling our compatriots for the
challenge of the moment, readying them
for the harsh tasks at hand, for the
herculean battle that more than ever is
the lot of modern man.
Here we shall forge iron, work
bronze, temper steel. Here will take
shape domestic utensils, tools for
workers, industrial machinery. Here
will be the cradle of the plow, the
loom, the locomotive, the sword. Here
vulnerable flesh will find armor, feeble
arms levers. Man's potential will
multiply, his efficiency will increase
limitlessly. O Teacher, who hath transformed our feeble compatriots into
giants, blessed be you a thousand times
over![10]

The Positivist Gómez

Halfway through the administration of Miguel
Abadía Méndez, in April 1928, people of Bogotá took
note of a letter from Alfonso López to Enrique
Santos, editor of the Liberal newspaper El Diario
Nacional.[11] The Liberal businessman and party
notable proposed that national problems be discussed
over the coming months in a series of conferences to
be held on Thursday evenings at the Municipal
Theater. Tickets would be moderately priced to
allow all citizens to attend. López included names
of speakers who had agreed to participate and their
chosen topics. Alejandro Bejarano would speak on
divorce, Luis López de Mesa on Colombia's international reputation, and Gómez on public works.
Alfonso López's Teatro Municipal conferences
were an immediate success. Colombia was in an
introspective mood during the late 1920s, and the
informal discussions of national problems appealed
to a broad cross section of the citizenry. There
was good attendance at the conferences held during
the month of May, and the barn-like municipal
theater was packed the afternoon of June 5 when it
came Gómez's turn to speak. His topic, public
works, seemed prosaic enough. But all knew his way
of making the most boring subject come alive--not
just come alive but set blood pounding in temples,
evoke hot verbal response and sometimes the threat

63

of physical violence; thus a hush of anticipation fell over the largely male audience as the handsome, portly Gómez rose to deliver what all suspected would be a memorable discourse. They were not disappointed.

Gómez's first Teatro Municipal speech created a sensation. Detractors blasted it as "negativistic and pseudoscientific," plagiarized from Revista de Occidente and Labor,[12] "full of contradictions and monstrous hyperboles,"[13] the product of "terrible determinism and out-of-date sociology."[14] The speaker was accused of employing oratorical devices "to create a profound spiritual depression in his listeners in order to make them more docile to the suggestions of his combative and destructive temperament."[15] "As Doctor Gómez spoke, I felt myself invaded by the tropics," wrote one listener[16]; another described his words as falling on a happy and confident town "like a tombstone."[17] Another expressed a widely held feeling that with the speech, "Doctor Gómez buried his political career under the heaviest tombstone."[18] That judgment appeared to be borne out when some weeks later members of Gómez's own party introduced a bill in Congress intended to make speeches critical of the fatherland punishable by a term in prison.

The speech, however, was also greeted with praise. The editorialist for El Diario Nacional found that Gómez had broken into a thousand pieces "the layer of collective idiocy that harbors the parasitic classes," and called his speech a welcome change from the constant, boring "rubbish" about Colombia's natural riches and glorious future.[19] Eduardo Santos, owner of the Liberal newspaper El Tiempo, lauded his courage in saying unpleasant things about his country, something that neither Bolivian essayist Alcides Argüedas nor Peruvian writer García Calderón dared to do. The owner and publisher of El Tiempo concluded that the speaker's "desolating words" inspired him to work harder to make Colombia a great nation.[20] Liberal El Espectador's editorialist wrote that while Gómez's words caused revulsion among his listeners, at the same time they caused our "intellectual elite to awaken from its current marasmus." The writer concluded that while Gómez's talk may have been full of pseudo-scientific and incorrect generalizations, the fact that no more than four men in the nation were sufficiently well-informed to refute him-- unlike in Europe or North America--provided lamentable support for his arguments.[21]

What did Gómez say to evoke these responses?
He began his two-hour lecture by informing the
audience that his goal was to help Colombia shed the
"vices" of hermeticism and silence. He wanted the
nation "to know itself." No nation lying at
Colombia's latitude had been the seat of a "true
culture," he said. Thanks only to the Andean
highlands running through parts of their territories
have Colombia, Venezuela, and Ecuador been able to
create cultures superior to those found in the other
countries lying at the same latitude: "Liberia,
Mandingo, Nigeria, Camarones, Niam-Niam, Chillurk,
parts of Abisinia and Somolia."[22] Unfortunately,
most of Colombia's 1.2 million kilometers fall outside of the cool, culture-producing Andean highlands. Although he knew the nation to possess
considerable natural resources, he reminded his
listeners that Colombia's coal, iron, and water
power were not being exploited, and that oil
resources were being exploited only for the benefit
of foreigners. Turning to the nation's racial
composition, he argued that Colombia's people
reflected the unfortunate consequences of racial
mixture, that the nation's predominately mestizo
population "combines the discordant qualities of
its ancestors": "It's enough to know that neither
in its Spanish ancestry nor in its African and
indigenous ancestry is our race apt for the creation
of either culture or independent, autochthonous
civilization."[23] Gómez next compared Colombia with
seventeenth century Spain, cursed with corrupt and
stupid rulers who brought the nation to ruin. He
continued the historical comparison, likening
Spain's Godoy, who lost Santo Domingo to the French,
with Colombia's Lozano Torrijos, who, he charged,
had recently negotiated away the Colombian Amazon,
and he harshly criticized the Abadía Méndez regime
for squandering natural resources. Concluding, he
asserted that Colombia is "a kind of immense green-
house;" because of this and in "these threatening
circumstances, we can't allow ourselves the luxury
of ineptitude."[24]
    The Teatro Municipal talk of June 5, 1928, and
its sequel, a rebuttal of his critics given on
August 3, were in the nature of secular homilies
aimed at awakening Colombians to their bad government. Colombia should not give away its valuable
possessions out of childlike ignorance as to their
true worth, he chided on August 3. It is an equally
serious mistake to be blindly optimistic about the
nation's prospects, for to do so only promotes "debt

prosperity" that is sure to leave foreign creditors
in possession of Colombia's wealth. He concluded
the second Teatro Municipal talk with an angry blast
at the national government and even the Jesuits for
having been unfaithful to their ideals and for
having lapsed into Spanish-like decadence bearing
frightful consequences for the nation. El Tiempo's
editorialist astutely interpreted Gómez's message in
his piece of August 4. He pointed out that Gómez
was calling attention to the "dense shadows gathering over the nation."

In his Teatro Municipal lectures of 1928,
Gómez clearly demonstrated the commingling of his
"liberalism" and his conservatism through modish
doctrines of positivist savor. The considerable
praise that his lectures received from members of
Colombia's Liberal elite underscores a point made
earlier in this essay--that Latin America's Liberals
and Conservatives found common ground in the
precepts of early twentieth century positivism.

Later published under the suggestive title
Questions on the Progress of Colombia
[Interrogantes], the lectures were a prescription
of what Colombia must do to cure its "spiritual
infirmity" brought on by bad government. The first
lecture began with a long introduction very much in
the conservative liberal tradition that had become
generalized in Latin America by the 1920s. It was
full of judgments on the uniqueness of Colombian
culture supported by a positivistic recitation of
empirical data. The pivotal first lecture was
delivered in a spirit of search for national origins
within an anthropological context. That approach
was informed by a tradition in late nineteenth and
early twentieth century European sociohistorical
writing dictating the search for clues explaining
"national personality." In such writing the theory
of "polygenism," holding that man was created as
separate races, the darker ones inferior to the
lighter ones, combined with Darwin's evolutionary
theory to make race seem the dominant factor in
national development. Gómez's remarks on the racial
character of Colombians that shocked many in his
audience were simply reflections of the dominant
strain in anthropological thought of his day.
Argentine scholar Carlos O. Bunge's assertion that
"race is the key, then climate, followed by history. . . . all are complementary, but blood, the
psychological heritage, is the mainspring of
events,"[25] is identical in spirit to Gómez's remarks
on race in the Interrogantes. The tendency to point

66

to physical environment as determining national
character, the principal point made by Gómez, was a
key feature of the cultural analysis supplied by
both García Calderón and Bolivian Alcides Argüedas.
When Argüedas attributed the Aymaran's harsh
personality to his equally harsh physical
environment, he drew from the same body of geodeterministic thought that moved Gómez to write "the
Indian race . . . seems resigned to misery and
insignificance. It is drugged by the sadness of the
desert, drunk with the melancholy of its highlands
and its forests."[26]

The striking, somber picture of Colombia, its
present state, and future possibilities sketched by
Gómez in his Teatro Municipal talks should not
obscure his purpose in presenting it. He intended
his lectures to be a clinical description of
national ills, complete with a prescription for
curing them. As he asserted in both talks, Colombia
was a "hothouse culture" requiring careful and
intelligent leadership in order to overcome her
imperfections.

Statements such as these suggest the attrac-
tiveness of racial and environmental determinism
among members of Latin America's intellectual elites
during the early decades of the present century.
Like other young men of his time, Gómez believed the
proposition that his nation could be made to progress and that insights from the infant discipline
called "social science" could be brought to bear on
the problem. In spite of its incompatibility with
his doctrinaire conservatism, and notwithstanding
his protests to the contrary, Gómez was not immune
to the dominant intellectual movement of his early
years.

Chapter V

ROMANTIC AND NATIONALIST ELEMENTS

The Romantic Gómez

Although Gómez argued that his thought was
rooted in strictest Roman Catholic orthodoxy--
willingly, joyously received from Jesuit mentors--it
is clear that his ideas were other than strictly
clerical and that his actions were not simply those
of a fanatic or a reactionary. But those other
elements of his ideology were difficult, perhaps
impossible, for Colombians to see after Gómez
launched his attack on Liberalism in 1932. His
fanaticism, exhibited during his battle to seize
control of the Conservative party, earned him the
nickname vaca loca* from partisan Roberto Urdaneta
Arbeláez, and even less appealing ones from
Liberals. In one short column written by El
Tiempo's "Fray Lejón" in 1936, Gómez was referred to
as "the great sick one," "the famous crazy," "a man
created for hatred and dictatorship," a "rabid
mastiff," "the hyena orator," and "the creole
Hitler."[1] No wonder that Liberals had trouble seeing Gómez as anything other than the "Monster" of
their bad dreams. He seemed beyond comprehension, a
malevolent evil force, at the least demented.

In searching out the secular sources of
Gómez's thought, it is helpful to return to the time
before he launched his early 1930s crusade against
Liberalism. It was then that the romantic, nationalistic Gómez, the student of art, literature, and
international affairs became, along with other young
men of his generation, an arbiter of national
politics and culture.

Gómez was a romantic. This is perhaps a risky
characterization, one that seems not to fit if we

---

* vaca loca: A type of firework that moves
rapidly and unpredictably across the ground,
emitting sparks, smoke, and loud noises.

define romanticism in the normal way as a spiritual and artistic movement in opposition to the ideas and postulates of the Enlightenment that reached its apogee in the early nineteenth century. Also Gómez was neither a European nor a contemporary of the famous European romantics. The characterization seems less indiscriminate, however, if we consider romanticism in the context of Western, as opposed to strictly European, history. One of the closest students of that phenomenon, A.O. Lovejoy, demonstrated that there was a "plurality of romanticisms," that persons of distinct cultures and time periods could be considered romantics if they rebelled against the eighteenth century prejudice that all phenomena are explicable through reason and mechanically derived laws.[2] The romantic movement was thus not limited by chronology or national boundaries. In this way, Lovejoy provides us an approach to understanding the romanticism of Gómez and a way of explaining how romanticism could flower in Colombia after the mid-nineteenth century. "The years between 1850 and 1890, which witnessed the growth of an abundant literature of a radical, romantic, and utopian character in New Granada (Colombia), are marked by an increasing French influence in national culture," writes historian Jaime Jaramillo Uribe. He supports his assertion with the words of José María Samper:

> The works of Victor Hugo and Alexander Dumas, of Lamartine and Eugene Sué influenced the social novel, poetry, and even books on political history. Two of the most influential works were Lamartine's <u>History of the Girondines</u> and Sue's <u>The Wandering Jew</u>. Modern Spanish poetry was also influential, especially that of Espronceda and Zorilla, works that awakened strong poetic sentiments in the youth.[3]

The social reforms undertaken by New Granada's romantic, radical Liberals inspired a reaction that resulted in the formation of the Conservative party. Conservatives, also imbued with romanticism, opposed the Liberal attack on tradition and objected to the Liberal assault on metaphysics, on revealed truth. Conservative party founders Mariano Ospina Rodríguez and José Eusebio Caro were hardly unique in their response to Liberalism. They merely formed the Colombian wing of the broad reaction to liberalism known as the Counter Enlightenment.[4] Gómez was part of that movement. He attended elementary and secondary school during the high tide of the Conservative-clerical assault on Enlightenment ideals in Colombia and was thoroughly grounded by his Jesuit professors in the writings of romantic conservatives like de Maistre, Bossuet, and Donoso Cortés. The young Gómez also read the novels of Dumas, Hugo, and Lamartine, though presumably he did so after school hours. Combine these intellectual origins with a volatile and emotional personality and what a student of nineteenth and twentieth century Colombian thought describes as the tendency of Colombians to romanticize intellectual constructs,[5] and it is possible to defend the characterization of Gómez as a romantic.

From his first moments as a public man, Gómez hurled himself into the Colombian political maelstrom with what might be called romantic abandon. A description of the early Gómez by Vicente Casas Castañeda begins, "All we childhood friends of Laureano Gómez were romantics." Casas went on to sketch Bogotá and the tertulia* of Gómez as he remembered them forty or more years later:

> We were a group of boys all bordering on adolescence, from all parts of the country. We gathered at the home of our future captain, attracted by the extraordinary prestige that the remarkable man had begun to exercise. . . . He sketched for us the idea of forming an academy and founding a newspaper. He talked of novels, poetry, of political and social consequences of the World War, and he spoke of the famous people who could be seen in those days in the streets of the capital.[6]

Gómez's later political campaigns were colored by the idealistic desire to navigate Colombia's stormy political seas with a defiance reminiscent of the protagonist in Espronceda's "Song of the Pirate." That image may well have occurred to poet Miguel Rasch Isla as he accompanied Gómez and other members of the Liberal-Conservative coalition who campaigned on behalf of Guillermo Valencia against

---

* tertulia: A social gathering, usually held at a private home.

Marco Fidel Suárez in the 1918 presidential contest. Rasch Isla observed the dashing young "human storm" as he fulminated against Suaréz and praised Valencia. He ultimately concluded that "what really inspired him was the romantic proposition of seeing the author of 'Rites' crowned with the laurels of victory." Recalling an essay in which Gómez praised the poetry of José Asunción Silva, Rasch Isla wrote of Gómez that "his soul is one of those that has a hidden, placid refuge where soothing colloquies with Eternal Beauty are conducted."[7] Who would deny the romantic content of Gómez's remark as he prepared to return from Europe in that eventful year of 1932: "I intend to throw myself into the whirlwind with no illusions. I return completely immune to disenchantment, through my resolve to have no personal ambitions."[8]

If Gómez was a romantic by intellectual, political, and cultural inheritance, as well as by temperament, so too was his romanticism nourished by ideological currents at large in Latin America during the first decade of the twentieth century. From Argentina to Peru to Mexico, young men of the intelligentsia mused on the mediocrity of mass society and its prosaic utilitarian philosophy and raised the cry for a "new idealism" to counter the antinational, anti-Latin spirit that grew in step with admiration for the United States and other "progressive" industrial nations.[9] José Enrique Rodó had provided the movement's ideological canon in his essay Ariel. Though never a declared arielista, Gómez shared spiritual kinship with members of the movement, contemporaries such as José Vasconceles and Francisco García Calderón. His condemnation of Marco Fidel Suárez and other admirers of the "Polar Star" (the U.S.A.) and his defiant rejection of positivism were repeated with equal fervor by the angry young men of Buenos Aires, Lima, and Mexico City. Gómez introduced his La Unidad editorial of January 30, 1915, entitled "Political Disinterest," with a paragraph clothed in "arielismo": "To speak of political disinterest in . . . this century of greed and egotism, when the crop that Jeremy Bentham sowed so long ago has been gathered in the granaries of the bourgeoisie, sounds to many like a romantic braggadocio, not favored by today's practical and positivist criteria; yet he who intends to construct a sound political edifice must make political disinterest his cornerstone." Nor was there a lack of sympathy and understanding between Gómez and the better known arielistas. The

Colombian politician knew and admired most prominent members of the movement and counted several of them as personal friends; for example, he was fond of quoting the works of José Vasconcelos, and the Mexican historian did not spare praise of his Colombian contemporary.[10]

Gómez's romanticism is further apparent in his belief in human individuality, the uniqueness of cultures and historic epochs, and the ongoing, linear development of history. It is admittedly difficult to separate his rationally derived Christian belief in the relativity of cultures and political institutions from his historicism. But to the extent that Gómez was sensitive to differences in peoples and nations, believed that individuals achieve fullest personal development through membership in organic communities, attributed significance to the working of "spirit" in history, and advocated the creation of an ideal society in Colombia, he was one with the romantic nationalists who subscribed to historicist canons.

It is through his belief in the creative and history-making capacity of the extraordinary individual that the romantic, historicist Gómez is most clearly perceived. Glorification of the individual was central to the romantic reaction to mechanistic, deterministic Enlightenment philosophy, as was the notion that some men are, by right of exceptional ability, destined to outstrip the rest. The view that certain men are endowed with heroic qualities that enable them to perform prodigious feats achieved its most complete expression in the works of Thomas Carlyle. Carlyle's theory of history captivated Gómez, who constantly drew upon it to justify his own belief that history is made by great men: "the great thinker Carlyle . . . said with absolute clarity . . . 'seek out the most capable, the most able man in any nation. Then grant him supremacy, render him unswerving reverence, and you will have acquired for that nation a perfect government'," he wrote in 1916.[11] Conversely, nations lacking great leaders could not hope to approach greatness of earlier times. Present-day North Americans, he opined, were pale imitations of honorable leaders like Benjamin Franklin and Abraham Lincoln. The passage of time changes peoples, making it impossible to recognize them as "members of the same race."[12] Gómez naturally attributed Colombia's problems to the lack of great men there. It seemed to him that for want of extraordinary leaders, life was boring in his country, a place where "the days follow one another with cruel monotony, grey and insignificant. One could say that we're a people without contemporary history . . . we have no history, but we're not happy either."[13]

In Gómez's view, three kinds of men are present in superior cultures: saints, heroes, thinkers and artists. Colombia had such men in years past, as he explained to the Senate in a speech titled "The Conflict of Two Cultures." He identified Simón Bolívar, father of Colombian national independence, as his nation's foremost hero. In comparison with Bolívar, another independence leader, Francisco Paula de Santander, was simply a mediocrity. (This was a taunt directed toward his Liberal colleagues, who regarded Santander as the historic founder of their party.) Continuing his panegyric to Colombia's great men, he asked rhetorically: "Has the United States of America produced anyone the equal of don Miguel Antonio Caro . . . what man as authentically wise as Rufino José Cuervo can the United States exhibit?"[14]

By the year 1928, Gómez's earlier pessimism over the lack of great men in the Colombia of his own era had somewhat abated, for he found an exemplary figure in General Pedro Nel Ospina. His essay "The Character of General Ospina" was a paean to the recently deceased former president under whom Gómez served as Minister of Public Works.[15] His spirits were further lifted by the example of Indian leader Mahatma Gandhi, a man who combined heroism and spirituality in a way that he found inspiring. Gandhi was to Gómez the ideal politician, honorable, ascetic, and endowed with a power of will that made the British tremble. Gómez placed a statue of Gandhi at the entrance of his study and once, in the early 1930s, threatened to lead his party in Gandhian passive resistance to the government of Liberal President Olaya Herrera. Never did he lavish greater praise on anyone than that bestowed on Gandhi, a man whose precept and example he defined as "Christlike."[16]

There are interesting parallels in the political thought of Gómez and that of Thomas Carlyle. The Scotsman developed his philosophy of the hero in history following the failure of parliamentary reform during the early nineteenth century. He longed for a new Cromwell to step in, clean British democracy's Augean stables, and harry Communists and other undesirables out of the land. Gómez, too, had the elitist's mistrust of democracy and believed a

74

hero was needed to provide the leadership Colombia
lacked. In the sturdy figure of Pedro Nel Ospina,
he found a peerless model, a man who "with hard,
uncompromising physical labor became the Colombian
who cleared more jungle and turned more primeval
forest into productive farmland than perhaps any
other." Citing Carlyle's study of Cromwell, Gómez
reminded that great men are silent, but they are the
salt of the earth. "Pity the nation where there are
few or none of those men--men like Cromwell and
Ospina."[17]
     Thomas Carlyle developed a dynamic conception
of history quite like that of the German romantics.
It was their belief that the spiritual life of a
people must be taken into account when designing
national institutions.[18] Organic community must be
respected if the desired coherence and permanence
are to be achieved. That was the same logic and
terminology that Gómez employed in explaining and
defending his "organic" constitutional reform of
1953. He asserted that an "authoritarian democracy"
was right for Colombia and that inorganic democracy,
the one-half plus one, was not. That sort of democracy was imported, alien, unnatural, and destructive
to national institutions. As early as 1921, Gómez
employed the Carlylian idiom in arguing that
national institutions must conform to national
personality. Carlyle, he said, depicts the hero as
the peerless leader in whose person are reflected
the principal ideas and institutions of his nation,
and whose genius leads his people along the path of
progress. While the chief goal of the English
thinker is that of praising heroes, said Gómez, "he
underlines the immediate and decisive influence of
institutions in the development of peoples, inasmuch
as those men were no different than those who gave
their respective nations the laws necessary for
their development."[19] His later remarks on the
failure of "mechanical civilization" in Colombia and
the world are closely attuned to Carlyle's belief,
stated a century earlier, that industrial society
destroys the "Moral Force" which is the parent of
all other force.[20]
     Biography was Gómez's preferred reading.
"We've had since childhood a passion for history and
for the Napoleonic legend," he admitted in one of
his El Siglo editorials.[21] But he did not limit his
study to books on the Corsican. Biographies of
Elizabeth I, Czar Alexander II, Charles V, Isabel
the Catholic, Justinian, Peter the Great, Julius
Ceasar, Alexander the Great, Charlemagne, and other

notables of history lined his bookshelves. Gómez was also intrigued by the lives of "great spirits" like Joan of Arc, Tolstoi and Dostoevski, and Mahatma Gandhi. He also studied the histories of persons with whom he felt no spiritual kinship: Rousseau, Voltaire, Erasmus, Hitler, and Mussolini. That reading was by personal inclination, carried out, one suspects, in the romantic hope that it might help Gómez identify the hero his nation needed: "One can only imagine what this country could be in the future if, through divine providence, a great man should someday appear among us."[22] Gómez never said that he thought himself to be that man, though some have read that into his youthful remark "I intend to be an important man."[23]

Nearly all of Gómez's reading in the area of social criticism was of the pessimistic variety--a romantic reaction to the Panglossian optimism spawned by Enlightenment rationalism. His speeches and writings were filled with references to works bearing titles like The Twilight of Civilization, The Decline of the West, The Crisis of Western Philosophy, and The Illusion of Progress. Among his favorite chroniclers of social decay were political writers Hilaire Belloc, Charles Benost, and Ernest Hello, and philosophers Nicholai Berdyaev, Vladimir Solevief, Jacques Maritain, Georges Sorel, and Oswald Spengler. When in a particularly gloomy mood, he reached back to the nineteenth century for citations from the pessimistic writings of de Maistre, Bossuet, Donoso Cortés, and Bonald.

It is significant that in none of his public expressions did Gómez cite that most devastating critic of modern society Friedrich Nietzsche. The point is instructive in that the writings of Nietzsche link the romantic revolt against modernity with the philosophy of violent nationalism given practical application by fascist dictators Mussolini and Hitler. Gómez was decidedly nationalistic, and he was also a romantic; yet unlike many contemporaries with whom he shared political affinities-- arielista José de la Riva-Agüero, for example-- Gómez never endorsed the extreme form of romantic nationalism known as fascism.

Gómez also distanced himself from reactionary writers Bossuet, de Maistre, and Bonald. Although on occasion he shared their pessimism about prospects for the human race, he never went so far as to endorse their absolutism. Throughout his life, he cleaved to the Suarezian social contract theory and the Catholic doctrine that citizens possess free will and a rational ability to select the form of government best for them. He firmly believed that history and personal idiosyncracy dictated that Colombia should be a democratic republic. Nor did Gómez fall into the papally condemned error of creating a "political theology" by which religion was used to justify a given form of government. De Maistre and Bossuet were reproached for viewing the church as an instrument of social control rather than as an element in the sacramental life of the community, and Charles Maurras was excommunicated for his positivistic advocacy of the church as an instrument of social control. Gómez espoused the orthodox view of the church as a chiefly sacramental institution.

Gómez's belief in free will, natural law, and human progress founded in reason made it impossible for him to view society as the instinctual, irrational organism posited by the European romantics. For him, society was not a biological organism ruled by instinct and reflex, but rather a corporatively constituted entity in which the individual lived in a state of creative tension, pulled one way by his anarchistic will and another by his common good-seeking rationality. These beliefs saved Gómez from falling into the unremitting pessimism of a Donoso Cortés or the nihilistic misanthropy of a Nietzsche.

Nor did the Middle Ages hold a special fascination for Gómez. While he considered himself a Thomist and thought in terms of an idealized society of order, his vision was forward looking and metaphysical rather than based on a false historical vision. His ideal was the Augustinian City of God, not the imagined medieval time of innocence and unity glorified by Novalis.

In sum, Gómez was not an extreme romantic. His thought was eclectic, and undergirding it were fundamental beliefs that kept him from joining the extremists who in the 1930s endorsed totalitarian solutions to social problems.

The Nationalist Gómez

The nationalism of Gómez was shaped by the sad events taking place in turn of the century Colombia. He remembered the late nineteenth and early twentieth centuries as a time of anxiety over the War of a Thousand Days, of despair over the loss of Panama to a foreign predator. His indignity was heightened in the years immediately following the loss of Panama by the spectacle of President Raphael

77

Reyes and Conservative party leader Marco Fidel
Suárez holding up the United States as a model that
Colombia should emulate in its movement toward progress. All of this rankled in the heart of young
Gómez, causing him to become a passionate and outspoken nationalist.
While the wound inflicted by Panama's force-
able excision was still fresh, Gómez was unstinting
in his criticism of the United States. In a June
17, 1912, La Unidad editorial concerning the proposed payment of reparations by the U.S. to
Colombia, he vented his anger against the Anglo-
Saxon republic:

> We have said before that the hand that
> pays us is the same one that has, on
> other occasions, thrown us a few crumbs
> to seal our lips, the same one that only
> yesterday strangled our sovereignty, the
> same one that even today hasn't troubled
> itself to hear our patriotic protest.

He concluded his editorial with a ringing challenge:
"Men who in your veins feel the fever of rebellion,
do not seek the friendship of the Yankee. . . . Let
the Russian come, or the Arab--welcome the Muslim if
you wish--but don't sell yourselves to the Yankee!"
By 1912 Gómez was beginning to voice his
antipathy toward Conservative party leader Marco
Fidel Suárez. Suárez has said, wrote the twenty-
three year old Gómez, that Colombia should follow
the "Polar Star." But that orientation, he
reminded, is what is going to cost Mexico the
formidable sacrifice that she is starting to make
even now. The United States has never wanted for
"brilliant sophistries" for use in exploiting Latin
Americans, sheltered beneath "the elastic Monroe
Doctrine, a banner of despolation every bit as
cynical as the one pirates flew from the masts of
their ships."[24]
Not long after that blast, Gómez placed the
question in broader context. In November 1912,
again writing in La Unidad, he interpreted the
actions of the United States and other industrial
nations in terms of economic imperialism. Is it
from a spirit of justice or simply for reasons of
self-interest and convenience that the Yankees want
to settle the Panama issue, he asked rhetorically.
Supplying the answer, he wrote that the North
Americans obviously were acting in the spirit of
their own national self-interest and most certainly

78

not that of Colombia. He went on to sketch the history of North American states, with special reference to the case of Nicaragua. Between 1908 and 1912, he recalled, the U.S. toppled several governments there in a successful attempt to control it. That tampering brought about a chaotic situation in Nicaragua that "has borne that nation to desperation and misery and has given the U.S. Department of State an excuse for inundating Nicaraguan cities with Yankee soldiers."[25]

Three years later, he turned his attention to the United Fruit Company and the implications of its operations in Colombia's Caribbean lowlands. In criticizing the power and privileges of that North American corporation, he anticipated by fourteen years the celebrated indictment of the company by Jorge Eliécer Gaitán following the massacre of striking workers in 1928. Gómez's editorial was prompted by the proposal of an official of United Fruit, one Mr. Marshall, that the government place his company in control of a local railroad. In the words of Gómez, such action would "signify the end of the banana industry in Colombia." United Fruit would have monopoly control over both the production and transportation of Colombian bananas. Acceding to the request of the North American company would also be a grievous infringement of national sovereignty.[26]

The support that Gómez and his newspaper gave the Central Powers during World War I must also be interpreted through his fear of British, French, and American military and economic might. Until its demise in mid-1916, La Unidad regularly carried lengthy reports on the war and even printed human interest pieces on war heroes and their families, provided by the German embassy. The paper's pro-German stance produced criticism from the pro-Ally majority in Bogotá. At length Gómez explained his apparent Germanophilia in an editorial of December 13, 1915, that he titled "The Convenience of a German Victory":

> Several times we've argued in this news-
> paper that Latin American nations should
> lean toward Germany in the present
> conflict, this because the victory of
> that nation would favor the autonomy and
> development of South American nations
> presently menaced by Yankee imperialism.

He added that all of the principal nations allied

79

against Germany--England, Italy, and France--had in recent years abused Colombia and her sister republics. Throughout the first phase of his political career, Gómez consistently employed a nationalistic idiom in his public expressions, speaking out against all who he thought were compromising Colombian interests through their venality or ineptness. That was the spirit in which he lectured fellow Conservative Insignares Piñeros in May of 1928: "A combination of three factors causes today's politico-financial entities to dwarf those of a century ago. They are as follows: the large number of government contracts, the cleverness of the business community, and the ineptitude of the government."[27] Some weeks later, in his first Teatro Municipal conference, Gómez earned the wrath of Fabio Lozano's sons by likening the diplomat, whose recently concluded boundary negotiations with Peru were praised in most quarters, to the infamous minister of Charles IV of Spain, Manuel Godoy. Fulminated Gómez.

> How many of our own Godoys are striving today for the title 'Prince of the Amazon,' the territory we've just lost, Only the Colombian people's profound ignorance of their traditions and their rights has permitted them to praise this new mutilation of national territory-- just as the crass ignorance of the Spanish people allowed them to exalt the destruction of their empire. Those who have applauded the treaty with Peru don't know what they're doing.[28]

A changing international scene caused Gómez to modify his nationalist ideas in succeeding decades; for example, his hostility toward the United States softened when, following World War II, that nation announced its intention to save the world from "Godless communism," a position that he applauded. But in spite of such changes in approach, Gómez, like most other Latin American conservatives, remained an outspoken nationalist.

Chapter VI

THE ATTACK ON LIBERALISM

Gómez versus the Colombian Liberal
Party, 1932-1946

The period September 1928 to June 1932 was
pivotal in the life of Gómez. He spent those years
in Europe with his family, living first as a student
and tourist, and later as Colombia's chief minister
to Germany. There he observed firsthand the tribu-
lations of Europe's democratic regimes and was in
Berlin during the emergence and rise of Adolph
Hitler and his National Socialist party.

As Gómez observed Germany's agony, he pondered
news reaching him from Colombia. His party split
its vote in the presidential election of April 1930,
allowing the Liberals to gain power for the first
time in nearly fifty years. The new President,
Enrique Olaya Herrera, launched a program of social
and economic reform as his copartisans flexed their
newfound political muscle at the expense of hapless
Conservatives.

Early in 1932, Gómez resigned his ambassador-
ship and returned home to oppose the new Liberal
party regime. His tenacious and ultimately successful campaign to drive the   Liberals from power
would become a central theme of Colombian history
during the 1930s and 1940s. Seen in broader
context, the battle of Gómez was the same as that
fought by all Latin American conservatives before
and during World War II as they labored to maintain
the coherence of their movement in a global setting
dominated by the death struggle between fascism and
liberalism.

In September 1928, Gómez and his family
departed Bogotá for their tour of the Continent.
It was a propitious moment for such a trip. Gómez
was by then thirty-nine years old, fresh from his
controversial lectures at Bogotá's Teatro Municipal,
and at the peak of his popularity and prestige. He
had served his nation in several diplomatic capaci-

ties, and while ambassador to Argentina earlier in the decade, he had broadened his knowledge through graduate study in public administration, economics, and the social sciences. But still he felt his education wanting. He was drawn to Europe, as he later explained, both by "an intense intellectual curiosity" and out of "concern over the contradictions and uncertainties of the contemporary world."[1] He sought to ease his anxiety by reflecting on what he referred to as "the gigantic tree of Western culture," particularly its French and Spanish branches, and he wanted to study firsthand the great debates shaking Europe and the world as the first third of the twentieth century neared its end.

Gómez's arrival in Europe coincided with a rush of decisive events. First came the economic collapse of 1929-30 that heightened social and political tensions all over Europe. Stalin was consolidating his hold on Russia--as Mussolini had four years earlier on Italy--and as Hitler was beginning to do in Germany. Spain was torn by debates between extremists of the left and right, and in faraway India, Congress Party President Gandhi served notice on Europe that colonialism was dying. France, the residence of the Gómez family during its first two years in Europe, was wallowing in corrupt and inept republican rule. Gómez mused on all this while hastening to make the most of his time away from Colombia. "Here time flies with distressing rapidity," he wrote a friend in May 1929, adding that "after many months here I feel as if I've just arrived." A bemused Alfonso López, in France on business at that time, commented on Gómez's efforts at self-improvement: "I see Laureano frequently . . . he continues to study."[2] Clearly under the spell of Paris, though put off by what he perceived as its inhabitants' aim to relieve foreign visitors of their money, Gómez penned glowing descriptions of his surroundings to friends back home:

> The quartier that so fascinates us is beautiful even from an external, superficial point of view. The Arch of Triumph, that presides over it, is perhaps the noblest and most harmonious monument in the world. It is located on a slight rise and dominates all the avenues that radiate from the plaza whose center it occupies. When seen against the sunset of these long spring

82

days, along the Place de la Concorde, or down the stupendous Champs Elyseés, it seems to symbolize Western man's most sublime achievement. The cupola, which reflects the pride and prestige of the Renaissance (and of which there are beautiful replicas in the Pantheon and the monument of the Invalids), yields to the suggestive power of the monument's silhouette--enormous yet elegant and graceful, outlined against the golden afternoon sky. There are moments when the sun, wrapped in its best purple mantle, shows through the prodigious curve. At that instant the Arch seems truly to be a portal to the immortal regions. . . ."[3]

In September of 1930, shortly after the fall of the Conservatives in Colombia and accession of Liberal President Olaya Herrera, Gómez was named Minister Plenipotenciary to Germany, and by October he and his family were ensconced in Berlin. Gómez presented his credentials to Marshal von Hindenburg the following month and settled in to oversee Colombian diplomatic and commercial interests. His diplomatic dispatches of 1931 and early 1932 are full of references to the steady gains of Hitler's National Socialist Party and the economic chaos that attended his rise. During this period, Berlin was moved by the story of a young man who murdered his wife and son and then committed suicide after discovering his younger son dead of starvation. In March of 1932, Gómez wired Foreign Minister Urdaneta Arbeláez of Adolph Hitler's attempt to force Chancellor Heinrich Brüning into ceding power to a right-wing coalition. He concluded his cable on an ominous note: "The atmosphere is charged with disturbing elements, both political and economic. The Continent's future is growing darker by the minute."[4]

The dispatch was one of Gómez's last from Berlin. Within two months, he tendered his resignation and returned home to occupy his newly acquired seat in the Colombian Senate. Gómez had profited from his trip. He would soon apply the lessons learned in Europe to Colombian problems.

During the fourteen years between his return and his party's victory at the polls in 1946, Gómez worked relentlessly and with remarkable energy to return the Conservatives to power. After seizing

83

control of the party through a series of punishing
Senate speeches against party members whom he called
collaborationists and traitors, he fixed his attention on the Liberals. He damned Olaya Herrera for
the widespread violence against Conservatives
attending the Liberal return to power. In 1934 he
published his indictment in a collection of newspaper pieces titled <u>Comentarios a un régimen</u>.[5] Next
he turned on his old friend Alfonso López. Though
it cost him a cerebral hemorrhage in early 1935,
Gómez led his party in intransigent opposition that
included electoral abstention through most of
López's formidable first administration. The
ostensible reason for abstention was the chief
executive's inability to control violence against
Conservatives in the <u>campo</u> and his reluctance to
reform electoral procedures as demanded by the
opposition. In the following administration, that
of Eduardo Santos (1938-42), Gómez allowed party
members to participate in elections, all the while
protesting the continued harassment of his partisans
by Liberals. The most notable incident of anti-
Conservative violence during Santos's term was the
police attack at Gachetá, Cundinamarca in early 1939
that left a dozen Conservatives dead. Gómez's anti-
Liberal campaign became shriller and more personal
when Alfonso López returned to the presidency in
1942. Three years later López resigned, leaving
young Alberto Lleras to complete his term. The
following year, Gómez engineered his party's recap-
ture of the presidency, thanks in part to Liberal
disunity. Perseverance had paid off. Conservatism
would dominate Colombia for the ensuing seven years.
    The written and verbal attack against Liberal-
ism that Gómez led between 1932 and 1946 had two
aspects. First was the frontal assault--an incessant pounding of the enemy political position during
the fourteen years of the Liberal reform.[6] His
second and much more subtle campaign was against
liberal ideas. By exploiting every flaw and inconsistency in philosophic liberalism, all the while
arguing the strengths of conservatism, Gómez aimed
to undermine the opposition's morale and inspire his
own forces. The success of his strategy was obvious
when a thoroughly dispirited Alfonso López left the
presidency in 1945, and the disoriented Liberal
party split its vote between Gabriel Turbay and
Jorge Eliécer Gaitán the following year.
    Before Gómez could get his campaign against
the Liberals underway in 1932, he had to secure
control of his own party. That meant removing

84

Antioquian politician Román Gómez from nominal Conservative leadership.[7] He did so with a ferocity that made the innocuous functionary, whom Gómez accused of trafficking with the Liberals, sound like a modern day Attila the Hun. The most famous portion of Gómez's indictment of Román Gómez is worth repeating here, for it conveys the tone and spirit of the verbal and written barrage that he would next direct against Liberals. With memorable apostrophe, he faced Román Gómez:

> You, Crispín, evil man--petty player in the cheap farce--violator of the Constitution and the Laws! You, Crispín, sly opportunist, who turns official influence to personal advantage, and to that of your relatives, followers, and lackeys! You, Crispín, beggarly seller of miserable properties, stolen from the afflicted who cry out from their prison cells! You, violator of sacrosanct private correspondence to promote your private business interests and your political machinations! You, Crispín, who clumsily conceals your true intent as you darken the corridors of the ministries, payroll offices, and government agencies, reaping the perquisites of a complacent administration to feed your immense horde of uncles, nephews and other relatives . . . You, Crispín, who profane the grave, that should be left undisturbed, to fling its ashes against me under the illusion that you can stay me on the path of justice! You, unimaginative calumniator, who has been unable to back your hateful charges except with nameless accusers! You, upon whose shoulders press, and will eternally press, the horrible tragedy of a reputation ruined by your venal crime that victimizes an innocent home! You, Crispín, whose very presence sullies the Senate, filling it with the shadows of your crimes--you have wanted to turn the Republic into an abject thing that we cannot venerate because you vilify and lower it with unmerited vainglory. The Senate will never again be great while you are seated here.[8]

With Román Gómez out of the way, the new
Conservative party chief began his assault on
liberalism. The titles and dates of some of his
incandescent political pieces suggest both their
content and the consistency with which Gómez
produced them: "The Futility of Violence," 1932;
"Chaux, or the Capitalist Bolshevik," 1934; "Under
the Power of Mr. Alfonso López," 1936; "The Right of
Collective Self-Defense," 1939; "Diatribe against
President Santos," 1940; "Denunciation of a
Minister-Contractor," 1941; "Symptoms of Decay,"
1942; "Letter to the Father of Chaos," 1943; "A
Miserable Humbug," 1945.[9] Each of these editorials
and speeches is a model of Colombian political
polemic.

Gómez's writings against philosophic liberalism are ideological in nature and are therefore more
important to this study than are his political
writings. At their most basic, they were aimed at
discrediting liberalism and everything to the left
of it, and at presenting conservatism as the best,
indeed the only, philosophy for Colombians. But
Gómez was careful to argue that true conservatism
did not embrace everything on the right. In an
important doctrinal speech titled "Our Ideological
Program," given at Chía on September 11, 1932, he
reminded his listeners that for genuine conservatives, nationalism is secondary to doctrinal purity.
Conservatives, he lectured, love the fatherland,
but only when it is a civilized, law-abiding one
where civil life is governed by constitutional
precept. The good conservative, according to Gómez,
"Loathes dictatorship, repudiates violence and brute
force; he makes himself a servant of the law, he
loves fairness, and he seeks justice against the
abuses of power, capital, and of elites whose
strength is founded in iniquity;"[10] thus, he sent an
unmistakable message to the fascistic "Leopardo"
faction of the party--a message that became clearer
in the ensuing months as he published searing criticisms of both Hitler and Mussolini.[11] He never
deviated from the doctrinal course set at Chía:
Colombian conservatism was both Roman Catholic and
republican.

His anti-Liberal pieces hammered at the
notions that liberalism had wrecked the modern world
and that if Colombians were not careful, their fate
would be that of unhappy Europe. These writings
fell into four categories. First were articles
holding up liberalism as harmful to modern man and
his world and arguing, at the same time, that only

conservatism showed the way to social salvation. The following titles are indicative of that genre: "Traditionalism versus Barbarism," "The Oppression of the Modern World," "Symptoms of Decay," "The Depersonalization of Life," "The Ruination of Mankind."[12] Related to these pieces are Gómez's writings on modern art as illustrative of the decline of Western civilization. Here we find his essay "Expressionism as a Symptom of Laziness and Inability in Art," and his articles ridiculing the modernist poetry of Colombian León de Greiff and Chilean Pablo Neruda: "A Literary Marvel: 'The Quadruple Ballad' of León de Greiff," and "Pablo Neruda, a Jokester."[13] Most numerous of Gómez's antiliberal pieces are those historical in nature, usually focusing on European history. Between June 11 and 26, 1940, we find six El Siglo editorials in which he almost gloatingly attributes the fall of France to liberal sins committed under the Third Republic.[14] The best concentration of such writing devoted to Colombian history are the eighteen El Siglo editorials appearing between February and June of 1940 under the collective title The Myth of Santander.[15] There he attacks the opposition by arguing that the man revered by Colombian Liberals as the historic founder of their party was no liberal at all. What then was Santander? Gómez concluded ringingly, "Santander was a jackal."[16]

Denunciations of liberalism as the deluder of Colombian politicians make up the third category of Gómez's punitive pieces. Here are grouped articles with titles like "The Bankruptcy of Liberalism" and "There Is No Escaping History," against Alfonso López's reform of the Constitution of 1886, and his heroic defense of the Concordat against Liberal modifications in 1942.[17] Related to these writings are Gómez's warnings against the dangers of moderation in the face of the Liberal threat, "The Moderate, Our Most Dangerous Enemy," and his insistence that Colombia's "Liberal Republic" was leading the nation to its doom: "The Disparagement of Authority."[18]

Finally, we come to his criticisms, cloaked in literary guise, of the morality of prominent Liberals and their government. In 1945 we find Gómez writing under his pseudonym Jacinto Ventura, gleefully describing seventeenth century Spanish decadence in "Backdrop," and illicit love and political assassination in "Royal Love Affairs, a Political Assassination in the Times of Quevedo."[19]

These labors had taken a heavy toll on Gómez's

health by 1946, but they had caused even more damage
to the Liberal regime. Early in that year he was
saying little about the upcoming presidential campaign but was secretly relishing the near certainty
that his personal ordeal of sixteen years was almost
at an end. His party still had not announced a
presidential candidate--Gómez assured the Liberals
that he would not run and claimed that he intended
to vote for the flamboyant antiestablishment
Liberal, Jorge Eliécer Gaitán. One afternoon in
February 1946, a group of Liberals and Conservatives
was enjoying the hospitality of Fernando Mazuera at
his hacienda near Bogotá. Talk turned to the
Liberal party split and whether or not Gaitán's
opponent, Gabriel Turbay, would withdraw from the
race. What was Dr. Gómez's opinion? "I don't know
if Turbay will withdraw. The only thing I'll bet on
is that he'll cry. . . ." "How so?" asked Abelardo
Forero Benavides. Gómez, outwardly annoyed, but no
doubt chuckling inwardly, responded "Cry, cry!
Don't you know what that is. Real crying. He'll
shed real tears."[20]
       True to his prediction, the Liberals lost the
presidential election of 1946. At the last moment,
Gómez engineered the candidacy of Mariano Ospina
Pérez, a distinguished industrialist from the
department of Antioquia. Ospina won with a plurality, and an embittered Gabriel Turbay departed
Colombia for France where he died a short time
later.

A Conservative Ideologist Interprets History

       By now the reader knows Gómez as a charismatic
conservative politican whose thought and actions
were motivated by a conviction that the best and
only course for Colombia was the one charted by the
Roman Catholic church in its philosophia perennis.
He knows too that Gómez led Conservatives in intransigent opposition to the Liberal party and liberal
ideas, ultimately becoming national president and
later losing that position following his attempt to
restructure politics and society along authoritarian
and "organic" lines. These facts are sufficient to
present Gómez in profile, but they provide at best
an incomplete picture of his thought. Only through
appreciation of Gómez as an ideological thinker can
he be understood.
       One of the peculiarities of Colombian histori-
ography is that Gómez's ideological nature has never
been thoroughly analyzed. This neglect is all the

more striking given his openness about his idiosyncratic view of the world. Gómez constantly
reminded audiences that his actions were determined
by Roman Catholic philosophy, described variously as
a "marvelous and harmonious structure," "a total
solution," or "a purifying fire," that gave him "a
conviction that is total."[21] He constantly urged
his followers to "see" present and past history as
he did, warning that not to do so would bring dire
consequences to the nation and to themselves. An
El Siglo editorial of June 21, 1942 provides a good
example of his evoking for his readers an ideological vision. "Blind is he who doesn't see that a
process is underway to liquidate an enormous accumu-
lation of injustices, depredations, and villainies,"
he wrote. "Humanity has been impelled toward positivist ends, with willful disregard of moral
precepts. . . . The crisis is underway and its
outcome isn't long in coming." Seven years later,
in a speech warning that Colombia was in danger of
falling to communist revolutionaries, he called it
the primordial duty of Conservatives to achieve a
"clear vision" of the danger in which the nation
presently found itself. "Not to see it," he continued, "to close our eyes before the acts that
oblige us to keep them open, would be a surrender of
such magnitude that history would judge most severely those of us who commit for the mental cowardice
of not wanting to see things as they are."[22]
    Evidence of the persuasiveness of Gómez's
vision lies in the enthusiastic way Conservatives
greeted his ideologically inspired harangues against
Liberals and liberalism and the vehemence with which
Liberals answered them. Hundreds of adulatory tele-
grams bearing the names of thousands of party
members flooded the offices of El Siglo following
every major speech by Gómez. Liberal outcry against
these same messages frequently surpassed their
acclaim by Conservatives. Following a 1942 Senate
speech in which Gómez stated that the Masons were
subverting Colombia and the western world, Enrique
Santos angrily denounced the remarks as "ravings,"
adding that "the attitude of the Conservative chief
is anachronistic, irrational, and puerile."[23]
Liberal rejection of the ideological Gómez reached
its extreme in 1942 when psychiatrist José Socarrás
concluded that he was insane: "In Gómez's mind,
misery and prosperity have alternately held sway,
independence and slavery, backwardness and progress,
peace and war in Colombia. Fortunately he's a
vacillating madman . . . and our intelligent people

are a little suspicious of his madness."[24] Socarrás perceived Gómez as an ideologist, but he saw only insanity in that fact. Journalist Luis Eduardo Nieto Caballero, the most perceptive of all Liberal Gómez-watchers, agreed that he was an ideologue, but did not go so far as to say that it implied insanity. "For him reality is something preconceived," wrote Nieto in 1942, "His mind feeds . . . on 'catatimic images,' that's to say altered according to the observer. His thought is vagrant . . . his mind has those light filters that only admit what accords with his temperament."[25]

The term "ideological" is not used lightly in describing Gómez's way of viewing the world. Rather it is used to describe a particular way of bringing the data of perception into accord with a preconceived and all-embracing design. Ideologies may vary, but in that they are held "ideologically," they share a fine uniformity that may be appreciated by examining several characteristics of ideological thought.[26]

First is the characteristic so astutely alluded to by Luis Nieto Caballero. The ideologist presents his system of belief as a thoughtful attempt to provide an explicit and coherent theory of man, society, and the world. It is an idealized way of seeing, a "total vision," to use Gómez's words. Second, one cannot perceive the world as the ideologist does unless he knows what that ideology is. This is to say that the ideologist cannot see the world as the nonideologist does. Nieto Caballero alluded to this feature of ideological thinking when he described Gómez as a man looking through filters "that only admit what accords with his temperament." We may also depict the ideologist as one who arranges the data of perception in accord with a preconceived schema or structure, from which it can be deduced that he sees what he believes he sees and does not believe what he sees;[27] thus, in 1942 Gómez professed to see a Masonic plot, and no one could convince him otherwise. In 1949 he warned that Communists were about to topple the government, though the communist legions that he constantly evoked were nowhere in evidence. Enrique Santos imperfectly understood this phantasmagorical aspect of Gómez's thought in 1942 when he called the Conservative's warning of Masonic conspiracy "child-like." Gómez responded in an El Siglo editorial titled "A Typically Masonic Newspaper," in which he pointed out in his accustomed manner that the Santos brothers were both Masons, and that their

newspaper El Tiempo was therefore a tool of the
international Masonic conspiracy. As such it was
undermining Catholic Colombia and pushing it toward
"rationalism" and "naturalism."[28]

An important consequence of the ideologist's
way of perceiving is his inability to communicate
meaningfully with anyone not sharing his vision.
Gómez was constantly at odds with prominent members
of his own party whose ideological position differed from his own. Augusto Ramírez Moreno and
Silvio Villegas are cases in point. Gómez considered them to be dangerous Conservative schismatics.
Gómez's heated denunciations of Mariano Ospina Pérez
after 1953 illustrate his shock and chagrin over
Ospina's apparent blatant disregard of ideologically
held principles that Gómez viewed as inflexible
determinants of Conservative orthodoxy.

A third characteristic of ideological thinking, apparent in the foregoing discussion, is that
an ideology cannot be challenged by facts, logic,
or competing theories. This is because every
phenomenon in society is assigned a significance
measurable in terms of the ideology itself, rather
than through some objective, empirical test tran-
scending it. Further, every political event,
regardless of its outcome, may be taken to confirm
the principles prescribed by the ideology. Gómez
interpreted Enrique Santos's irate denial of Masonic
conspiracy as proof of the Masonic subversion. Had
Santos and El Tiempo kept their silence, Gómez would
have labeled that an equally strong proof of their
conspiratorial intent.

A corollary to its imperviousness to logic is
that only when an ideological program is applied can
it be shown to all to be deficient. It was not
until 1953, therefore, when Colombians embraced the
Rojas dictatorship in order to rid themselves of
Gómez and his visionary constitutional reform, that
it could be demonstrated that the Conservative
leader's program was unworkable.

When the political discourse of a nation is
highly ideological, as was Colombia's in the first
half of the twentieth century, there is great
likelihood of civil strife. Ideologies are exclusive, encompassing visions of reality that leave no
ground for compromise or accommodation. They can
only rebut one another in a polemical fashion. As
an ideology has no validity for those who refuse to
accept it, the ideologist can do no more than accuse
the nonbeliever of "false consciousness" and restate
his argument in ever more forceful terms. The

nation so unfortunate as to find its citizenry divided along ideological grounds, as was Colombia in the century prior to the Violencia, can anticipate civil war.[29]

In the 1930's and 1940's, before the Violencia, his fall from power, and the Rojas dictatorship convinced Gómez that he must abjure polemics, the Conservative leader spent much time and energy supplying an intellectual basis for his ideology. In this Gómez was following the logic that the successful defense of an intellectual position requires a credible academic foundation; yet there was irony attending that enterprise. In that Gómez, like all ideologists, wanted to prove the validity of an intellectual construct lying beyond empirical tests, he attempted what was logically impossible. Unable to weigh all evidence in a spirit of scientific inquiry, he simply searched for evidence that seemed to support his dominant hypothesis. In this sense it may be said that ideologists "use" academic disciplines to "demonstrate" the validity of their beliefs. We find Gómez citing the Old Testament, Sullust, Tacitus, Voltaire, Renan, Michelet, Rochefort, Saint Jerome, and Max Nordau in a single page of his speech on the Masonic conspiracy.[30] Even so, acceptance of his argument required a leap of faith that only his fellow ideologists were able or willing to make. To make the leap easier, Gómez employed the popular devices of ideological argumentation: colorful metaphor and emotional hyperbole. In his Senate speech on Masonry, for example, Gómez informed his fellow senators and the nation that liberal philosophy "is the desert, is anguish, is absolute darkness," that ignoring the "Jewish danger" is "to surrender the nation to the Jews," that "Masonry is . . . exclusively the enemy and persecutor of Catholicism"[31] thus, he was able to convey a sense of urgency that could not have been transmitted through normal discourse.

Of all the tools available to Gómez in arguing his position, history proved the most useful. As ideologists have before and since, Gómez employed history to enhance his vision of the present and to strengthen his co-ideologists' faith in the vision. Laureano Gómez was a past master in the use of history to buttress his ideological vision, as the following discussion demonstrates.

Gómez loved history, which he called "life's teacher."[32] He claimed to be happiest when ensconced in his large library, poring over a recent history of France or Spain, a biography of Henry VIII or Erasmus or Cardinal Richelieu, or studying a philosophical treatise that illuminated history in a way that he found particularly convincing. But apart from the personal satisfaction that he gained from wide-ranging reading, he always turned to history for help in proving the validity of his world view. For Gómez "the marvelous mirror of history" shows us "the direction of our journey and the things we've encountered along the way."[33] The metaphor could not be more appropriate. Gómez the ideologist saw in the mirror of history a body of information that explained and supported what he had always known to be true. All the more important, it helped him show Colombians that their history was part of a greater whole, that their problems were not unique: "for the reflective man, critical reading of newspapers is really the study of the most recent page of universal history," he told his followers in January 1938, adding in a later speech that "the present turbulence in Colombian life is merely an episode in the universal drama."[34]

The idea that the western world was in a state of crisis suffused the political message of Gómez as well as his interpretation of history. In his view, the crisis was born of a steady deterioration of fundamental values dating from early in the six-teenth century and reaching its culmination early in the twentieth. "Today there are threats to all that Western culture represents--to all the liberties, rights, and preogatives that we, as free men, love," he told the nation in a radio address of 1949. Unless right-thinking, patriotic Colombians rallied to his cause, the forces of darkness would triumph and would "force humanity into a slavery worse than that of barbarian times."[35] It was a message he had been repeating for many years. "Our labor is great," he had said a decade earlier, "the fatherland is compromised, these days are tragic and apocalyptic, because catastrophe approaches!"[36] His diagnosis of the crisis and his prescribed cure were always the same. The West is in decline, he argued, because "today's world has strayed from Catholic doctrine and has substituted for it those imbecile principles of 1789. That's the reason the world is hemorrhaging today."[37] The challenge could be met only if Colombia and the West returned to the old morality informed by Christianity's _philosophia perennis_, as articulated in conservative political philosophy.

Gómez's view of history may be described as

linear and theological. Like all orthodox Christians, he rejected the notion that history repeats itself, no doubt basing his belief on the concept that Christ died once for man's sins and will not die again.[38] That being the case, it follows that any doctrine of eternal repetition in history is invalid. Proponents of Christian theology believe that history is a manifestation of the will of God who created man in His own image, and therefore human history has a divinely inspired purpose. The Christian historian must strive to understand that purpose. But man cannot hope to understand fully God's intent, and he must therefore seek the answers to his teleological questions indirectly through an examination of human actions that is oriented by reference to God's commandment that man pursue moral ends. Just as St. Augustine told Christians to behave as though they lived in the city of God and the saints, rather than in the city of sinful man, he directed the Christian historian to judge man's past by transcendent moral standards. In this way St. Augustine set for Christian historians like Gómez the metaphysical task of determining the working of divine providence in the conflicts between the two cities.

Without directly acknowledging the sources of his metaphysical view of history, Gómez abundantly testified to its Augustinian origin. In a speech of 1934, he cited Hegel's History of Universal Philosophy in arguing that cultural history is the study of man's progress toward moral perfection, toward the "objectification of the spirit." The linear, metaphysical, and theological perspective of Gómez, which may be called an Augustinian-Hegelian view of history, is clearly seen in the speech. He asserts that all notions of justice, morality, and liberty emanate from the "world of the spirit," a realm not shared with lesser creatures that are governed by blind, instinctual urges. The human mind, guided by the Spirit, which is God's spirit, is capable of discovering eternal truths. In this scheme of things, man creates the state as a step toward helping him objectify the universal values that he has discovered through rational means.

Through his reading of Hegel, Gómez also found a way both of updating his Augustinianism and bringing his antiliberal historicism into line with orthodox Catholicism's demand that the faithful believe in divinely inspired eternal and universal values. He could argue that man can move toward realization of such values along particularistic

94

lines. As he explained it, "civil and political
culture in different nations is measured through
examination of the formulae their people employ for
reaching universal ends with the least possible
detriment to the liberties, prerogatives, and rights
of individual
citizens."[39]

In summary, Gómez viewed history as a progres-
sion toward ends that man cannot know with certainty
but can interpret and understand through the moral
precepts contained in Christian doctrine. These
beliefs colored his interpretation of the crisis of
contemporary civilization, a crisis whose origins
can be found in Western man's progressive distancing
from Christian morality. Understanding this, and
the fact of Gómez's ideological nature, enables us
to survey meaningfully his vision of history.

For Gómez, history was all of a piece, a great
book, some of whose chapters were "luminous," others
"dark," others "uncertain." Within that context, he
saw Western man passing through three distinct
epochs upon each of which he passed judgment. The
first embraced everything prior to the advent of
Christianity, when man's anthropomorphic vision of
the universe hobbled his spirit by depriving him of
knowledge of life's supreme and transcendent
values. That was followed by the Christian epoch,
when Western man received the ethical foundation
upon which he could begin to construct a godly and
humane civilization. It was a thousand year "noon-
time" of "spiritual and mental unity" that would
have lighted the way to perfect peace had not
northern Europeans willfully destroyed that unity,
ushering in the third historic period. The third
era was a lugubrious time when an increasingly
secularized western world lost its moral bearings,
passed from schism to atheism to revolution, and
made of contemporary history a time of permanent
crisis. Gómez described contemporary men as "mad,"
victims of a "horrible nightmare," brought on
because "they no longer know where they come from,
or what should be the rhythm of their lives, or the
course of their destiny."[40]

As one who believed that the only true
civilization was the one founded on Roman Catholic
precepts, Gómez spared few words and little sympathy
on pre-Christian societies. At best, as when
discussing the ancients, he described their benigh-
ted state patronizingly, sometimes even objectively.
At worst, as in his remarks on pre-Colombian
Americans, he implied that they lived as little more

95

than beasts prior to the coming of Europeans and their faith. Gómez saw the ancients as men of limited vision, enclosed within an "anthropocentric vault" where, he wrote, "there were no transcendent horizons. All ideological vistas were limited by closed curves whose very nature made any escape toward the transcendent impossible." At length their closed system proved insufficient: "the moment came when pagan wisdom showed signs of decrepitude because its system turned out to be lacking, incoherent, incapable of solving the enigmas of daily experience." At length the antiquated philosophy fell to pieces. Gómez likened its demise to that of an exploding dirigible "that disappears, devoured by flames, leaving nothing more than wisps of smoke and a few fragile struts, twisted and charred."[41]

Luckily for the ancients, a better faith soon replaced their shattered world view. As Gómez explained it, "the appearance of Christianity upon the earth saved man from the sink of mundane naturalism, interrupted the enervating movement around hollow, unsound principles." Christianity was likened to a purifying wind that had saved mankind from natural reason, "the great intellectual catastrophe that had squeezed the human spirit like grapes under the implacable winepress."[42]

Gómez was unwilling to admit that indigenous Americans possessed any real culture prior to the advent of Christianity. They were people of a land that "had vegetated for centuries in a fog of barbarous primitivism." He was speaking not only of the Colombian Indians. He cited Mexican writer and politician José Vasconcelos in asserting that the Aztecs not only practiced barbarous human sacrifice, but oppressed surrounding tribes reducing them to slavish servitude. Neither in Mexico, nor in Peru, nor in Colombia was the destruction of native American culture any great loss: "nothing was lost, because there wasn't anything worth saving. In nations such as ours, it is impossible to find positive traces of any true pre-Colombian civilization," he wrote. Those unfortunate lands remained sunk in barbarism until Europeans arrived bearing "the most glorious and noble culture conceived by the mind of man: Roman Catholic Spanish culture."[43]

Christianity, then, was the great civilizer of mankind. It unified European peoples and gave the savages of the world something worth living for. In Gómez's view, Christian Europe found its most sublime expression in imperial Spain of the sixteenth

96

century. The Spain of Ferdinand and Isabella and of the Hapsburg monarchs Charles V and Philip II was "a work powerful in its homogeneity of conception, its realization of high ideals, its faithfulness to Roman Catholic ideals of hierarchy and moral values, and in its exaltation of human intelligence and valor," all of which led Gómez to state that "the Spanish empire forms one of the most important chapters in human history."[44] His perception of sixteenth century Spain was not entirely idealized. He did admit that some pages of the glorious chapter were marred by the same "stains and blemishes" that mark the history of every people in every epoch. But the overall picture was exhilarating. The Hapsburg monarchs showed admirable ability in "understanding the sixteenth century Spanish spirit. They became the faithful interpreters of the Spanish soul, Christian in essence and democratic in form."[45] Nobility of spirit and greatness of soul were qualities shared by the mighty and the humble alike. Even the foot soldiers who served under conquistadores like Cortés, Pizarro, and Jiménez de Quesada had achieved "an extraordinary cultural level . . . in the porticos of the cathedrals where, filled with emotion, they listened to the performance of the autos." Ultimately all this was owing to religion, orthodox Christian religion. The Spanish monarchs and their subjects lived their "golden century" because they, more than any others, had created a state predicated on the eternal principles of Catholic political doctrine. Gómez saw creation of the Spanish empire as a collective expression of the common good, as defined in the light of Catholic, universal values. The men of the Siglo de Oro, imbued as they were with the sublime precepts of their religion, made up "a superhuman generation--they became almost semi-divine." Whether in the fields of art, architecture, literature, or drama, or in the creation of empire, they "reached heights never equalled after that time."[46]

Understanding this idealized vision of sixteenth century Spain helps us grasp Gómez's interpretation of greater European history. With powerful metaphor, he depicted the modern period as a time when fallible men willfully ignored divine principles, suffering definitive punishment in the process. He usually began his somber march through history by describing the events of December 10, 1520, when Luther publicly burned Pope Leo X's condemnation of his teaching. Gómez described it as

97

"that tragic day, as painful for Catholicism as it was fateful for all of Europe."[47] Luther's posting of his ninety-five theses on the church door at Wittenberg and his subsequent rebellion against papal authority set into motion a series of events that "led northern Europe into revolt against its glory and destroyed all possibility of spiritual and mental unity for humanity; it threw the Continent into a thousand vicissitudes."[48] Men like Luther and Erasmus ("that monk fled from the monastery") were bad Catholics, types seen frequently in history, who, after having defined a position and having sworn to defend it, "think nothing of going over to the opposite party."[49] But much more than simple acts of insubordination and bad faith, their rebellion represented the attempt to have relativism and rationalism triumph over divinely inspired truth: "In their satanic struggle, they created a doctrine according to which everything had to be examined and no lasting judgments made. With that kind of doctrine, Protestantism tried to slow the efficacy of Christ's liberating work."[50]

The Reformation was modern man's first step away from traditional wisdom and transcendent sources of knowledge. The next stopping point was the Enlightenment, a time of "deliberate and systematic misleading of public opinion on moral and intellectual values--truly a pact with the Devil."[51] Voltaire, Diderot, and Rousseau were, according to Gómez, the oracles chosen to structure government policy during that epoch "falsely called one of 'enlightenment'."[52]

These pernicious historical movements--the Protestant Reformation, which was "a sedition of the individual against the species," and the Enlightenment, with "its stubborn attacks on the existing order"--fed the popular desire to replace the rule of reason with rule of the will. The people eagerly seized on Rousseau's notion of the general will and mythified it, making it an instrument for achieving the "one-half plus one" that allowed simple majorities to control representative bodies. The one-half plus one soon passed from popular myth to universal superstition. Rousseau's idea became a "marvellous talisman for achieving universal happiness." But the liberty, equality, and fraternity that synthesized Rousseau's message were fraudulent:

the years have revealed that it was a meaningless slogan, because the liberty

98

brought by the French Revolution
destroyed true equality and replaced it
with scandalous and intolerable
capitalism, the creator of economic
slavery. The rivers of blood produced
by modern wars find their source in the
one flowing out of the French
Revolution. Mankind's greatest
slaughters followed the proclamation of
'liberty, equality, and fraternity;'[53]

thus, Gómez could conclude that the French Revolution failed because it never bought mankind a single
day of the liberty and dignity that it had so
cavalierly proclaimed. "The Revolution brought only
tyranny and the degradation of man."[54]

Enlightenment ideas entered Spain with the
Bourbon kings of the eighteenth century, destroying
the traditional principles that had made the Spanish
empire robust. Gómez accused the Bourbon monarchs
of having brought despotism to Spain. Their ideas
were exotic to the Spanish and led to "annihilation"
of the traditional Christian juridic concepts of the
Hapsburg kings. As they imposed their arbitrary
rule, the Bourbons "spread an enervating, ultimately
lethal venom throughout the organism" that was
imperial Spain.[55] Charles III destroyed Spain's
"enchantment," the "spiritual link that had long
guided the relations between the monarch and his
subjects."[56] That spiritual bond was, according to
Gómez , fragile yet integral to maintaining the
empire, and infinitely more effective than the mere
physical presence of military administrators.

Gómez's view of the early colonial period in
Colombia paralleled his idealized vision of
Hapsburg Spain. He painted a glowing, even roman-
ticized picture of sixteenth century New Granada,
according to which the Conquistadores travelled to
America principally to Christianize and civilize her
peoples. To support his view, he pointed out that
as soon as the native peoples were subdued, they
were baptized: "The water and the salt bore prodigious supernatural virtue, as well as America's
juridic order."[57] Within the Church all men were
brothers. For Gómez, that fact rendered absurd the
notion that the idea of human equality was unknown
prior to the French Revolution: "The Revolution's
pretentious arrogation of a concept that, having
already been invented, could not be invented a
second time, was one of the poisonous lies so
calamitous to contemporary humanity."[58]

As in Spain, Enlightenment ideas worked their mischief in Spanish America. In a 1940 El Siglo editorial, Gómez gave an economic interpretation of the subversive process. He traced the attack on Hispanic America's "spiritual empire" to eighteenth century Bourbon commercial imperialism. "Seen from this perspective," he wrote, "Colombian history has been nothing more than a chronicle of persistent, furious attacks by an external enemy, aided and abetted by Colombia's native sons."[59] One notable foreign enemy of the Hispanic tradition was Fiscal Moreno y Escandón, the royal official who attempted to reform the educational system of colonial New Granada along antischolastic lines. Moreno's actions were, according to Gómez, typical of the foreign-inspired innovations that were perverting national customs. As he put it, the plan of Moreno y Escandón exacerbated old problems and didn't contribute anything new. Rather, it served merely to disorient several generations of students who were taught Voltairian encyclopedism by "weak-minded types of sectarian temperament."[60]

Gómez attributed Colombia's instability in her early national period to misguided patriots whose "constitutional delirium" contradicted "the principles of order and hierarchy, of virtue and merit" propounded by Spanish scholastics like Vitoria, Soto, Molina, Suárez, Mariana, and others.[61] These errors brought the disasters of the Patria Boba, when Colombia was wracked by civil war, and all that followed. The Constitution of Cúcuta of 1821 played a special role in Gómez's interpretation of the early national period. He called it "the mother of all our calamities," saying that the liberals who controlled the constitutional convention "suffused the document with Santanderist and Masonic principles that opened the way for later antireligious agitation."[62] To that document he traced one of Colombia's greatest plagues, "inorganic universal suffrage . . . [that] goes against the nature of society."[63] The Constitution of Cúcuta enshrined the false Rousseauian dogma of the general will, which represented "the consecration of positivist laws--any sort of laws--and their ascendance over moral laws."[64]

Between 1821 and 1886, right-thinking Colombians struggled to preserve their traditional beliefs in the face of foreign-inspired Liberal subversion. All the nation's problems were seen as products of Liberal perfidy. The civil war of 1839 was called a logical consequence of the

100

revolutionary teachings of the Santanderist faction, while the "Liberal revolution of 1849" was brought about by a "reactionary element that sought the support of the mob . . . in order to win its support in the name of tyranny and bad government." The barracks coup of 1854 was "simply another example of Liberal morality." The Constitution of 1863 rounded out the Liberal program of _lese patria_. Gómez judged it as "the keystone in the Liberal revolutionary arch." That constitution, also known as the Rionegro Constitution, was seen as enshrining the notion of demagogic popular sovereignty that eventually bore Colombia to extremes not dreamed of even by the French constitution makers of 1793. "In the period that followed," concluded Gómez, "our republican traditions disappeared and with them the fundamental principles of social organization. . . . Such was liberalism's destructive work."[65]

Colombia was lifted from the depths of degradation in the 1880s when Núñez and Caro launched their program known as the Regeneration. Gómez described that moment as one in which the nation was awash in the blood produced by incessant civil war and chaos created by an ineffectual federal political system of liberal inspiration. Crime abounded, human rights were routinely violated, and the nation was in economic ruin. But thanks to the work of those clear-eyed Conservative patriots, wrote Gómez, Colombia entered a period of peace "so enduring" that "even the most prescient of our predecessors would have been amazed."[66]

The chief juridic expression of the Regeneration was the Constitution of 1886, referred to by Gómez as "the most eminent product of our national wisdom," and the "foremost conscious synthesis of the Colombian juridic personality." Speaking in Manizales in 1936, he lauded the document and its authors, under whose auspices Colombia entered the twentieth century. The Constitution of 1886, he said, was drafted neither in the spirit of German idealism nor in that of Anglo-American positivism. Rather, it fell somewhere between those "frozen extremes." The wise constitution makers loved liberty as well as order, and they stabilized the republic, leaving fallow ground for both tyrant and anarchist. Thanks to their "prodigious work," the factors of dissolution and decadence were overcome: the "lethal and terrible influence of the tropics," the exceedingly mountainous nature of national territory, the "ethnographic deficiencies" of the population, and the frivolity and volubility of

Colombians--elements "that combined to make Colombian history either a chain of infamous tyrannies or a succession of disorders that could easily have robbed us of our independence, returning us to the yoke of foreign domination . . . . Our prosperity is owed to the Constitution of 1886."[67]

Gómez was ten years old when the twentieth century began, and before the first decade of the new century ended, he had set his political course. His coming of age thus coincided with the change in global history noted by Virginia Woolf and others. As Gómez fought to establish himself in the world of Colombian politics, he struggled to understand what was happening beyond national boundaries and to reconcile it with his beliefs. When he departed for Europe in 1928, "disconcerted by the contradictions and uncertainties of the contemporary world,"[68] he had already meditated on the works of early interpreters of the new age--Spengler, Berdyaev, Bergson, Maritain, Sorel--reading which in combination with what he saw in Europe convinced him that the modern age was one of acute and dangerous crisis. Following his return to Colombia, he often voiced this belief. "Throughout the contemporary world and in our unfortunate nation as well, there is nothing more than superficiality and vanity," he said in a speech of 1936. Today, creative energy is at a low ebb, said Gómez: "It seems that beauty and glory have disappeared from the earth; first Russia, next Spain. Now it seems that France is entering that funeral period that signifies a slide toward barbarous tyranny."[69] Two years later he blamed the crisis for the fact that "today humanity is the victim of a terrifying nightmare."[70] The sense of crisis that Gómez shared with so many others of his generation colored his perception of twentieth century history and undergirded his interpretation of it.

In keeping with his methodical personality, prescriptive nature, and position as Conservative party leader, Gómez explained the problem of modern society to his followers and told them how it must be solved. That is precisely what he did in a series of political speeches delivered in Colombia's major cities between September and December of 1938. Each speech, broadcast over national radio and printed in El Siglo, treated different aspects of the contemporary crisis. But the solution was always the same: If Colombians wanted to save their nation from chaos, they must cleave to the philosophia perennis of Roman Catholicism, and battle the designated evils with evangelical zeal. His address to the Conservative convention of Nariño, titled "The Oppression of the Modern World," contains his assessment of the problem of contemporary history. He began by citing Jacques Maritain to the effect that human intelligence was under attack by the very forces it had itself unleashed. Through his excessive rationalism and disparagement of transcendent truths, said Gómez, modern man has plunged the modern world into chaos. In Colombia, he continued, only the Conservative party "has seen with luminous clarity the gravity of the hour and has dedicated its power and prestige to the great battle against diabolical powers."[71] Only the Conservative party gave modern man the "precise, sure rules, founded in the perfect logic of truths that satisfy the eternal certainties of the human mind."[72]

Thus did Gómez teach history to his followers. The vision he presented them was one of organic, hierarchical Catholic certainty informed by ethical verities, placed in jeopardy by a relativist, inherently immoral modern world.

Possessing a doctrinally coherent philosophy and an unquestioning view of the past was all the more important as the decade of the 1930s progressed. During that time, Latin American conservatives like Gómez found it necessary to defend their position on two fronts. To the left was liberalism, the old nemesis. On the right was fascism, a competing ideology of great potential danger to political conservatism. The democratic right's struggle to maintain doctrinal and political coherence during the clash between liberal democracy and fascist totalitarianism would preoccupy its spokesmen for nearly two decades.

Chapter VII

BETWEEN WORLD WARS: LATIN AMERICAN
CONSERVATISM EMBATTLED

Dilemmas of the Non-Facist Right

The years between World War I and the end of
World War II were a time of troubles for all Latin
American conservatives. Throughout the period,
militant competing ideologies appeared destined to
make the conservative vision of harmony and hierarchy a quaint anachronism. In Mexico the party of
the Revolution was in firm control; in Peru the APRA
party seemed on the verge of seizing power and
implementing its program of radical reform; and in
Colombia the Liberal party was ascendant. Marxist-
Leninist parties were making gains everywhere in
Latin America, drawing sustenance from the global
economic depression of the 1930s. More troubling
were movements on the radical right. The fascist
program was one of order and discipline predicated
on a corporate organization of society akin in some
respects to Catholic principles of social organization. The success of authoritarian regimes in
Spain, Portugal, Germany, and Brazil attracted less
orthodox conservatives.

Latin American conservatives of the interwar
period were faced with the unpleasant and difficult
task of fighting the competing ideologies on two
fronts. They did so, as did Gómez in Colombia, by
retreating to their most secure, indeed their only
true bulwark, that of the philosophia perennis.
Party leaders lectured that fascist systems robbed
man of his individuality, his dignity, and his
humanity; and at the same time stressed the conservative values of order and discipline. The decade
of the 1930s found them accentuating hierarchical,
organic, and antimajoritarian aspects of conservative thought, and elaborating corporative schemes of
social organization. It was a strategy that
effectively undercut the fascist position.

Hot rhetoric characterized the conservative

105

assault on liberal ideas and on those to the left of liberalism. Conservatives never tired of charging that liberalism had failed, that the recent war was the price England, France, and Germany had paid for selling their souls to laissez-faire capitalism. They damned liberalism for its anticlericalism and blamed liberal economic policies for the worldwide depression of the 1930s. They even blamed it for the rise of fascism and communism, claiming that in jettisoning the ancient moral verities and replacing them with Godless utilitarianism, liberals had ushered in an age of moral relativism whose logical denouement were the dictatorships of Mussolini, Hitler, and Stalin.

Anti-Americanism was another weapon of conservative counterattack. As World War II approached and Pan-Americanism became the order of the day, conservatives warned that close ties to the Americans threatened national integrity. Yankee imperialism, they claimed, lurked behind the honeyed phrases of hemispheric solidarity.

A program of social activism also marked the conservative response. It drew inspiration from the Papal encyclical Quadregisimo Anno, issued by Pius IX in 1931. That document recapitulated Leo XIII's assertion that Catholics be sensitive to the social problem, and it praised the work of socially concerned Catholics whom he described as "those chosen men whom we have termed auxiliaries of the Church."[1] The poor must be helped, said the Pope, but in such a way as to preserve the common good and to guard against the individualism and collectivism that cast the unwary "upon the shoals of moral and juridical and social modernism."[2] Latin American conservatives, particularly the younger ones, were attentive to the challenge. They saw in it a way to make their thought relevant to twentieth century social reality.

The conservative fight to defend their philosophic position met with mixed success. Their policy of "defensive righting" and the stress on nontotalitarian aspects of conservative belief saved most of their partisans from the fascist heresy. The growing tendency of forward-looking conservatives to meet rather than to resist the challenges of rapid social change invigorated a message that by its nature could be neither utopian nor revolutionary.

But Latin America's conservatives paid the price for defending their doctrinal position. In stressing the antimajoritarian, corporative, and

hierarchic elements in their thought, and in opposing close collaboration with the United States, they
opened themselves to the charge that they favored
fascist dictatorship. To the untutored ear,
conservative denunciations of egalitarianism and
majoritarian democracy and their calls for spiritual
unity among Latin peoples sounded like pleas for
solidarity with Nazism. The movement toward greater
social activism also helped to split conservatism.

Growing Division in Conservative Ranks:
The Chilean Case

The developments sketched above were perhaps
clearest in Chile, a country whose political climate
was in a state of ferment during the years between
the wars. Conservatives there lost few of their
number to fascism, yet their party became badly
divided nonetheless. The writings and careers of
Alberto Edwards, Jorge González von Marées, and
Eduardo Frei serve to illustrate this process.

Alberto Edwards Vives was one of the most
prominent spokesmen of the Chilean Conservative
party during the first third of the twentieth
century. Best known for his opposition to the
domination of national politics by a mercantile
elite that he called "la Fronda aristocrática," he
advocated a return to the rule of a virtuous elite
not corrupted by that "Jewish disdain for everything
that is not gold."[3]   Large doses of authority and
the "natural hierarchy" of organic society were
Edward's remedies for Chile's ills. As he put it,
"religious discipline, the traditional habit of
obedience, and the spontaneous submission to hierarchy are prebourgeois phenomena. They exist in
greater or lesser degree in all civilizations and
times." The advent of modern society led to the
decay of old patterns of discipline and obedience,
and with it, social dissolution or the appearance of
totalitarianism; thus, Edwards could conclude that
"in order to exist, society needs chains, spiritual
or material. Liberty and organicism are incompatible terms."[4]   In spite of his aristocratic
disdain for both the masses and the nouveau riche,
Alberto Edwards was not of a totalitarian turn of
mind. He took pride in the fact that until they
lost "the traditional habit of obedience, the people
of Chile were different. That is to say they were
submissive and disciplined, respectful of power and
of social hierarchy. We were the English of
America!"[5]

If Edwards Vives represented the traditional "old guard" of Chilean conservatism, Jorge González von Marées and Eduardo Frei Montalva were the "angry young men" on his right and left. González founded the Chilean National Socialist party in the late 1920s, making authority, antiliberalism, and nationalism the chief planks of his party platform. Whereas Edwards advocated the rule of a virtuous, Portalian elite, González located his agent of social control in corporatism. He would replace Chile's parliamentary democracy with a "functional political structure" whose supreme administrative organ was a supreme council whose members held lifetime tenure.[6]

"We are Fascists," wrote González, "without that signifying in any way that we intend to copy Italian or German fascism. Our movement is characterized by its essentially nationalist tendency."[7] Indeed, his party's nationalism rivaled its authoritarianism. Writing in 1940, he made clear what he perceived to be the greatest threat to Chilean integrity: "The greatest enemy of Latin American unity is the so-called Pan-Americanism. That is the exclusive creation of the United States for maintenance and increase of its influence over our republics. There's nothing more to Pan-Americanism than geographic proximity."[8]

Like González, Eduardo Frei was a nationalist, though one more attuned to Chile's role in a region threatened by the superior power of others. Writing in 1942, Frei warned that "when influence is distributed and power blocks formed, the result is that hegemonies are established or confirmed. This continent stands like a solitary prisoner. It awakens many appetites and serves to compensate some for their losses [in other parts of the world]."[9] Like his fascist contemporary, Frei warned that Chile needed greater economic development if she were to stave off foreign predators and the privileged national elites "who commit sins against society," in the process "injuring the spirit of the people and degrading the national soul."[10]

Where Eduardo Frei differed sharply, indeed fundamentally, from both Jorge González von Marées and Alberto Edwards was in his anti-authoritarianism. Frei not only failed to stress the traditional conservative values of order and hierarchy in his pronouncements, but he stressed the very majoritarian principles that were anathema to conservatives of the old school. "America," wrote Frei, "is a land of democracy and hope. The dictatorships that

108

we've known differ from those seen in Europe. They do not manage to destroy our elemental [democratic] sentiment."[11] He went on to call Chile the Latin American nation whose democracy had evolved more than any other, and whose mission was to support less fortunate sister states in their movement toward viable representative government.

Frei and the other young men of Chile's conservative left wing tempered their progressivism by couching it in terms of Christian community. That was nowhere more apparent than in the "Declaration of Principles" that Frei and his colleagues wrote when they inaugurated a group called Chilean Youth in 1935. The young conservatives (Frei was twenty-four at the time) affirmed their belief in

> Christian spirit and nationalism . . . a National state that is organized hierarchically . . . defense of liberty within order . . . defense and protection of the family, society's fundamental unit . . . corporative organization of society . . . the hierarchical and disciplined organization of our young people.

Members of the Juventud Conservadora concluded their list of eighteen guiding principles by pledging "abnegation and sacrifice in the service of Chile and of God."[12]

Within two years, Juventud Conservadora would break away from its parent group, the Chilean Conservative party, to form a new party called the Falange Nacional. In time it would become the Chilean Christian Democratic party. But through it all, the bond of Christian organicism would provide a common link uniting not just Chilean conservatives but their copartisans throughout Latin America.

The experience of Chilean conservatives was markedly like that of others elsewhere in Latin America. During the interwar period, Ecuadorian conservative leader Jacinto Jijón y Caamaño defined his party's ideology in terms of rather orthodox Christian Democratic theory.[13] In Mexico Manuel Gómez Morín launched the party of Acción Nacional as a traditionalist, nonfascist, anticommunist, and antitotalitarian alternative to the party of the Revolution (PRM).

The Chilean scenario was also being played out in Colombia, where conservative "young Turks" like Silvio Villegas suggested a fascist alternative to the orthodox leadership of Gómez. To Gómez's left, there were Conservatives associated with the more progressive "Nationalist" faction of the party.

But in Colombia the left-right division within conservatism was not apparent until well after World War II. This was largely due to the power of the personality of Gómez and to the intensity of the orthodox position.

Gómez Answers the Fascist Challenge

During his years as Colombia's diplomatic representative in Germany (1930-32), Gómez had the opportunity to observe the tactics of Adolph Hitler and Benito Mussolini at close range. When he returned to Colombia in mid-1932, he was resolved to immunize his party from fascism and to caution against allowing traditional freedoms to be swallowed up "in a holocaust to the new idols."[14] Gómez referred to Hitler's Nazis as "bolsheviks of the right" and in 1935 judged the Führer to be a criminal: "The morality that condemns the methods used by Hitler will continue intact when nothing is left of the dictator save bitter memory . . . . Hitler is not a great man. Germany will not pass through the doorway of crime to dominate mankind."[15] He was no more charitable to Mussolini, whose violent tactics merited similar condemnation:

> The moral question is foremost. Power acquired through violence, material victory achieved through bloodshed and institutionalized upon the ruins of human dignity and liberty, cannot yield blessings. The appearance may be lavish, the facade imposing, and the overall impression one of permanence. But universal human experience reveals that it will last one human lifetime-- two at most. Then will come the inevitable fall. We know, well we know, that it is thus.[16]

It was very much in Gómez's political interest to condemn the right-wing totalitarians. A significant faction within his party was drawn to fascism, and he waged a continuous struggle to keep them from further weakening the collectivity. In an El Siglo editorial of 1937, he lectured a wayward party member who had suggested that fascism would bring infinite well-being to Colombia, taking the unprece-

110

dented step of defending the French Declaration of the Rights of Man. That document, he wrote, "is supported by a wholesome philosophy . . . and undeniably remains the basis of the rights of the citizen." He went on to point out that the chief evil of the French Revolution was the hypocrisy of the revolutionaries themselves, whom he called "pseudo-humanists."[17] During a doctrinal speech of June 1938, Gómez warned Conservatives of the dangers of extremism, pointing out that rightist dictatorships, such as those of Mussolini and Hitler, extinguish human liberty quite as thoroughly as do dictatorships of the left: "A turn to the right implies the destruction and death of liberty. The dictatorships holding sway in several important nations offer material well-being in exchange for bondage."[18] Four months later, he rebuked Sinforoso Ocampo, a prominent party member from the department of Caldas, for breaking party discipline. When Ocampo proposed the names of several Fascists for election on the Conservative party ticket, Gómez asked if he really intended to nominate persons who had allowed themselves to be

> infected by the ridiculous neo-nationalist epidemic that tries in vain to tarnish the free and glorious image of traditional conservatism, replacing the party with the cult of the dictator? Do you intend to disturb the admirable discipline and doctrine of our party in pursuit of . . . the miserable [fascist] theory that intends to destroy liberty, replacing it with tyranny and despotism . . . ?[19]

For some twenty years, Gómez found it necessary to defend himself from Liberal charges that he was a Fascist. In a Cámara debate of 1926, Representative Carlos Arango Vélez implied as much when he attacked Gómez for citing Oswald Spengler's "fascist" work The Decline of the West. Gómez dismissed the charge, remarking that Arango obviously was not familiar with Spengler's work.[20] During the 1930s and 1940s, the Liberal indictment grew more intense. Time and again Gómez explained that his position was anti-dictatorial and pro-democratic. In a 1943 interview by a reporter from El Liberal, he responded to the question of whether he endorsed the idea that Spanish-American nations should form a Hispanist, Falangist league, by saying that as a spiritual force, Hispanism needed no institutional formalization. He added that Falangism "is an accident," and that Hispanism would exist regardless of Spain's political system. He went on to point out that talk of fascist fifth column activity was a Liberal and North American ploy to maintain hemispheric solidarity in wartime. In response to the question of whether his party had moved to the right during the twentieth century, he answered "neither to the right nor the left. It remains the same because it is a doctrinal party."[21]

As events in Europe led that continent into World War II, Colombia's Liberal governments warmly supported the Allies and cooperated in stamping out fifth column activity, both real and suspected, within national boundaries. Heavy-handed actions against German nationals, including the blacklisting of many businesses owned by Germans, brought protests from Gómez. He pointed out that German commercial firms were not necessarily connected with the Nazi regime, and that tyrannical actions against noncombatants contradicted Allied claims to be fighting for freedom and democracy. Gómez also protested U.S. Ambassador Spruille Braden's mixing in national politics and sending false reports of Nazi activity in Colombia. While criticizing what he considered excessive North American influence in Colombian affairs during the war years, Gómez insisted that he was not antiAmerican. He stated his position in the following terms:

> We have said that we're friends of the United States and thus we will be. American capital, energy, and talent are necessary for our progress; they are very welcome and we receive them with open arms. But at the same time their capital must be respectful of Colombian sovereignty; it must obey our laws; it must seek cordiality and not . . . unjust advantage.[22]

The Liberals used Gómez's announced neutrality to good advantage in the political battles of the late 1930s and early 1940s. They tarred him as a Nazi sympathizer and happily depicted him as an enemy of democracy. Casual observers of the Colombian scene in turn transmitted that view to the wider world. The popular North American journalist John Gunther said of Gómez, "he is a typical politician of the extreme right, and we shall find one

112

of him--with identical stigmata--in almost every
South American country . . . . His ideas, his
instincts, his sympathies, are all bitterly anti-
United States."[23] Gómez denied such charges when he
was able, doggedly cleaving to his position that
Colombia's proper course in international relations
was one of strict neutrality. He recalled that
shortly after the outbreak of war, his newspaper
condemned Hitler's aggression against the European
democracies. What he opposed, he went on to say,
were those Colombians who

> began to voice theories that we consid-
> ered false, unpatriotic, and danger-
> ous--theories holding that 'national
> sovereignty is a purely metaphysical
> concept . . . .' We proclaimed a policy
> of neutrality, following the example of
> President Concha in the time of the
> Great War.[24] We spoke in favor of a
> wise and prudent policy that was neither
> Caesarist, or Germanophile, or reaction-
> ary; and that never showed partiality to
> the Central Powers.[25]

One of Gómez's hottest replies to Liberal
charges that he was a Fascist occurred at the end
of 1943. Minister of Finance Carlos Lleras, a
diminutive man nicknamed "the microbe" by the
laureanistas, had referred to the supposed Nazism of
the Conservative leader. Gómez responded as
follows: "It's easier to discover a microbe, fatten
him up, and sell him to the government, than to
prove our adhesion to Nazi ideas. Mr. Lleras had
not even begun his activities as a financier, nor
had El Siglo begun publication, when we protested
the first crimes of the Axis." He went on to remind
readers that his book El cuadrilátero was the first
in Colombia to criticize Hitler and Mussolini, and
that the volume evoked warm praise from prominent
Liberals. He rested the case for his antifascism
with another dig at Minister of Finance Carlos
Lleras: "May the midget of our finances donate his
blood for lifesaving transfusions with the same good
will with which he discovers, fattens up, and sells
a microbe! Only then will we believe in his sincere
adhesion to the cause of the democracies."[26]

Gómez versus Philosophic Liberalism

If Gómez believed that fascism and national socialism were destined to fail because of their violation of moral laws, he was no less certain that liberalism was doomed because of its grave philosophic defects. Since liberalism infected a great number of Colombians, he knew that he must do what he could to lessen the impact of their error. He had never hidden his antiliberalism, though he chose not to belabor it during the 1920s when he allied himself with the Liberal party to attack more effectively the Conservative old guard. But during the 1930s, when he was Conservative leader, he projected a vision of recent Colombia that placed full blame for national problems on the opposition. He depicted pre-1930 Colombia as a utopia of peace. "Perfect peace reigned following the War of the Thousand Days," he once reminisced, pointing out on another occasion that while the Conservative old regime made mistakes, its record in the area of civil guarantees was "almost perfect."[27] It made no difference that Liberals cited abundant proof of Conservatives' use of force to maintain their control of power prior to 1930. To Gómez it was not that way at all. His inability to see Colombian political violence as an institutional problem sprung from national political pathology enabled him to fix as its cause what he believed was the defectiveness of liberal philosophy itself. He could, therefore, explain that under the administration of President Enrique Olaya Herrera, the nation experienced "the introduction of assassination as a permanent recourse" because Olaya was not "a man of deep convictions or of broad and coherent philosophic thought." This was because rather than having spent his years abroad in Europe where he might have learned some fundamental values, he had lived in the United States where he "absorbed the values peculiar to North America."[28] Gómez depicted Liberals as "ignorant barbarians, hirsute and frenzied, with coarse stones and brutal flint hatchets," whose lack of ideological consistency allowed them to fall into "a materialistic, mechanistic style of life."[29]

That characterization applied equally to Colombian and to European liberals. Through the decade of the 1930s, Gómez evolved the theory that liberal ideas were directly responsible for the rise of fascism. He first expounded that notion in 1934 when he ascribed Hitler's rise to the fact that dur-

114

ing the nineteenth century, Germans adopted Kantian "scientifism" and turned their backs on Roman law with its inflexible moral standards.[30] He portrayed European liberals as inept persons who had stumbled out of "the intellectual desert of the left" to impose a parliamentary tradition that produced great discontent that in turn brought "the reaction, personalism, and authoritarianism that today dominate some of the world's leading nations."[31] His conclusion was that because liberalism paved the way for tyrannies of both the left and right, it was an ineffectual social and philosophic doctrine and for that reason was supremely dangerous.

Historical analogy was one of Gómez's favorite devices for demonstrating the validity of his thesis that liberalism was a great threat to Colombia and the world. It seemed perfectly clear to him that Alfonso López, leader of the eclectic "Revolution on the March," was no different from the European liberals who were leading their respective nations toward disaster. Spain presented the best case for comparison. At the turn of the century, that country was a peaceful and progressive place. Its king, Alfonso XIII, relied on the sound advice of Conservative party leader Antonio Maura, and together they worked to implement programs of moderate social and political reform, programs that Gómez claimed had influenced his own political thought. "The generation to which we belong," he wrote in an El Siglo editorial of 1937, "first entered public life under the influence of ideas developed in the Motherland . . . . Maura embodied our deepest ideals."[32] Maura's fall in 1909 and the subsequent disappearance of the Spanish Conservative party were seen by Gómez as representing the "death of the principle of political authority" there. More than that, it was "suicidal" for Spain or any other country to lose its Conservative party.[33]

Gómez used the Spanish Civil War of 1936-39 as an example of what lay in store for Colombia if its "liberal revolution" were not cut short. Writing as much about Colombia and Alfonso López as about Spain, he described how a "mediocre intellectual" named Manuel Azaña won the presidency in 1936, thanks to extensive vote fraud and the help of a leftist popular front coalition. Afraid to be labeled a "reactionary" by his supporters, the weak Azaña, in fact only a figurehead president, agreed to preside over a thoroughgoing national revolution. His program involved "the looting of private property for use by the affiliates" and other such

115

assaults on Spanish society.[34] Both Azaña and his chief minister Casares Quiroga were docile servants of communist colleagues who were busy implementing instructions sent to them from the Third International in Moscow. Noncommunist members of the popular front protested that the government had no army capable of withstanding the subversive leftist threat, but their warnings were ignored by Azaña and Casares Quiroga. Only the revolt of General Francisco Franco thwarted what certainly would have been a complete takeover by the Bolsheviks. To make sure that Colombians did not miss the point he was making, Gómez carefully spelled it out:

> In Colombia we already have the popular front. I invite everyone . . . to seriously consider the picture of a nation at risk and to consider whether it is possible that we lose our liberty and fall to the same amorphous tyranny that bloodies and dishonors Spain.[35]

Fifteen months before Franco's triumph, Gómez expressed his great pleasure that Spaniards had rallied to the defense of their country. In his speech of January 29, 1938, bearing the significant title "The Decadence and Grandeur of Spain," he said the following:

> There is no historical example of spiritual aridity like that of Spain under liberalism. The people's will was rendered impotent, and their bodies bent beneath the yoke of barbarism. . . . Spain was dominated by a communist revolution, dominated more completely than she was by the Moors. . . .
> Praised be God who allows us to witness this unexpected moment of national transformation! Praised be the events that, day by day, cause to well from deep inside us the fervent salute: Up with Catholic, imperial Spain![36]

Contemporary French history also served Gómez as a beacon illuminating the Colombian case. When Paris fell to the Germans in June 1940, he greeted the event with a series of El Siglo editorials in which he argued that the true France, the nation of Joan of Arc and Charles Martel, of Racine and Rabelais, of De Maistre and Bourget, of Delacroix and Rodin, still lived. What had fallen to Hitler's armies was nothing more than the "juridic" France of the corrupt Third Republic, a "regime of blood and pus."[37] He saw the six decades of the Third Republic as a classic example of how a proud people could be brought low by liberalism. The march that culminated with Nazi armies goosestepping through the Arc de Triomphe had its beginning in the eighteenth century when that Christian nation began to follow Voltairian precepts instructing that man should "laugh at things divine."[38] During the nineteenth century, she allowed herself to become "contaminated with all those venomous intellectualisms that had destroyed her traditional soul, her beautiful Christian soul. Rationalism made her a hollow shell, without faith."[39] Gómez called the fall of Paris a preventable tragedy: "All was announced--by the men of the right. But the left turned a deaf ear. What is worse, they were voluntarily deaf. They are to blame for the blood, the tears, and the desperation of these hours."[40]

As always in Gómez's interpretation of current events, there were implicit and explicit cautionary messages for Colombia. Beware of those who spout false doctrines, he warned, for they excite the masses and lead them toward that abyss called "revolution on the march."[41] Learn from the sad lessons of France, the nation that jailed Charles Maurras, "the most fecund thinker of the contemporary period." When "communism and socialism won control of the French government, Maurras was thrown into jail. Months later the rotten husk that was the Third Republic fell before the German invasion."[42]

Russian history also served Gómez as an object lesson in his campaign against liberalism. His favorite case in point was Alexander Kerensky, the politician whose February Revolution preceded by a few months that of the Bolsheviks. In an essay titled "Kerensky, the Talker," he was none too subtle in likening the failed Russian reformer to the Colombian liberal "revolutionary," Alfonso López: "The chief of the Russian government, following the proven rule of all [liberal] revolutions on the march, made constant concessions. . . . Meanwhile, Lenin, with his small slanting eyes and his prominent cheekbones, laughed at the harmless verbal furor."[43]

In a later speech, titled "The Most Dangerous Enemy: The Moderate," Gómez made even more explicit his argument for the virtue of extremism in pursuit of a just cause. The moderate, said Gómez, is

117

always closer to his neighbor on the left than to
his neighbor on the right. As it is always easier
to descend than to ascend:

> one needs more ideas, more courage, more
> virtue, and more moral energy to defend
> order than to destroy it. This is why
> the worst enemy of civilization is the
> moderate. The Marxist, who attacks head
> on, may be repulsed and cast aside. The
> moderate doesn't seem to attack and
> therefore doesn't arouse suspicion. One
> doesn't take, with him, the indispens-
> able precautions. Nevertheless every
> day he surrenders some outpost or
> precinct of the venerable fortress.[44]

The "Enemy Within": Masons, Jews, Communists

From his attack on moderates who were uncon-
scious collaborators of the left, Gómez moved on to
those groups he claimed were active conspirators
against civilization. Like most ideologists, Gómez
was inclined to interpret historical events in terms
of conspiracy theory. The concept of conspiracy
served as a lubricant that helped him fit what was
inexplicable or illogical into his paradigmatic
vision of the world. Gómez blamed three groups for
the alarming decay of Western society: Masons, Jews,
and Communists.

Anti-Masonic pieces constitute a significant
portion of Gómez's earliest political writings. He
dedicated numerous editorials in La Unidad to the
theme that Masonic lodges, "synagogues of Satan,
that connive to lure away the followers of Christ,"
were subversive and should be declared illegal in
Colombia.[45] He considered the order to be overtly
antireligious, and its members all deserving of
excommunication. He justified his charges by pointing to the Masonic-inspired program of church-state
separation in Third Republic France. In later years
he expanded accusations of conspiracy in his anti-
Masonic remarks by linking Masonry to international
communism, reasoning that there must be a connection
since liberal Masonic doctrines were so useful to
the Communists.[46] Though he condemned the brutal
fascist takeover of Ethiopia in 1935, he also noted
that "the great misdeed that Mussolini committed in
international politics is being exploited by Masonry
around the world." The charge was documented
through reference to "the specialized magazine

118

Judenkener."[47]

Gómez was equally outspoken in his indictment of Jews as subverters of the Catholic world view. While willing to praise "the admirable Israelite vigor" that enabled the Jewish people to preserve their identity under conditions that had destroyed other ethnic and religious groups, he indicted them for "their egotism and exclusivism, their implacable and cruel greed, their self-assurance, and their methods of organization and work."[48] In one of his earliest political campaigns, that exposing the greed of Muzo emerald mine directors, he won applause with a reference to Colombian businessmen who allowed themselves to be hoodwinked by Jewish bankers in London: "Shylock, the avaricious and mysterious Jew, who is the Emerald Company, has masked himself with the national flag."[49] Underlying his anti-Semitism was a hostility sprung from what Gómez perceived as the Jewish intent to lead Christians away from their religious beliefs. This explains his blast at Stefen Zweig for writing a biography lauding the Catholic schismatic Erasmus: "one must not forget that when the above mentioned Jewish publicist undertakes the study of someone, he entertains a preconceived notion that he pursues in detriment to the truth. Zweig is not a historian, but rather a covert polemicist harboring the rationalist bias of his race."[50]

The specter of communist conspiracy against Colombia, a theme present in Gómez's writing from the 1930s, loomed ever larger to him as Marxism gained global popularity during the twentieth century. In the late 1920s, when he joined the Liberals to attack Abadía Méndez, Gómez scoffed at the president's reference to the "communist menace." He called it a "scapegoat phrase" and agreed with Liberals who denied that María Cano, Torres Giraldo, and "two dozen agitators" posed any threat to the nation.[51] By the late 1930s, however, he included Communists as part of the infernal triad dedicated to destroying Western civilization. By the 1940s, they had eclipsed both the Masonic and the Jewish in Gómez's hierarchy of threats to the nation. He warned that with the war at an end and with Moscow reviving the International, Colombians must "prepare to defend the statutes of civilization against this dangerous resurgence of the totalitarian hydra."[52] To reinforce his words, El Siglo began publishing a series of gruesome photos purported to depict Spanish Catholics executed by Communists during the civil war.[53]

Gómez's views on the Masonic-Jewish-Communist conspiracy are revealed in his Senate speech of 1942 titled "Masonry and Its History."[54] He prefaced the lecture on history with a vignette describing his meeting with president-elect Eduardo Santos shortly before he took office in 1938. In reply to Santos' question on what the Conservative party wanted of the new administration, Gómez replied that his co-partisans were most interested in guarantees that violence would not be used against them. "Next," said Gómez, referring to the fact that Jewish refugees had been given jobs in the Ministry of Education, "I spoke of our concern over the insulting spectacle of national education being turned over to some foreign Jews expelled from other nations for bad behavior and for perverse teachings, and I told him that we want to free education from Masonic influence." At that, said Gómez, Santos exchanged a knowing glance with Carlos Lozano who was also in attendance. "Naturally they smiled," he continued, "and I heard the words that are invariably spoken: 'Masonry is foolishness, of absolutely no importance; to my way of thinking, it has absolutely no influence or transcendence; Masons are just men who get together to dine. What they do has no significance whatsoever. Any concern about them is banal.'"[55]

After establishing that he knew the Liberals did not take his fears seriously, Gómez proceeded with the introduction to what stands as his only sustained effort at explaining his complicated conspiracy theory. Sometimes, he said, Catholics suspect that their religion is no longer valid. When they begin serious study of those traditional beliefs, they come upon "a cloud, a mist that obscures the principles of Catholic philosophy, seemingly relegating them to the past and robbing them of validity for the present age." There is a plethora of books and learned disquisitions, he continued, "that indirectly refute Catholic philosophy as an outdated thing on the verge of disappearing altogether."[56]

When arriving at the understanding that many consider his philosophy outmoded, continued Gómez, the troubled Catholic turns to the body of thought that has apparently invalidated his own--perhaps others have discovered the flaw in Catholic logic? He undertakes closer examination, searching for answers to his questions. But what does he discover?

He discovers greater, more fundamental
faults than the enemies of Catholic
philosophy have revealed to him. He
ends up with nothing. He becomes a
tabula rasa left with nothing more
than naturalism or sterile, rigid
rationalism that preserves certain
external appearances, but that doesn't
speak to the innermost human conscience,
to intelligence in repose, to the soul's
serenity . . . He finds himself in the
desert, in anguish, in absolute darkness![57]

This was the way Gómez introduced his speech
on the Masonic-Jewish-Communist conspiracy. It was
an argument founded on the belief that if rational
man rejects the only perfect and satisfying philosophy of life and chooses instead to follow another
that on thoughtful examination turns out to be a
fraud, a false philosophy that has managed to
deceive the majority of mankind--a majority that
admittedly is not particularly astute--then, Gómez
the ideologist believed, some dedicated, intelligent, and infernal force must be to blame.
    According to Gómez, the studious person of
scientific temperament will discover that in the
modern world there are three sources of the current
malaise. The first is a universal phenomenon--
almost as universal as Catholicism--and that is
Judaism. The second is communism, a philosophy
capable of providing a doctrinal base for the great
mass movements of contemporary history. Third, and
finally, is a social phenomenon at once open and
hidden, "acting in almost all historical episodes of
the various nations but denying and hiding its role
in them; it has determined the twists and turns of
history at decisive moments, all the while denying,
I repeat, that it has intervened in those events.
This phenomenon is Masonry." The naive or uninform-
ed may smile, may deny that this is the case, but
his disbelief springs from "a voluntary or involun-
tary ignorance. There is no other explanation."[58]
    As one who thought in terms of hierarchies, it
was natural that Gómez should perceive the conspiratorial forces as a hierarchy. Standing at the top
was Judaism: "The phenomenon of Judaism is primordial; it is antecedent." The Jews were a
remarkable but thoroughly pernicious race, argued
Gómez. He cited numerous ancient and modern
authorities on the subject, concluding that one

121

could go on nearly infinitely in that vein: "there
is almost no thinker of substance who hasn't had to
consider this, because it is a problem with which
humanity has always lived." He went on to cite
Saint Jerome's description of the Jews as a
"lugubrious, miserable people, yet a people failing
to inspire pity." The chief characteristic of Jews,
continued Gómez, is their lack of a fatherland:
"They live in a nation and seem to be citizens of
it. But they really aren't citizens!" Given the
fact that they are scattered throughout the world
and have dedicated themselves to intellectual
pursuits, "they have the art and skill of appearing
to be the only thinkers on earth, the acme of wisdom
and literature, the sum total of everything; and
thus they pervert the judgment of the world."[59] To
underline his point that Jews were an essentially
disruptive force in any nation state, he cited his
own experience with them. Gómez described once
being struck by a phrase that he attributed to the
writer Max Nordau: "Christians, your mentalities
are unlike ours. We aren't German, or English, or
French. We are Jews." Gómez then recalled his own
perception of the Jewish presence in German life
during the early 1930s:

> While representing a relatively small
> proportion of the German population,
> they managed to become the bankers, the
> journalists, the owners of theaters, and
> the foremost physicians. They held
> almost all posts in the liberal profes-
> sions, owned the principal stores.
> Absolutely everything was dominated by
> Jews![60]

In the view of Gómez, there were only two
alternatives: "Either turn the nation over to the
Jews, or expel them." Expulsion was the solution of
several of the world's greatest rulers, most notably
Isabella the Catholic. Gómez claimed to have an
"unrestricted admiration" for Queen Isabella. When
she decided that Spain would not prosper unless her
Jewish population were expelled and then acted on
her decision, the results were, according to Gómez,
phenomenal:

> In the course of just a few years Spain
> passed from being a nation torn by
> discord, to the leadership of European
> nations . . . It was necessary to exile

122

the Jews! How it must have afflicted
her Christian soul; how the indispensable laceration must have pained her!
Nevertheless she did it; and when she
did it, in exercise of her authority, it
was, in my opinion, an indispensable
act.[61]

Given the fact that the world's Jewish
population is rather small, Gómez continued, "it
needs channels of influence--a means of dominating
and vanquishing its adversaries. . . . They can't
do it by themselves . . . They need a polity, a
tactic, a method. For this reason the communist
doctrine appeared in the world." Communism, second
in Gómez's hierarchical triad, was called by the
Conservative leader "a Jewish creation, completely,
totally. Jews were its creators and its first
proponents; they were its philosophers, its exposi-
tors; in communist theory there is no intellectual
influence that springs from any other source; all
was born there." By gaining control of the dispossessed with promises of the redistribution of
wealth, and by robbing them of their faith in things
divine, "Judaism, working behind communism, achieved
a domination that otherwise would not have been
possible."[62]
    The 1917 Bolshevik revolution in Russia was,
according to Gómez's analysis, "a Jewish phenomenon." Trotsky, Kamanev, and the others used aliases
for their real names which were Jewish. "I have a
book," he continued, "listing the leaders of the
Soviet Union. With the exception of some four, or
five, or ten, all of them are Jewish."[63]
    Gómez concluded his 1942 Senate speech by
explaining his view on how Masonry related to
communism and Judaism. Communist doctrine is not in
itself sufficient to guarantee the world domination
that Jews desire. They must have a mechanism by
which they can gain access to the upper echelons of
society. That mechanism exists and is of their own
creation: "Masonry is a typically Jewish creation." Proof of that assertion, said Gómez, is
found in the Masonic rite itself:

The words, much of the ceremony, the
candelabrum they use, many of the
emblems, even the name itself [is
Jewish]. Masons refer to themselves as
the congregation of Hiram, and it is
said that Hiram was the architect who

123

built the Temple of Solomon--Jewish, of
course --and from this comes the
denomination 'Great Architect of the
Universe.'[64]

Gómez went on in this vein, citing a book titled
La_verdad_israelita called El_Israelita, to
demonstrate that Masonry was Jewish. "And why has
Judaism created Masonry?" he asked. "To influence
decisively the march of the world!"[65]

After establishing his case, at least to his
satisfaction, Gómez went on at some length expound-
ing his conspiratorial interpretation of the
Masonic-Jewish origins of the French Revolution,
Colombia's chaotic nineteenth century history, and
the loss of Panama. He concluded the speech by
citing many of Leo XIII's condemnations of Masonry
as an enemy of Catholicism and warning that Colombia
was Mason-Jew-Communist-ridden. He ended his Senate
speech with the following clarion call: "You must
understand that the nation has great enemies. But
as I told you one year ago, it is mistaken to
believe that the enemy is without. The true, the
fearful, the definitive enemy is here within!"[66]

Chapter VIII

"LIBERAL/PROGRESSIVE" AND "TRADITIONALIST"
CONSERVATIVES: CONFLICT AT MID-CENTURY

The Split in Latin American Conservatism
Viewed Empirically

Defeat of the Axis powers in World War II
freed Latin American conservatives from the
unenviable task of simultaneously combatting rival
ideologies on both the left and right. With fascism
discredited, conservatives such as Colombia's Gómez
could lower the level of polemic. He abandoned his
shrill anti-Masonry and anti-Semitism and concen-
trated on protecting his nation from what he
perceived as communist subversion of the status quo.
As Gómez and others like him sought to control
social change, his more liberal-minded copartisans
argued that conservatism must move leftward if it
were to remain a viable sociopolitical philosophy.
They called for a doctrinal reorientation that
generated two decades of acrimonious debate between
"left" and "right" conservatives.
In several Latin American nations, the process
of ideological realignment was quite open. In
Chile, for example, the debate between members of
the "traditional" Conservative party and those of
the "progressive" National Falange, later Christian
Democratic party, generated a large body of writing.[1] Elsewhere, national events of greater moment
took precedence, as in Colombia where Violencia and
a military coup overshadowed the personal and philosophic differences separating Conservative party
leaders Gómez and Mariano Ospina Pérez. In other
nations the process by which the painful reorientation occurred must be gleaned from the writings of
individuals and from official publications of
national conservative parties.
The literature produced by the debate between
traditional and progressive conservatives is useful
to the student of twentieth century conservative
thought in several respects. Of greatest concern

125

to the present study is the way it delineates the nature and intensity of disagreement between the two factions, as well as the common ground they shared.

Careful reading of the literature of post-war conservatism reveals that it contains three clusters of related ideas. The first consists of all reference to nonrevolutionary strategies for improving the lot of the ordinary citizen. Here it is referred to as the complex of "liberal/progressive" ideas. The second, the "traditional" conservative cluster, is made up of word and phrases stressing the maintenance of existing society and the reconciliation of social change to the preservation of the status quo. The third cluster of ideas originates in sociopolitical teachings of the Roman Catholic church. For that reason they are referred to here as "religious" elements of conservative discourse.

Predominating in the "liberal/progressive" category are themes of majoritarian democracy and parliamentarianism, hostility to authoritarianism, and economic themes such as calls for increased economic development and protest against Latin America's economic dependence. Anti-imperialist statements are likely to occur. Prominent too are calls for greater social justice for the disadvantaged of society. These concerns may be voiced in the abstract or may take the form of endorsement of educational and agrarian reform and policies favoring workers. There are also likely to be strictures concerning the social function of property. During the two post-war decades, the progressive conservative was likely to sprinkle his writing with distinctly nonconservative elements such as calls for accommodation with those holding liberal or socialist ideas, or outright endorsement of some liberal or socialist ideas.

The traditionalist cluster includes anti-communist and antiliberal ideas, the latter sometimes in connection with anti-capitalist statements. The idea of hierarchy is prominent in the second cluster, and reference to "natural order" and to distributive justice is frequent. Such phraseology is often elitist and antiegalitarian in tone and content. The traditionalist endorses antimajoritarian democracy through advocacy of indirect parliamentary rule or corporative schemes of representation. References to democracy are couched in terms of authority; hence, terms such as "the rule of law," "social order," "discipline," and "order" occur frequently, along with praise of

126

the armed forces and occasional calls for censorship in the interest of social harmony. Political centralism is endorsed, and federalism is scorned. Included among "traditionalist" conservative ideas are nationalist ones of a historistic cast. Those tend to accentuate national uniqueness in terms of narrow republicanism--as opposed to locating the national interest in international or global terms.

Included in the "religious" cluster are references to Catholicism and the universality of its values, to the need for close ties between church and state, and to the importance of religious content in education. All references to social and political harmony, to the reconciliation of class conflict, to the conciliation of human differences, to Christian communitarianism, to the common good and the need for sublimation of individualism are also grouped in this category, as are references to private and public morality and virtue. Statements of a spiritual nature, of belief in ideas and ideals, are assigned to the religious category, along with references to the organic nature of society, the social nature of man, and primacy of the family in society.[2]

The three cluster concept can be used to help illustrate the breach in Latin American conservatism following World War II. Chile again provides an excellent example. In the year 1959, two Chilean conservatives, Eduardo Frei, just six years away from becoming his nation's first Christian Democratic president, and a charismatic university professor named Jorge Iván Hübner Gallo, published statements arguing the progressive and traditionalist conservative positions.

Eduardo Frei's "The Road to Follow" was clearly "liberal/ progressive," full of calls for national economic development, social justice, and democracy. It was also heavily anti-authoritarian.

Christian Democracy is ready to take its stand on an economic position, lending its ideas to the economic development of Latin America, to increasing rates of capital investment there, to changing its agrarian and economic structures, and to changing the structures of international commerce that are stifling all our peoples.

Addressing the social problem, he asserted that

127

Chileans had been separating themselves from the poor for too long: "in this hour we cannot vacillate. . . . We believe that the hour of justice has come, and as that great Uruguayan, de la Torre Muller, said: 'There is one generation to defend liberty, there is another to achieve social justice.'" Frei concluded his address with the ringing call "let us raise our voices in a single cry, all our arms in a single battering-ram, because we wish to cast off the night of America and give to the peoples true justice, full liberty, cleanness of action, and devotion to a noble cause."[3]

Hübner Gallo's essay was equally impassioned but entirely different in tone, stressing authority and hierarchy in a context of Christian community. Natural reason and natural law, wrote Hübner, form the ideological basis of traditional conservatism. "These are the concepts of God, State, and Social Order." He went on to explain that "the conservative groups in each country are not class parties, united by senseless economic interests. Rather, they are groups that embrace, as a synthesis of the entire nation, members of all the social strata, united by a common longing for the public welfare."[4]

Hübner's hottest blast was reserved for the Christian Democrats, a fact which makes the essay particularly useful in helping to define ideological space between left and right conservatives in Chile of the 1950s.

> Like their counterparts in France [they] began by professing a true idolatry of democracy, liberty, and human rights, inspired directly by secularist liberalism. They do not try to temper majoritarian democracy in any fashion so as to render it legitimate and acceptable. They think of the rights of the individual rather than of the common good. They do not contemplate organizing suffrage upon a logical, hierarchical basis, but are content to rest it upon a foundation of equalitarianism; nor are they willing to place upon liberty the restraints demanded in the interest of morality, goodness and truth.[5]

Hübner ended his indictment with a particularly damning charge: "Their ideology rests neither upon the glorious Aristotelian-Thomistic tradition, nor

128

upon pontifical teachings. Instead, it is rooted in the liberalism of the French Revolution, poorly disguised by the varnish of Christianity concocted by the philosophical talent of Maritain."[6] In spite of the notable differences in the Frei and Hübner essays, there is also an area of agreement in them. That is in the cluster of ideas pertaining to religion. For Hübner, conservatism "is essentially a spiritual movement [which] proclaims above all its faith in God, the church, and religion, which are the immovable bases upon which social life should be founded."[7] Frei describes Christian Democracy as follows:

> a philosophy which interprets man, which inspires poets and dramatists, which is capable of engendering a conception of art, which centuries ago built the Gothic cathedrals, and which in this century can inspire new forms of human creativity. This is a philosophy which can speak to youth, separating them from vice and purifying them in the strength of a great idea.[8]

The left and right of Chilean conservatism clearly found their common ground in the Catholic philosophia perennis.

A simple count and cataloging of the ideas contained in the Frei and Hübner essays help clarify the nature of their ideological thrust. Such survey reveals that more than half of Frei's remarks (54 percent) fall into the "liberal/progressive" category, while virtually none of Hübner's remarks (1 percent) touch on economic, social welfare, or majoritarian issues. But the figures are far from suggesting that Frei was a liberal in 1959 and Hübner a conservative without social conscience. More than 40 percent of Hübner's remarks are couched in the language of Christian humanism, as are nearly one-third of Frei's.

When the technique described above is applied to other examples of conservative writing of the post-World War II period, a similar left-right split is revealed. Conservatives who were influenced by Christian Democratic ideas, or forced leftward by a dominant liberal or radical party, as in the cases of Alceu Amoroso Lima of Brazil and Manuel Gómez Morín of Mexico, expressed their conservatism in liberal/progressive terms. Others, such as Nicaraguan Conservative party leader Carlos José

129

Solórzano and long-time Chilean Conservative party leader Sergio Fernández Larraín, felt no compulsion to do so.

Reasons for the breach in the Latin American conservative establishment are not to be found only in pressures external to national conservative parties, or to the lure of Christian Democracy. They are seen too in the personalities of individual conservatives. Examples of this generalization can be found in Colombia where conservatives Mariano Ospina Pérez and Gómez were elected president in 1946 and 1949, respectively. The political atmosphere in Colombia was explosive over the entire period of the Ospina and Gómez presidencies, and both men struck exceedingly conciliatory notes in their inaugural addresses to the nation. For all of that, however, when studied closely and when their content is analyzed, their presidential messages reveal significant differences. Gómez was able to strike a liberal/progressive note in just 14 percent of his address, while Mariano Ospina Pérez was able to do so to the tune of an astonishing 65 percent! Meanwhile, Gómez articulated themes of traditional conservatism in 53 percent of his inaugural message, while Ospina did so in just 5 percent of his. The open split between Gómez and Ospina in 1953 was nothing more than the formalization of fundamental philosophic differences that had always separated the two men--indeed, had existed in Colombian and Latin American conservatism from the late nineteenth century.

The following chart, based upon analysis of the content of doctrinal statements by eight prominent Latin American conservatives, suggests the extent to which copartisans were divided by the liberal/progressive and traditionalist dichotomy. But perhaps more suggestive is the degree to which both left and right conservatives found common ground in Roman Catholic social philosophy.

Content Analysis of the "Liberal/Progressive,"
"Catholic," and "Traditional" Social
Ideas of Selected Latin American
Conservatives, 1946-1962[9]

Group One: Liberal/Progressive Conservatives

	Percent "Lib/Pro"	Percent Religious	Percent "Traditional"
M. Ospina	65	30	5
A. Lima	43	33	24
E. Frei	54	31	15
M. Gómez Morín	41	50	9
Average Grp. I:	54	36	10

Group Two: Traditional Conservatives

	Percent "Lib/Pro"	Percent Religious	Percent "Traditional"
C. Solórzano	26	16	57
L. Gómez	14	33	53
S. Fernández L.	2	27	71
J.I. Hübner G.	1	44	55
Average Grp. II:	12	30	58

The nature and extent of the split in
conservative ranks during the twenty years following
World War II was clear. The succeeding two decades
would reveal the extent to which the liberal/
progressives would carry the day.

"Traditional" Conservatism Ascendant in Colombia

Conservative party victory in Colombia's
presidential election of 1946 signified the triumph
of "traditional" conservatism in that nation.
Mariano Ospina Pérez was, it is true, a moderate.
But he owed his office to Gómez, the traditionalist

whose clever strategy of promoting the mild mannered Ospina insured their party's victory over the divided Liberals.

Tragically for Colombia, ongoing political tensions and social pressures rooted in rapid social modernization combined to create sporadic civil war in the countryside. That conflict, called the Violencia, led to a collapse of Colombia's traditional political system during late 1949 and to the temporary end of civil government in 1953;[10] thus, the moment for Conservative return to power was hardly propitious. Ospina's moderate regime and the more conservative presidency of Gómez that followed were destined to fail. The ill-starred interlude of Conservative party rule ended with the military coup of Lieutenant General Gustavo Rojas Pinilla on June 13, 1953.

The story of Gómez and Colombian conservatism during the late 1940s and 1950s is not one of political or ideological triumph. It is, rather, the account of one traditional conservative's search for an ideologically consistent cure for what he perceived to be his nation's chief problems. It is also a case study of the traditional conservative critique of mid-twentieth century society.

Between the Conservative return to power in 1946 and the military coup of 1953, Gómez moved farther to the right in his thinking on society and politics. Events taking place both in Colombia and internationally explain this shift. No sooner did President Ospina Pérez take office in 1946 than reports of political violence began reaching Bogotá from the provinces. Gómez sought an explanation for this phenomenon that grew worse each month, finally resulting in the long-lived Violencia.[11] First, he attributed the trouble to Liberal perpetrators of electoral fraud. Then, when that explanation seemed insufficient, he implicated the entire opposition party. As he phrased it in the title of a speech delivered in November 1947, "The Liberal Party is Responsible for the Violencia."[12] Events surrounding the assassination of Jorge Eliécer Gaitán on April 9, 1948, during which enraged Liberals, blaming Gómez for ordering the murder, destroyed the Conservative leader's home and newspaper and drove him into exile, convinced Gómez that foreign subversives were the ones responsible for Colombia's ills.[13] Foreign Communists and domestic ones as well were attempting to bring about revolution through collaboration with Liberal party members where possible and were otherwise using the Liberal

132

opposition to further their ends. Newspaper editorials written by Gómez following the infamous "9th of April," bearing such titles as "Trails of Death," "National Catastrophe," "Colombia's Dishonor," and "Colombia at the Crossroads," proclaimed his conviction that Colombia was on the verge of changing in a disastrous, revolutionary way.[14]

When Gómez returned home some thirteen months after the Gaitán assassination, he did so grimly determined that Colombian civilization should be saved and that he would be its savior. "I return . . . like a soldier," he told supporters on the eve of his departure from Spain.[15] In a speech given two months later, he assured his followers that "only death can seal my lips."[16] By October 1949, Gómez had his party's presidential nomination and the following month was elected to succeed Ospina Pérez. Liberal party leaders, angered over violence against their rank-and-file and over Ospina's declaration of a state of seige shortly before the election, refused to participate in the voting. In the eight months preceding his inauguration, Gómez grappled with a thorny problem: How could he halt national dissolution without betraying his oft-stated belief in democracy? His public statements left no doubt that he felt this could be done. In January 1950, in a speech titled "Democracy under a New Regime," he began unfolding a plan for revitalizing Colombia's democracy, nearly done to death, as he explained, by the excesses of Liberal parliamentarians and a crazed proletariat. His plan had two parts: first, a restructuring of Colombian democracy along organic lines, and second, a rejection of majoritarianism--the "one-half plus one" against which Gómez had vociferated for more than a decade. Rule by majority, complained Gómez, had become a blunt instrument with which the Liberal party (that he insisted was a minority party) imposed its programs upon the nation in clear violation of moral law and the common good. By voiding most of the Liberal legislation passed since 1936, Colombia could be saved.

To Liberal eyes, the Gómez plan to conservatize Colombian institutions was at most dictatorial and at the least paradoxical and wrong-headed. The political restructuring he proposed was at base corporative, uniting democratic and antimajoritarian principles. As such it represented the culmination of a long meditation by the new president on the nature of democracy. The history of that meditation bears recounting, for it parallels the disillusion-

133

ment with majoritarian democracy that conservatives were experiencing elsewhere in the Western world.

Gómez had always insisted that he was a democrat and that his country was irrevocably so. In 1915, for example, he stated that he was convinced that "genuine democracy is the only solid basis for a sane polity." Twenty-four years later, he opined that both his nation and his political party were "profoundly and intimately . . . democratic." Twenty-three years after that, he remarked that he opposed the notion of a coup d'etat in Colombia because "I have faith in democracy, and that is what the nation needs."[17] He also vigorously insisted that dictatorial government could never work in Colombia. In late 1936, when Mussolini and Hitler were in the flush of totalitarian vigor, Gómez wrote that dictatorship was not a healthy form of governance. He added that the proper formula is the one proclaimed on Colombia's national seal: Liberty and Order.[18] Eight years earlier he had lectured one of his own party members about the Conservative's faith in democratic principles. The Conservative, he said, holds that "a good government need be neither omnipresent, nor arbitrary, nor all powerful. . . . On the contrary, it is full and public debate that permits national leaders to destroy the mistrust their enemies have of them."[19]

When he began his critique of liberalism during the 1930s, Gómez found it necessary to examine his belief in democracy more closely. He was forced to confront the fact that the democratic principles in which he believed sprang from the liberalism that he abhorred and that he held responsible for the contemporary crisis in Western society. How could he define democracy in a way that was compatible with his belief in government by a moral and intellectual elite, a way that would sustain him in his battle against liberal majoritarianism? In characteristic fashion, Gómez attacked the problem logically and methodically. First, he stated his conviction that democracy, in its present form, had failed. Democracy, he observed, was a concept sprung from nineteenth century liberalism. When liberalism failed, then its "legitimate daughter," democracy, was necessarily degraded too. Nineteenth century liberalism could be summarized, according to Gómez, in two words: "liberty and equality." But over time the order of the two words was reversed, giving preference to the second. Democracy became associated with emancipating the masses from their poverty. "Socialism sprang from this inversion of terms. It was a legitimate child of democracy in the same sense that democracy was child of nineteenth century liberalism."[20]

Liberals had so abused democracy that rather than allowing it to be a liberating force, they made of it a destructive one that filled the masses with communistic passion. With the problem defined thusly, Gómez went on to the task of explaining how Conservatives could save democracy. There are, he wrote, three ways of understanding that concept. First, there is democracy as a social tendency, that quality described in papal encyclicals as inspiring one with the desire to give the working classes, "oppressed more than ever by the modern world," not just a reasonable standard of living but justice as well. Second is political democracy, understood in the sense propounded by Aristotle and Thomas Aquinas as merely one form of government possible under law, available to different peoples in accord with their level of development and with the laws governing their respective nations. Finally, there is "democratism," or Rousseauean democracy "that desires to make a religious myth of the word, to make of it a sort of lay divinity in order to substitute it for belief in God and in the supernatural."[21]

Conservatives, argued Gómez, fully endorse the first two definitions of democracy, but they abhor the liberal doctrines of "absolute liberty" and "extreme individualism" that allow the strong of society to exploit the weak. Consequently, they endorse the movement to grant social justice to the dispossessed of the earth and to pursue democracy in its political sense:

> The laws of history admit only democratic and republican government on Colombian soil. Any other physiognomy of state or system of institutions is exotic to us and repugnant to the most deeply rooted sentiments of Colombians, and is incompatible with the primordial exigencies of our philosophic convictions. In this sense the Colombian Conservative party is deeply democratic. By the same token, Conservatism abhors the "democratism" that has its origin in Rousseau's teaching. . . . The Colombian Conservative party feels profoundly distanced from totalitarian

135

theories and practices that immolate
liberty and human dignity before an idol
no less insatiable than the bloody
Moloch of antiquity: the God-State. We
Conservatives believe in a different
God, one who promulgated laws . . .
entirely different from the iniquitous
and cruel ones of the "multitude god" of
the oppressive and tyrannical
God-State.[22]

Even before his ascension to power, Gómez had
openly pondered how he might cure democracy without
killing it, from time to time giving hints about the
course of his thought. In 1946 he opined that "if
democracy is to succeed, it's necessary to stride
through open spaces."[23] Six months earlier, in an
El Siglo editorial titled "The Ill Repute of Power,"
he suggested what those "open spaces" might be. He
began by quoting Spanish conservative Vásquez de
Mella's assertion that "democracy will always
triumph, but in its hierarchical form, not in its
equalitarian form." Then Gómez posed a rhetorical
question:

Is it really democracy that is practiced
by those who find themselves in power in
Colombia? Here the political descend-
ants of Rousseau have managed to deform
our institutions . . . in order to
pander to the masses who become drunk
with power for the convenience of a few
opportunists. . . . This is the rotten
scaffolding of the democracy that
governs us--a democracy sustained by the
humble, based in trickery, and exploited
by the elite with oligarchic tactics.

The course of action was clear: "an infection must
be cauterized if one is to avoid frightening
consequences." In other words, Colombia's
"egalitarian democracy" must give way to
"hierarchical democracy."[24]

Metaphysical Imaginings and Visions of Harmony: The Abortive Constitutional Reform of 1953

A constant theme in Colombian history has been
that of attempts by political leaders to impose
wildly varied, often utopian systems of government
upon the citizenry. Gómez was in step with this

national tradition in attempting to force his particular ideological vision upon the populace.[25] The Conservative party leader's attempt at harmonizing national society under neo-Thomist corporative forms took shape in a thoroughgoing constitutional revision known as "the Reform of 1953." That revision was never effected. Gómez was driven from power shortly before the new corporative charter was to take effect.

The abortive Reform of 1953 merits study for at least two reasons. First, it illustrates the tendency of Colombian (and Latin American) leaders to try to objectify metaphysical constructs. Second, it provides an excellent example of the sociopolitical thinking of Latin America's traditional conservatives at the midpoint of the twentieth century.

The political idiosyncracy of Colombian leaders has been much noted. Attempts to characterize or describe it run from Francisco García Calderón's subjective "they fight in Colombia over ideas; their hatred has a religious character. Colombian political parties have fixed programs, and in the quarrel over inflexible convictions, they become Byzantine and then destroy themselves," to Colombian sociologist Orlando Fals Borda's interpretation, set forth in his book La subversión en Colombia.[26] It is not the present writer's intention to rework the terrain of political utopianism in Colombian history, but rather to explore briefly the characteristics of mind that moved Colombian and other Latin American leaders to try to force their diverse population into idealized structures of utopian design. The point of reference is Gómez who struggled throughout his lifetime to impose his own idealized plan, made manifest in the Reform of 1953.

The attempt to sketch the broad outlines of a mind, in this case the mind of Gómez, is begun with reference to equally broad hypotheses about the several modes of human thought. It has been suggested that a mind can be understood by investigating the way it conceives and imagines the universe. This is the argument formulated by a number of noted philosophers, among them A.O. Lovejoy and Albert North Whitehead.[27] They further postulate that when exploring the subject of universal vision, it is possible to place all human beings into two categories, the first "classical" and the second "romantic." The person of classical turn of mind is a seeker after the eternal, the unchanging, and the harmonious, who recoils from change and decay.

Persons of classical orientation lean toward coherent and exact relationships that encompass all of experience, omitting nothing. The romantic is bolder, a risk-taker who revels in change. He is daring in outlook and quick to reject both protection and authority. He is a seeker of variety, plurality, and even disorder--all qualities antithetical to his opposite, who craves unity and ideal exactness. Clearly, Gómez was a "classical"-minded man who perceived the universe in terms of harmonious eternal verities. That was apparent in his first El Siglo editorial. There he described El Siglo contributors as persons "who deduce with closed logic, perfect harmony, and seductive rational exactitude the luminous system of rights and duties that sustain and nourish the human personality."[28] Gómez's rejection of everything in Hispanic culture that lacked the requisite harmony and coherence is clear in his assessment of a famous work by Mexican muralist Diego Rivera: "The work is in its entirety motley, exotic, incoherent, and without grandeur. It shows the symptoms of decadence to a much greater degree than do the mosaics of San Vitale de Ravenna."[29] Expressive both of the classical mind's satisfaction with its perfect vision of the universe and its hostility toward the romantic-minded is the profession of faith that Gómez made in the Colombian Senate in 1942: "We Catholics, who possess a total system, a philosophic doctrine, and a political system, are able, as studious men, to coolly debate our principles with those who follow other systems. . . . We are right; we do not doubt."[30]

Another way of exploring an individual's thought is through examination of his ethical stance. If we can understand the criteria upon which he bases his understanding of proper human conduct, then we can understand a great deal about him. An individual's moral stance can be appreciated through examination of how he deals with two ideas spanning the greater part of moral philosophy: the concepts of the "right" and the "good."[31]

The "good" in human experience involves the satisfaction of desires and aspirations; the "right" deals with modes of organization, the rules and regulations by which society is organized. Moral philosophers explain that there are two major frameworks by which individuals typically orient their pursuit of morality, as defined by their ethical system. The first is called the "goal seeking" framework. The "goal seeker" looks to human nature to understand man's basic goals and strivings. He assumes that human appetites point the way to what is good for society, and that the proper task of the moral person is to help human beings achieve the good life. To put it another way, the goal seeker sees the moral process in terms of pleasure and pain, means and ends. He looks to desire, aspiration, and pleasure as essential vehicles for achieving morality. He is ever searching for strategies to help his fellow humans lead their lives in accord with his particular ethical system.

The person who embraces the juridical framework sees ethics as a system of laws or rules enjoined upon human beings. He speaks in terms of "moral law" and argues that man has the inherent rationality to understand the "divine will," or the "natural order." The concept of the "right" dominates this conceptual framework. A virtuous person is defined as one who consciously obeys moral laws. When the moral philosopher of juridical orientation speaks of the "good," he usually does so in terms of the moral good, and not of good in the physical sense, satisfying the desires of men. By basing moral behavior on the individual's rational acceptance of what is declared to be right, as opposed to what brings pleasure, the juridical-minded employs guilt, shame, and awe to enforce morality as he has defined it. Morality is not conceived as a means of achieving an end, but rather as a fundamental principle of human behavior expressed in terms of universal rules of personal conduct. The juridical-oriented person secures obedience to moral law with threats of ultimate punishment that evoke anxiety and pangs of conscience.

The foregoing conceptualization of approaches to morality allows us to place much of what we know about Gómez in a comprehensible context. Gómez was a model of the juridical temperament. He steadfastly insisted that divinely inspired moral laws necessarily undergird all others. Were that not the case, a law could not be considered valid. He told members of the Supreme Court in his presidential inaugural address of 1950:

> He who has just taken the oath before
> you is a man of firm convictions, who
> has tried over the course of his life to
> discover justice in social and political
> matters, this without cleaving to the
> formalism through which positivist law
> tries to interpret . . . the eternal

principles of moral law, consubstantial
with human nature.[32]

Gómez's conviction that man possesses the
ability to approach moral perfection through
exercise of his rationality is apparent in his
perception of Colombian society. Those who are
truly virtuous, who are cognizant of and obedient to
God's law, approach saintliness, while the others,
the morally disinterested and the vicious, inhabit
the lower reaches of society. In one of his more
memorable pronouncements on the subject, Gómez
likened society to the space described by a child's
whirling jumprope. The space at either end of the
catenary shape is tiny, relative to the great volume
at its center. Gómez saw human society as shaped
the same way. At one pole is saintliness, at the
other is sin: "At the distinguished saintly end are
found the men of sublime and heroic virtue; at the
other extreme are found bad men." Moving away from
either pole toward the wide part of the catenary,
said Gómez, the intensity of both virtue and vice
diminish. Finally, one reaches the center of the
volume "where rest the immense mass of men, almost
indifferent to the antagonistic principles of vice
and virtue, drawn toward one or the other extreme
only by chance."[33] This was a Thomist vision of
society predicated on the notion of human inequality
and hierarchy. "I speak in the name of the principles of Catholic doctrine that are expressed in the
philosophic works of Saint Thomas, who tells how a
state must be organized," Gómez told Darío Echandía
in a Senate debate of 1942.[34] Dante gave literary
expression to the Thomistic vision of society in the
Divine Comedy. There he described the ordering of
souls in Paradise, where each found its place in
accord with its capacity to love God. The spirit of
God's love unified the hierarchy, stilling each
soul's desire to move upward and winning its
acceptance of the divine order. This vision of
harmony and perfection appealed to the juridical-minded Gómez who described it in a Senate debate
of 1940:

Man, according to Dante, is part of the
cosmos. He is linked to the hierarchy
of the universe. . . . Man is not an
isolated being. Rather, he is part of
the greater hierarchy, having an end and
a destiny, and having certainty of both
his past and his future.[35]

140

Throughout his career, Gómez waged an unending battle against the forces of immorality that were robbing Colombia of her virtue--"the great battle against infernal powers," as he once termed it.[36] His idealized fatherland was of the harmonious sort posited by the moralist of juridical orientation. It was a republic in which the citizenry enjoyed liberty within order and was governed by "the hierarchies derived from virtue and the intelligence that coexists with merit."[37]

Liberals who faced Gómez in congressional debate or who tried to answer his polemical outpourings with empirical fact found his mystical metaphysical approach to politics particularly vexing. How was a liberal-minded twentieth century politician to answer charges that his philosophy was "in profound error . . . error that consists in refusing to recognize truth and in insisting in believing fiction,"[38] or that the Liberal party under "a rain of empty formulae, labored and ill-conceived," had perverted "the natural and obvious sense of things;"[39] or that his party had originated in "a veritable pact with the devil," one that produced "cursed fruit . . . a hurricane of skepticism, of fascination with things foreign, and of blasphemy?"[40]

Nor did Gómez limit his invocation of metaphysical ideals, spiritual constructs, and diabolical nether regions to his antiliberal blasts. Rather, such terminology suffused all of his thought. In art criticism, he was likely to pass judgment on the work in question in accord with its conformity to "the categorical imperatives of life and morality."[41] In his essays on history, he was likely to find the cause of some major event, World War II, for example, in the loss of a people's "spiritual unity."[42] When speaking of a subject dear to his heart, the Conservative party, he was wont to employ metaphysical absolutes: a "perfect peace" would reign in a society organized in accord with Roman Catholic philosophy;[43] Conservative party members could afford to scorn biological laws because "the excellence of our goals separates us from the ordinary and binds us to the spiritual,"[44] strict adherence to Conservative principles would repair "the disfigurement of the national soul" inflicted by liberalism.[45]

In employing metaphysical imagery, Gómez placed himself in a tradition of discourse that had been in decline for some three centuries. Scholastic thought, with its strong otherworldly cast,

141

came under devastating attack in the seventeenth and eighteenth centuries. By the nineteenth and twentieth centuries, reasoning that smacked of scholasticism usually evoked amusement rather than scorn; thus it is no wonder that Gómez's critics usually dismissed out of hand or simply ignored his oratorical flights into the world of imagination. When they did bother to remark on his metaphysical imagery, they attributed it to Gómez's "medieval" mentality, to his inability to adjust to modern reality, or to the fact that he was mentally unbalanced. The Liberals based their scorn on a respectable body of philosophic opinion. An empirical, scientific age pushed metaphysics entirely outside the field of human knowledge, labeling it an irrational form of wish-fulfillment. Persons of otherworldly bent were said to be helpless neurotics lost in a consoling fantasy world, or paranoids seeking refuge from fears lying beyond the reach of reason and fact.

Gómez never commented directly upon his use of metaphysical constructs, nor did he bother to respond to those who did. When forced to say something about his personality, he invariably responded with the verse from Thomas à Kempis, "You're no better because they praise you, you're no worse because they revile you: you are what you are."[46]

The metaphysical turn of mind peculiar to ideological thinkers is not without its defenders. Modern philosophers Henri Bergson and Martin Heidegger have rejected the claims of logical positivists that metaphysical visions are nothing more than expressions of an emotional state. Rather, they see such expression as indispensable to human existence, leading to acquisition of knowledge of fundamental philosophical questions that are inaccessible to the logical analyses of the empiricists. Philosopher Ernst Cassirer provides another approach to appreciating metaphysical thought. Cassirer describes man as a symbol-creating animal who typically uses his imagination to help him understand the world and to act within it.[47] While the symbols employed by the metaphysician may not be understood in the same way as those used by the scientist or the historian, they do serve the same function. That is, they help the individual organize and understand what he perceives around him. All evidence points to the fact that this is the way Gómez employed metaphysical expressions in his debates with Liberals, in his exhortations to the Conservative faithful, and in his abortive constitutional reform of 1953.

Gómez returned to Colombia in mid-1949, invigorated by a positivist commitment to action and burning with the desire to save the nation.[48] That conviction is transparently clear in every public utterance he made between June 1949 and his inauguration as president on August 7, 1950. As members of the opposition Liberal party began to perceive the outlines of the Gómez reform, they reacted with shock and anger. So controversial was it that more than twenty years later, the reform, which provided for popular election of president, legislature, and municipal councils, was tarred as "totalitarian" and "anti-democratic," an intellectual offshoot of "Nazi-Fascist Falangist ideology."[49] That reaction, both immediate and retrospective, is reminiscent of the response to Gómez's celebrated Teatro Municipal talks of 1928, used by detractors to prove that Gómez had become a liberal.[50]

The Reform of 1953 was highly prescriptive in nature. It attempted to institutionalize authoritarian rule by a moral elite through construction of an elaborate, interconnected network of social controls.[51] Those controls, designed to favor and promote the growth of social solidarity, were to have been benign in nature. The document at large reflected both Gómez the engineer, whose vision of a progressive Colombia so fascinated Liberals early in his political career, and Gómez the authoritarian and organic social theorist who drove Liberals to distraction after 1932.

Gómez took great pains to stress the superiority of corporative government. As he awaited his inauguration, he published several newspaper pieces in which he explained this belief. Just because some totalitarian regimes made use of corporative organization, he wrote in January 1950, there is no reason to conclude that corporatism is a totalitarian system. On the contrary, corporative organization may be chosen for any government whose leaders value efficiency and progress. Corporativism, wrote Gómez, is that political form through which democracy finds its most sublime expression.

Gómez argued that when national legislation is formulated by elected representatives from distinct occupational groups--labor unions, farmers, industrialists--the quality of representative government is improved:

> popular representation ceases to be
> quantitative, becoming, instead,

143

qualitative. Instead of reflecting amorphous groups of twenty thousand or more inhabitants, representation is based on the individual's economic activity, corporation or guild membership. Nothing, is more friendly to labor unions than is corporatism; thus nothing is more democratic.[52]

As a sort of postscript to his paean to corporative government, Gómez repeated his old indictment of majoritarian democracy--rule by the "one-half plus one":

> What is clear is that the system of popular representation that was a millstone around the neck of the republic for so many years must be substituted for something better. It is the hope of all Colombians that past congresses, which neglected their legislative duties, preferring instead to usurp powers of the chief executive . . . never again return in their old form.[53]

The Reform of 1953 was drawn up by a constituent assembly composed of Conservatives who were willing to carry out the president's wishes. That it was an accurate reflection of Gómez's thinking can be seen in his message to future members of the assembly. That speech, written in late 1951, is the reform of 1953 in outline. One of its most important paragraphs contains a concise statement of Gómez's thought on the democratic process:

> Universal suffrage is good and on occasion irreplaceable; for example, it serves very adequately as a means of selecting the national president, because at that moment it precisely fulfills its natural function, which is that of assaying public opinion.
> Universal suffrage may also be the most advisable way for partially selecting the legislative branch of government, in order that the elemental and primary desires of the masses have adequate expression in the laws of the nation.
> But we cannot generalize the concept

144

to the extreme of subjecting all the
nation's business to majority vote.
Majoritarianism is inegalitarian. It
levels down and submits most administrative decisions to a nontechnical process
that runs contrary not just to public
advantage but to basic common sense.[54]

The document produced by the constituent
assembly selected by Gómez was, in final analysis, a
diverse collection of political ideas. On one hand
it must be viewed against the backdrop of political
disintegration and civil war--the Violencia--
plaguing Colombia during the late 1940s and early
1950s. On the other it can be seen as a traditional
conservative's last best attempt to preserve an
idealized Colombia that had existed only in his
metaphysical imaginings and visions of social
harmony.

Many of the document's provisions reflect the
spirit of anxiety, idealism, and self-deception in
which it was drawn up. For example, we find the
projected reform incongruously providing for direct
popular election of the president (Title XII,
Article 114) and other public officials, thereby
preserving hallowed democratic traditions, while at
the same time stripping Congress of most of its
traditional deliberative functions (Titles VII, IX,
X). Meanwhile, near absolute control of national
affairs was placed in the hands of the president and
his inner circle. The crisis atmosphere surrounding
the Gómez presidency is reflected in provisions that
can only be termed oddities in the context of
twentieth century constitutionalism. In addition to
the provision that Congress must vote "only in
reference to the common good" (Title XI, Article
105), the common good was to determine the degree of
freedom allowed business and industry (Title III,
New Article). Class conflict was anathematized, and
social harmony lifted up as the ideal in what stands
as the most ingenuous article of the entire document: "The Colombian state condemns class struggle
and promotes social harmony under the shelter of
justice" (Title IV, Article 1). Rivaling that
article in idealism was the one reflecting the
notion that, given society's organic nature and the
fact that the family rather than the individual is
the fundamental social unit, heads of families are
juridically superior to unmarried adults. It
stipulated that married men be permitted two votes
in elections for municipal councils, and that

145

married women be allowed double representation pending the enactment of appropriate legislation (Title XX, New Article).

Gómez's constitutional reform testified to its progenitor's faith in economic planning. An entire new section was drawn up describing the functions of a new cabinet-level National Economic Council that would oversee all matters related to economics and economic planning. Several months before the reform was to go into effect, Gómez penned a newspaper piece describing the benefits that he hoped economic planning would bring to Colombia. Written in a retrospective vein, as though composed in the year 1962, it supposed that economic planning would end fraud and errors in the carrying out of public projects, and that public monies would be spent on the basis of need rather than of patronage.

The portion of the Reform of 1953 relating to economic planning was truly forward-looking. The depoliticization of public works projects through submitting proposals to study and approval by scientists, engineers, and foreign experts, and funding of such projects through loans from international lending agencies did in fact come to pass in Colombia.

Other provisions reflecting the reformers' spirit of eclecticism in matters economic included special economic protection for families, prohibited child labor, guaranteed a minimum wage, promoted cooperatives, and barred government contractors from holding certain political offices within six months of signing the contract. All of these provisions were in harmony with the article stating that "the economic system is founded in free enterprise and individual initiative, exercised within limits of the common good" (Title III, Article 32).

The best image of Gómez the authoritarian idealist, the traditional conservative activist, the progressive of medieval orientation, is the one projected by Gómez himself at the conclusion of the 1952 essay on what he believed Colombia would be after ten years under the benign and curative reformed constitution:

> The most admirable thing about the constitutional revision of 1953 was not the reforms themselves, but rather it was the wise and noble spirit of justice that inspired it. Careful attention was paid to the dictates of

146

experience, the tireless planting of
what for so long has been sown midst
fallow furrows of grief. A strict sense
of responsibility for the delicate task
they carried out enabled the constituent
assembly to realize a sober, sensitive
labor that animated and gave impulse to
the formidable progress that Colombia
proudly reveals in 1962. Statesmen
whose norm was strictest administrative
propriety, whose minds and consciences
were profoundly Christian, achieved
success in bringing stability, peace,
and greatness to Colombia. They saw to
it that the nation's institutions and
their functioning earned the respect of
all and became worthy of universal
emulation. Colombia knew how to free
itself from the anguish and uncertainty
that afflicted the world. Now the
nation is rich and happy, with wide and
promising vistas before it.[55]

Gómez and his constitutional reform are best
understood in the context of that broad offensive
against secularization and erosion of traditional
social forms appearing in the West late in the
nineteenth century and gaining momentum in the early
twentieth century. He and many others attempted to
posit workable alternatives both to the world of
bourgeois capitalism and to the solution offered by
socialists. The French rightist Charles Maurras
drew upon the same metaphysical absolutes and evoked
the same vision of social decay and impending doom
as did Gómez in rallying partisans to the barricades
in defense of national virtue. British conservative
Harold Macmillan's comment that he hoped to bring
labor "more and more into active partnership [in
industry] on the basis of a policy which sought to
serve the common interests of both management and
labor," is difficult to distinguish in form or
content from Gómez's stated desire to "reestablish
harmony between labor and management on a basis of
mutual understanding, respect, and harmony; this to
insure . . . that modern industrial society doesn't
end up recreating slavery."[56] It is doubtful that
L.S. Amery's proposal that the British Parliament be
modified by adding a third house made up of representatives of business and labor could be closer in
spirit to Gómez's plan to make the Colombian Senate
a semi-corporate body. These plans of parliamentary

147

reform were old when first proposed in Great Britain and Colombia in the mid-twentieth century. They were simply restatements of the conservative desire to heal societies split by industrialism and threatened by class war.

North American political philosopher Walter Lippmann invested as much energy as Gómez in identifying the malaise of the age and suggesting cures for it. In his book The Public Philosophy, he argued that there are universal standards of behavior to which man must adhere lest the world be rendered hopelessly chaotic. His evocation of Platonic ideals calls to mind Gómez's "categorical imperatives of life" that man must follow if he is to create the "good society."[57] Other North American philosophers have been as insistent on returning to the Platonic Aristotelian, Thomistic vision of world order. Eric Voeglin and Leo Strauss are two contemporary thinkers who insist that society will be set right only when mankind embraces a rational cosmology informed by the eternal principles described in natural law.[58]

Contemporary history reveals that Gómez was squarely within Latin America's authoritarian tradition. The region never shed its patrimonial character bequeathed by sixteenth-century Iberian colonizers. Whether claiming to stand for the Revolution, the military, democratic republicanism, a "Third Force" or "Justicialism," or the philosophia perennis, Latin American national leaders have tended to be caudillistic authoritarians presiding over highly centralized nations. Still, like most other Latin Americans, Gómez believed unabashedly in democracy. When in power and before, he racked his brain for a way to reconcile that principle with those of order and hierarchy. The resulting semi-corporate constitution that crowned his efforts is no more odd or incongruous than the corporative one-party system that has ordered Mexico's quasi-revolutionary society for well over half a century.

Gómez attempted to address Colombian problems in accord with national realities as he perceived them and within the context of powerful cultural uniformities shared by all Latin American peoples. Everything he did throughout his career reflected his desire to bring change to Colombia in a way that he felt to be in the best interests of his people and in harmony with his own ideological, conservative view of what was proper for the nation. He never ceased reminding his fellow citizens that their destiny was, in essence, in their own hands, that they must seek their own solutions to their own peculiar problems. But let Gómez state his idea in his own words:

> What do we see when we gaze upon ourselves? We see that we belong to a moral and intellectual complex. We find that within the context of universal history, we're closer to some [cultural] traditions than to others. We are members of a distinct culture. It's not Japanese or Chinese, or Hindu, or Slavic, or Germanic, or Anglo-Saxon. There are saints and heroes in our history who are ours alone, and who move us more profoundly than do the great figures of other cultures. We possess thinkers and artists who communicate beauty and emotion to us much more intensely than do other artists and intellectuals. Our consciences shout the truth that there are . . . things that speak clearly to our ears, without need of intermediaries.[59]

Chapter IX

THE LAST YEARS OF LAUREANO GOMEZ

Antideterminism and Its Consequences

The years between the fall of Gómez in 1953 and his death in 1965 were perhaps the most eventful ones in his political career. Old and sick when unseated by military coup, Gómez might have accepted defeat, spending his remaining years in comfortable repose. But that scenario was hardly acceptable to the flinty individual Colombians knew as "the Monster." Gómez battled back from his Spanish exile, ultimately helping to topple Rojas Pinilla. Almost incredibly, he did so by joining forces with his old enemies, the Liberals. Together with Liberal party leader Alberto Leras Camargo, Gómez helped craft the bipartisan accord known as the National Front. In so doing, he insured that his faction of the Conservative party would remain a force in national politics.

Gómez's sudden conversion to bipartisanship was greeted cynically by many Colombians. They called his turnabout proof that Gómez would gladly sacrifice ideals to gain power. They said he would stop at nothing to unseat General Rojas and to strike at his chief rival for Conservative party leadership, Mariano Ospina Pérez, whom he routinely blasted as a traitor for collaborating with the government of Rojas Pinilla.

This is not the place to address the complexities of Colombian politics during the last years of Gómez, or to assay the old Conservative's complex motives for his reversals of long-held positions. But it is germane to set forth the intellectual sources of those changes.

Inconsistencies in Gómez's thought sprang in part from the fact that he was not a determinist. Though he occasionally drew from deterministic theories, he rejected them overall as incompatible with his linear view of history, with the Roman Catholic doctrine of free will, and with his belief that men make history and that great men shape it. His antideterminism is quite apparent in his essay "The Character of General Ospina" written just months before his Teatro Municipal lectures of 1928--lectures that many Colombians denounced as abjectly geodeterministic. In it Gómez labeled as "obsolete" both the geodeterministic theories of Frederick Ratzel and the "ambitious constructions of sociologists and cultural geographers."[1] He expressed the belief that a nation's greatness stood in direct proportion to its wealth in creative and dynamic individuals.

The rejection of determinism gave Gómez a flexibility in his approach to national political problems disconcerting to those who thought that as an ideologist he was incapable of creative thought. In fact his historicist, even relativist, belief that human society changes and that men, through their creative energies, change their social institutions in accord with objective conditions peculiar to their culture, was quite compatible with his idealized vision of what Colombian society should be. His belief in the timelessness and universality of Roman Catholic values did not clash with his historicism. The one was a Platonic concept, an ideal of perfection to strive for. The other allowed man the freedom to bring himself and his society into ever closer conformity with the ideal-- this through understanding the unique features of his history and culture; thus Gómez could argue in 1938 that democracy is a political institution whose precise form and function must be determined by each people "in accord with the level of its development and national characteristics."[2] In 1952, when trying to convince Colombians that they would be best served by a semi-corporative political system, he couched his argument in solidly historicist, nondeterminist terms:

> Political science is eminently relative. No system created by the human genius is optimal, infallible, and of universal utility. Nor is any system created for the direction of human community lacking in partial advantage or good ideas for solving determined problems. The art of the statesman consists in selecting, among the beneficent methods available, the one that best accords with the idiosyncracy of the nation where it is to be applied.[3]

That this significant feature of Gómez's belief fell outside the liberal/ conservative/ communist paradigm caused no end of confusion among Colombians. When, in 1955, rumors began circulating that the exiled Gómez was calling for a national referendum on the dictatorship of Rojas Pinilla, his detractors hooted that he had experienced a sudden "conversion" to democracy. Some weeks later the Liberals admitted with apparent surprise that Gómez had consistently endorsed the practice of democratic election for filling a variety of public posts.[4] Even so, the Colombian public did not appreciate that Gómez's call for elections was consistent with his conservative and his historicist principles.

The four year Spanish exile was not entirely unpleasant for Gómez. There, surrounded by his family, he spent most days reading, writing, taking afternoon strolls, and pondering his fall. All the while he remained active in Colombian politics, sending home a steady stream of letters in which he denounced the military government at home and all who collaborated with it.[5] The heated nature of those epistles, circulated clandestinely when necessary and openly when possible, made it clear that he had lost none of his old combativeness nor his conviction that he was the legitimate leader of Colombian conservatism; yet for the very predict-ability of their tone and content, the letters from Spain were deceptive. Gómez was undergoing a shift in political attitude. The metamorphosis did not reflect a change in his fundamental beliefs, but it did represent a reversal of his lifelong approach to the conduct of Colombian politics. He was adopting the position that Liberals and Conservatives must cease the old, polemical debate on their philosophic differences and instead must work together to heal the body politic.

In absence of any explanation by Gómez of this change, we cannot know with certainty the process through which he decided to make peace with the Liberals. But there is ample evidence to help us explain it. Principal among the causal factors were the Violencia and the dictatorship of Rojas Pinilla. From the beginning of the Violencia, during the administration of Ospina Pérez, Gómez was horrified that his countrymen could commit atrocities upon one another in defiance of the Christian principles by which Ospina, and later he himself, guided the nation. Throughout his presidency, Gómez explained the Violencia as a fiendish lawlessness carried out by Liberals, Communists, and common criminals.

Later, from Spain, he observed that Rojas Pinilla too was unable to quell the bloodshed. The General was reduced, as Gómez had been, to labeling the violentos (perpetrators of Violencia) criminals and Communists and using the army in a futile attempt to restore order. The humble people of the Colombian countryside continued to die by the tens of thousands.[6] Gómez mused on this and at length reached his conclusion: the Violencia was not the responsibility of Liberals, or Communists, or of common criminals--and it was certainly not his fault, as many Colombians averred. It was a product of the old political sectarianism. Colombia must kill sectarianism to end its Violencia and must restore the traditional parties to their places of preeminence.

But how could that be done with power in the hands of a military strong man? Gómez was sure that the Rojas Pinilla regime would not last long. After all, every Colombian schoolboy knew that "Colombia is sterile ground for dictatorships," a phrase Gómez had repeated frequently over the years. From the first day of his fall, he had done nothing but work to bring Rojas down. All that was needed was a rapprochement of the Liberal and Conservative parties, something that, if difficult, was still not impossible to achieve. Since their formation a century earlier, the parties had frequently joined forces to unseat dictators. But once the parties were returned to their traditional dominance, how could they be kept from lapsing into old habits that had produced the rural warfare? That was the real problem. The solution came to Gómez one day early in his exile. He was reading Reinhardt Dozy's History of the Moors in Spain when he happened on the chapter describing a plan by which Christians and Moors alternated in the rule of Spain, all the while dividing bureaucratic posts between them.[7] Christians and Moors, Conservatives and Liberals-- the analogy must have made Gómez smile.

The story of Colombia's National Front need not be retold here. Suffice it to say that the epochal agreement, drawn up in Spain by Gómez and Liberal Alberto Lleras Camargo, provided for alternating Liberal and Conservative presidencies, and equal division of lesser political posts. Colombian politics would operate under terms of the National Front compact until the year 1974.

Rojas Pinilla fell in 1957, and the following year Alberto Lleras Camargo was sworn in as the first of four presidents to serve under the bipartisan accord. Gómez spoke at Lleras' inauguration, giving one of the most notable speeches of his political career. The speech was the antithesis of his other discourses, focusing on the themes of harmony, cooperation, mutual understanding, and the laying aside of old hatreds. But even more remarkable was the fact that for the first time, he admitted that the partisanship that for forty years had found its most perfect expression in Gómez was wrong:

> When we have been able to kill the sectarianism among us, we will be on the verge of achieving harmony and peace . . . . We have all erred. But the cruel hand that oppressed us made us understand our error. It caused us to turn our backs rapidly and decidedly on the old methods of political battle and to give ourselves over to this generous and fecund task aimed at fundamentally correcting the political life of our nation.[8]

For the rest of his life, Gómez was true to those sentiments. He steadfastly supported the Frente Nacional, and as he predicted, the Violencia ended during the time of political power-sharing. In his last years, Gómez found fault with much that transpired under the Frente Nacional. But he never pronounced his judgments in the old polemical terms. Once he made up his mind about something, he rarely changed it.

Nearly as striking as his conversion to bipartisanship was the shift in Gómez's attitude toward the United States. It was emergence of the United States as the world's leading anticommunist power that changed his perception of the nation Gómez had once called Colombia's worst enemy. American diplomats listened closely as Gómez discussed communist subversion within the Liberal party--an ironic change from the days when U.S. ambassador Spruille Braden told his government, on Liberal authority, that Gómez was the Colombian most dangerous to American interests. Gómez's change in attitude toward the United States was nothing short of breathtaking. After the tragic Bogotá riot of April 1948, he frankly endorsed an intimate relationship with that nation in the interest of providing a united front in the Cold War that raged at that time. In a nationally broadcast radio

address delivered a month before his election as
president, Gómez spelled out his thinking on the
United States, international communism, the Liberal
party, and their relationship as he perceived it.
First he praised the U.S. for having achieved the
highest levels of economic prosperity and political
stability of any modern nation. Then he described
the threat to that well-being posed by "the disease
of communism that detests prosperity and seeks only
ruin and desperation in order to stimulate the
hatred of some men for others." Gómez lauded the
action of the United States in seeking to have all
American states outlaw their communist parties. It
was that initiative by the United States, said
Gómez, "that produced the communist uprising of
April 9, 1948, whose authors have been shown to be
international Communists."[9]
      During the four years that Gómez spent in his
final exile, he modified other ideas that he had
vigorously supported in earlier times. When he
returned to Colombia, he no longer argued that the
best way to save the nation from communism was by
harassing the Liberal party. His conversion to
bipartisanship was no less notable that his endorsement of liberal economic developmentalism and inter-
nationalism. In an interview of May 1958, he
clearly indicated these changes. Gone was the
arielista rhetoric about Latin American spirituality
and the need to oppose destructive materialism. Now
he discussed regional problems and prospects in
economic terms. He became interested in the notion
of a Latin American common market, whose effect
would "make us much less dependent on the nations of
other continents." His view of the United States
was more balanced and judicious than at any other
time: "I observe with pleasure a modification in
U.S. policy with respect to the Latin American
nations. The U.S. seems convinced of the benefits
of economic collaboration with us." When asked by
the interviewer to comment on the relative merits of
capitalism, socialism, and communism, his response
was surprisingly mild: "One cannot adhere to a
single school of economic thought. True wisdom is
being able to select from the different systems in
accord with what is best for each unique nation."[10]
      Gómez's responses in the 1958 interview indi-
cated that he believed the world was fundamentally
different from when he entered political life. That
was what he said two years later when describing his
thinking on Colombia in the international setting:
"The international structure of the world has

changed fundamentally in recent times." He added
that the "new modalities" of international political
organization had made the diplomacy known earlier in
the century obsolete. Colombia must not hesitate to
adopt the new political styles. Gómez made specific
reference to the European Economic Community, saying
that Latin American nations should forget old rival-
ries and outmoded isolationism and unite to form
their own economic community.[11]

At the end of his life, only the essential
religious ideas of Gómez remained unchanged. All
the others had undergone a long metamorphosis that
in some cases reversed them and in others caused
them to disappear altogether. But this does not
mean the Conservative held his ideas lightly.
Rather, it signifies that the thought of Gómez
evolved along with the century--a century unique in
the rapidity and profundity of change in all areas
of society and in all parts of the world. Gómez
possessed certain fundamental metaphysical beliefs
that he followed unswervingly throughout his life,
yet he remained acutely aware of national and international intellectual and socioeconomic developments. It was his ability to maintain deeply held
beliefs while accepting changing social conditions
that accounts for his durability as a Colombian
political leader.

Gómez, His Ideas, and His Uncertain Place in Colombian History

The luxuriance of Gómez's thought, his
combative nature and propensity to personal attack,
his use of exaggeration and colorful metaphor, his
sophistic reasoning and logical inconsistencies, his
fanciful historical comparisons and the awe that he
inspired in political friends and foes alike all
combined to make him a difficult man for most
Colombians to understand. This dearth of understanding among people of his own nation is not
entirely Gómez's fault. His fellow citizens rarely
commented critically or objectively on his pronouncements or considered whether his ideas might in
any way be compatible with their own. This failure
to perceive Gómez with a degree of objectivity and
understanding, either when he lived or afterward,
has not been good for Colombia, for it implies that
an important part of recent national history is
dimly seen, or not visible at all.

Gómez was responsible for at least some of the
confusion surrounding him. On one hand he suffered

the logical inconsistency that plagues those who try
to interpret the world through an all-encompassing
ideology. On the other, and much more damaging to
the cause of understanding, was the punishing way he
used words. To Gómez the ideologist, words were
weapons used in fighting for the just cause. He
honed them to a razor edge and wielded them in
political battle with the verve of the medieval
crusader who resolved to slaughter as many of the
enemy as possible before being himself cut down. In
fact Gómez used crusader terminology to describe his
use of words in political debate. "Today one must
learn to wield the invisible but no less cutting
sword of words, which wounds the adversary more
severely than does the weapon of steel," he said on
one occasion.[12] On another he asked:

> and what is martyrdom but the highest
> expression of selflessness? Let the
> politician-knight who enters the lists
> of his noble profession, armed with the
> Idea, first cloak himself with the red
> tunic of disinterest--this even before
> he straps on the helmet of reason,
> embraces the shield of truth, grasps the
> sword of honor, puts on the spurs of
> constancy.[13]

Even more revealing was a remark Gómez made during
the year 1940: "The impact or effect of my words are
of no importance to me. This is because I never
speak with the objective of achieving a determined
reaction. Rather, my words spring from an unfailing
sincerity."[14]

Even had Gómez delivered his speeches drily
and with irrefutable logic, it is doubtful that the
Liberals would have given him a fair hearing.
Neither set of antagonists was capable of objectivity under the superheated political atmosphere of
Colombia in the 1940s. Political polarization
heightened in the course of the twentieth century,
spurred on by the growth of national government.
Bigger government meant more government jobs, and
the fate of persons holding those jobs rested on the
success of their party in presidential elections.
The Liberal bureaucrat who knew with certainty that
he would lose his job in the event of a Conservative
electoral triumph was not interested in what Gómez
had to say. His only desire was that his political
patrons should prosper and that he retain his
sinecure. Spoils system politics and lack of a

tradition of compromise meant that it was not in the
interest of Liberals and Conservatives to understand
one another. The opposite condition prevailed. It
was thought necessary for each side to make the
other seem as odious and unhuman as possible to keep
the electorate's interest high; and so, Gómez
painted Liberals like Alfonso López, Carlos Lleras,
and Darió Echandía as enemies of Catholicism, as
Masonic destroyers of faith and family, intent on
corrupting the nation and handing its people, bound
and defenseless, over to the powers of darkness.
The Liberals found it equally convenient to depict
Gómez as a jackbooted Fascist anxious to impose a
medieval authoritarianism upon Colombia. After
snuffing out all human rights and negating social
gains achieved since independence, a demented,
sinister Gómez would refurbish inquisitorial
dungeons and set fanatics to tormenting Liberals.
Such political myth-making was the opposite of truth
seeking and worse than lying. Lies could be dis-
proved, but the myths created by Colombia's political elites lived on to the nation's detriment. They
flourished in the ambience of hyperbole and extremism that fatally weakened Colombian democracy during
the first half of the twentieth century.

The failure of Colombians to perceive Gómez
accurately or to comprehend what he said objectively
is only partially explained by partisan exclusivity
and ideologically impaired vision. There was a
factor that, while linked to the first two and
sharpened by them, was not dependent upon them.
That was the lack of a critical tradition in
Colombia. Gómez was not understood by his friends
or enemies simply because there was no desire on
their part to do so. The unwillingness of Colombians to examine critically ideas and opinions at
variance with their own may perhaps be explained as
a psychocultural phenomenon, an analysis that is
beyond the scope of this history of ideas. The
present writer can only point out its existence and
explain its significance in the context of this
study. In Colombia's compartmentalized society,
politically active citizens knew what they believed
and what was in their best interest, and they made
it their business to seek out others with whom they
agreed. In accord with their hierarchical and
authoritarian tradition, there was always a recog-
nized leader whose opinions and dictates they dared
criticize with the certainty of being declared
schismatic and summarily expelled from the group.
The only safe alternatives were to agree whole-

heartedly with the leader's ideas or to remain
silent. This was hardly a mechanism for keeping a
political leader like Gómez from adopting extreme
positions, as he frequently did. To attempt mean-
ingful criticism, as did Augusto Ramírez Moreno in
1936, was to be excommunicated from mainstream
politics. It scarcely need be added that there was
no intergroup criticism, only polemical attack,
disparagement, and negation of the competing ideas.
To be a follower of Gómez meant writing panegyrics
that bore titles like The Good Government of
Laureano Gómez, or The Paradigm: A Small Biography
of a Great Man, or Laureano Gómez, or Tenacity in
the Service of Justice and Fatherland.[15] To be
against Gómez meant penning diatribes with titles
like The Victims of Doctor Laureano Gómez, or
Laureano Gómez, Psychoanalysis of a Resentment, or
The Monster.[16] The lack of a tradition of reasoned
political criticism in Colombia was sufficient in
itself to guarantee intentional ignorance of what
Laureano Gómez stood for.
    Examples of uncritical perception of Gómez
abound. Conservative followers of Gómez prided
themselves that their copartisans believed in the
caudillo "with blind faith," and viewed him with
what can only be termed adoration. In 1934 one of
his followers described Gómez as "paladin of conservative principles, of administrative pulchritude,
of intransigent Colombianism, of clean elections,
and of social guarantees and individual rights."[17]
The following year another opined that "Laureano
Gómez, with his word and gesture, and with his
doctrines, has come to be . . . the culminating
figure of our politics."[18] At the same moment,
Liberals were declaring that "Laureano Gómez has
never been a man of ideas," calling him a "politician without convictions . . . without manliness."[19]
Even more harmful to understanding was "friendly"
negation of his ideas. In 1942 Alfonso López
advised his colleagues "not to worry" about Gómez's
El Siglo editorials because he knew that the Conservative chief didn't really mean what he wrote.[20]
Then there were those who changed their opinion of
Gómez in midstream. Luis Eduardo Nieto Caballero
was guilty of this. In 1928 he described the
Conservative as one of the most valuable elements in
Colombia's democracy, only to do a complete about
face six years later, when he referred to "the ugly,
small, hunchbacked soul of Laureano Gómez . . .
this spongy Hitler . . . ."[21] Thirty years later,
Carlos Lleras did much the same thing when he joined

Gómez in working to establish the Frente Nacional
not long after having made headlines by saying,
"With Laureano Gómez we'll never negotiate . . .
the Liberal dead will rise up and cry 'cowards! You
can't make pacts over our bodies!'"[22]
The final, inevitable result of the failure to
judge Gómez critically is uncertainty over his place
in national history. When informed of Gómez's
death and asked to assess his significance, Alberto
Lleras waffled. The Liberal who knew Gómez better
than most could do no more than say "it's hard to
make an objective, sure judgment. But it's impossible to deny the greatness of someone who moved his
people to the extent that they either fought him or
followed him."[23] At the end of a long, exhaustive
study of the Conservative party during the years of
Gómez dominance over it, a foreign scholar was
forced to admit that:

> if [Gómez] represented real needs and
> articulated genuine feelings, it is
> unclear what they were: and if he did
> not, then it is equally unclear how he
> managed to remain leader--if disputed
> leader--of an opposition party in a
> two-party system for fourteen years with
> little more patronage at his command
> than a newspaper office that he
> shared.[24]

Such uncertainty about a man who played an
important and highly controversial role in Colombian
history is unfortunate. That Colombian political
elites destroyed their democracy and then stumbled
into civil war and dictatorship in part because of
their refusal to understand one another's views is
tragic. What is done cannot be undone. But harking
back to the notion that one must study history in
order not to repeat it, it is best to consider the
historical Gómez, putting the mythical Gómez to
rest. For Colombians, it is time to undertake the
patriotic act of viewing Gómez critically, of
understanding his conservative ideas and their
origin.

Chapter X

LATIN AMERICAN CONSERVATISM SINCE THE 1960s

From the 1960s to the Present

Gómez, peerless leader of Colombia's traditional conservatives, passed from the political
scene at a time when all Latin American conservatism
was moving toward the center of the political spectrum. The striking moderation of Gómez's last
public statements are properly seen as reflecting
this broader trend. This is not to say that the
"liberal/progressive" and "traditional" division has
disappeared. It is just that there has been a
marked tendency for present-day articulators of the
conservative position to speak much of economic
development and social justice, and little of order
and discipline.

Numerous examples from contemporary Latin
American politics support these generalizations. In
recent years, Christian Democrats Luis Herrera
Campíns and Lorenzo Fernández of Venezuela, Conservative Belisario Betancur of Colombia, and
Christian Democrat León Febres Cordero of Ecuador,
all won presidential elections or came close to
doing so while mounting campaigns of a populist
nature. Lorenzo Fernández nearly won the Venezuelan
presidency in 1973 while calling for state ownership
of basic industries, ideological pluralism, and
universal social justice. Belisario Betancur who,
significantly, was in his youth a staunch follower
of Gómez, successfully campaigned on a program that
included promises of free university education and
low-cost housing "without down payment." Febres
Cordero, whose opponents characterized as a "right-
wing populist," won his 1984 presidential race
pledging to reconstruct Ecuador by opening a "great
front for union and sacrifice in which no one feels
a member of either right or left."[1]

Their populist leanings notwithstanding, there
is little doubt that Latin America's conservatives
remain committed to their fundamental principles.

163

Analysis of their messages reveals that while there is much in them that is liberal, even socialist, they are more fundamentally conservative; for example, Belisario Betancur's 1982 work _De cambio, cambio!_ (_Change, for a Change!_) is overwhelmingly a call for social reform and structural change in Colombia, as well as an indictment of social inequity there; yet Betancur's is not a demand for revolutionary change. Neither does he point fingers, or assign blame for Colombia's social problems. His activism is noncombative, even benign. The following passage from _De cambio, cambio!_ illustrates its author's feeling that Colombia's problems should be handled through collective, harmonious effort, a notion quite consistent with conservative philosophy:

> My challenge is aimed at promoting social mobilization, human inventiveness, and collective solidarity. It must do so if we are to make the most of one of the stellar moments of contemporary life. . . . My words must not be received as a threat but rather as an invitation to a decisive endeavor that will change our traditional patterns of life.[2]

There are certain litmus tests that can be used to determine the conservative content of writing on contemporary Latin America. They consist in noting the presence of certain words and concepts that are both basic to the conservative idiom and that also stand as "code words" implying much beyond their actual meaning. One such concept is that of the "common good." The term connotes a belief that human society, governed in accord with divine law, is a harmonious one whose members enjoy justice that is distributive in nature. By implication, the term stands for hostility to the liberal state, especially to liberal individualism which is seen as antithetical to the common good; thus when we read that Mexico's Partido de Acción Nacional (PAN) demands that the state "be an authentic expression of all the people," and that the end of the state is "the realization of the common good," we have reason to suspect that PAN is a conservative party. When we find fully one-third of PAN's party principles phrased in terms of the common good, we may conclude that the men and women of PAN are most certainly conservatives.[3]

Frequent use of organic terminology and the
couching of calls for change in terms of social
harmony, unity, and solidarity are indicators of
conservatism, founded in the notion of Christian
community. Former Venezuelan President Rafael
Caldera made that connection clear when he described
his party's program as "inspired by Christian
principles that accentuate the human being . . .
[and] that attempt to bring about social justice and
human solidarity."[4] It scarcely need be added that
the harmonious, communitarian approach to man in
society is implicitly hostile both to liberal individualism and to the notion of class conflict
posited by dialectical materialists.

Another sort of language pointing to a conservative stance is that dwelling upon religion,
morality, and virtue. Rafael Caldera's assertion
that his party exercises power "within the moral
order," and Colombian writer Mario Laserna's remark
that the state's duty is to order the human community and to insure "its physical and moral unity" are
indications of the conservatism of the two men. As
code words, their moral/religious terminology
implies a criticism of relativism and of the moral
laxness and the loss of ethical standards seen by
conservatives as characteristic of our era. At a
more fundamental level, they represent criticism of
the process of secularization set into motion by the
Enlightenment--a process blamed for modern man's
loss of virtue.

Conservative thinking on property has changed
in recent decades. Today there is general agreement
that the social function of property overrides its
private function: "Private property isn't an end in
itself. . . . It must be regulated in accord with
exigencies of the common good," reads a portion of
the statement of principles of Mexico's Partido de
Acción Nacional.[5] But this is far from saying that
conservatives are moving toward accepting socialists
tenets. Colombia's conservatives make that clear in
a 1973 statement having overtones of supply side
economics: "To counter the left's call for distribution of scarce resources, we propose a policy of
stimulating production. This, combined with equitable distribution of resources, constitutes the
basis of authentic social justice."[6]

A notable characteristic of Western conservatism is its flexibility: that is, the ability of
conservatives in Europe and the Americas to adapt
their thought and program to changing social conditions, all the while striving for the maintenance of

social order and stability. Latin American conservatism provides an excellent example of such
flexibility through its adherence to the principle
of subsidiarity, which is the doctrine that inter-
mediary organizations have a right to independence from the state. One of the most authoritative
comments on the principle is that found in Pius IX's
encyclical of 1931, Quadregisimo Anno.

> It is wrong to withdraw from the indi-
> vidual and commmit to the community at
> large what private enterprise and
> industry can accomplish . . . it is a
> disturbance of right order for a larger
> and higher organization to arrogate to
> itself functions which can be performed
> efficiently by smaller and lower
> bodies.[7]

The smaller bodies to which the Pope referred were
labor unions.

The principles of subsidiarity have served
Latin American conservatives of both left and right.
During the government of Eduardo Frei, left wing
"populist" factions within the Chilean Christian
Democratic party lobbied strenuously for the right
to create autonomous rural unions. Echoing Pius IX,
they cited the principle of subsidiarity in arguing
their right to pursue anticapitalist and communi-
tarian-socialist approaches to social change.[8]

At the other extreme are conservatives such as
those represented by the Nicaraguan Conservative
party. Confronted by a socialist government that is
less than sympathetic to their doctrines, they
insist on their right to form groups and associations whose interests are contrary to those of the
government. Their philosophic underpinning is the
principle of subsidiarity, and their chief interest
group is the Nicaraguan Conservative party.

For one conservative party, Mexico's Partido
de Acción Nacional, the principle of subsidiarity
plays a key role in its program. The principle
serves PAN leaders with a viable rationale and
strategy for opposing the hegemonic Partido
Revolucionario Institucional (PRI). Without citing
the principle of subsidiarity, Manuel Gómez Morín
clearly had it in mind when he lectured a PAN
convention on "the imperious necessity of decentral-
ization," which he called one of the bases of democratic society. He continued his none-too-subtle
indictment of PRI, pointing out that independent

corporate institutions are "the ones most denied and persecuted by dictatorships." Such subsidiary bodies, he concluded, must "be protected because thus and only thus can society and the individual exist."[9]

Conclusion

The writings of notable Latin Americans, from José Enrique Rodó and Miguel Antonio Caro, to José Vasconcelos and Alberto Edwards, to Alceu Amoroso Lima and Laureano Gómez, to Rafael Caldera and Eduardo Frei demonstrate that there is indeed a coherent, continuous conservative tradition in their part of the Western world. Their writings, and those of like-minded contemporaries, reveal much more as well. They suggest the changing shape of conservative thought over the past century.

Around the turn of the century, there was a rough agreement among conservatives that their chief duty was to continue their traditional defense of the church and opposition to liberal-inspired secularization. At the same time, they were aware that the world was being transformed under an avalanche of scientific discoveries, and they were anxious that their tradition-bound societies change with the times. It is, therefore, quite understandable that many Latin American conservatives should fall under the sway of positivism, a philosophy whose stress on order and progress offered them a way of coming to terms with the modern era. Their attempt to reconcile nineteenth century concerns with twentieth century realities would eventually lead to a major reorientation of conservative thought.

The years between the world wars were difficult ones for Latin American conservatives. Confronted by competing ideologies on both the left and right, they faced the task of simultaneously dealing with both. Defeat of the Axis in World War II and the concomitant discrediting of fascism eliminated the ideological challenge from the right. But the effort to formulate a viable response to liberalism and socialism widened the breach in Latin American conservatism that had been visible for thirty years or more.

Following World War II, the historic division between conservative traditionalists and those of a more progressive turn of mind became formalized. In some countries, that process took place through the formation of Christian Democratic parties. In others, it occurred through splits in traditional

167

conservative parties. Christian Democrats and those like them drew inspiration from Papal encyclicals dating from Leo XIII's _Rerum Novarum_ of 1891. More recent Papal pronouncements, especially John XXIII's _Pacem in Terris_, issued in 1963, were influential among conservatives looking for doctrinally acceptable ways of promoting social change.

The post-war division in conservative ranks was rooted in many things--personal antipathies, differences in constituencies, inherited grudges. But more divisive were essential differences in outlook and personality. Conservatives who saw it their duty to preserve the traditional social order against change, especially that threatened by liberals and socialists, assumed a stance of "defensive conservatism." Those who failed to find apocalyptic implications in ideological challenge from the left, and whose chief concern was changing society rather than preserving its traditional form, found comfort with the group described here as "liberal/progressive."

There has been a decided shift in conservative thought over the present century. Four generations ago, conservative leaders tended to be traditionalists. Today the situation is reversed with liberal/progressives in the forefront. The shift has been a gradual one, but one nonetheless evident in the public statements made by conservatives themselves.

More significant is the way conservative ideas have not changed. Throughout the period surveyed, Latin America's conservatives have consistently and uniformly couched their language in terms of the Catholic social philosophy that orients them and anchors their thought. Whether they are traditionalists like Jorge Hübner and Laureano Gómez, or liberal/progressives like Eduardo Frei and Belisario Betancur, the two kinds of conservatives share common ground of a fundamental sort. The emphasis of their message may shift, as it certainly has over the century. But in that they remain faithful to a shared philosophy. One can conclude that the ideological center of their thought continues to hold.

NOTES

Introduction

1. José Luis Romero, ed <u>Pensamiento conservador,</u>
   <u>1815-1898</u> (Caracas: Editorial Arte, 1978) is
   an anthology of conservative writing from all
   parts of Latin America. Nearly all other
   studies focus on a single notable thinker,
   Carlos Valderrama Andrade's <u>El pensamiento</u>
   <u>filosófico de Miguel Antonio Caro</u> (Bogotá:
   Instituto Caro y Cuervo, 1961) being a good
   example; or they contain information on Latin
   American conservatism in conjunction with
   other subjects. Charles A. Hale's <u>El</u>
   <u>liberalismo mexicano en la época de Mora,</u>
   <u>1821-1853</u> (Mexico City: Siglo Veintiuno
   Editores, 1972) is such a work. It contains a
   great deal of useful information on Lucas
   Alamán and the course of early nineteenth
   century Mexican conservatism.

2. José Luis Romero, <u>El pensamiento político de</u>
   <u>la derecha latinoamericana</u> (Buenos Aires:
   Editorial Paidos, 1970) attempts to cover the
   whole subject, while Gastón Cantú, ed., <u>El</u>
   <u>pensamiento de la reacción mexicana; historia</u>
   <u>documental, 1810-1962</u> (Mexico City: Empresas
   Editoriales, 1965) and Alfonso Noriega, <u>Pensa-</u>
   <u>miento conservador y conservadurismo mexicano</u>
   (Mexico City: Universidad Nacional Autónoma
   de Mexico, 1972) offer surveys of the subject
   within one nation.

3. Useful recent studies of these sorts include
   the following: William Rex Crawford, <u>A</u>
   <u>Century of Latin American Thought</u> (Cambridge,
   Mass.: Harvard University Press, 1963);
   Harold E. Davis, ed., <u>Latin American Social</u>
   <u>Thought, the History of Its Development since</u>
   <u>Independence, with Selected Readings</u>
   (Washington: The University Press of
   Washington, D.C., 1961); Harold E. Davis,

Latin American Thought: A Historical Introduction (Baton Rouge: Louisiana State University Press, 1972), Revolutionaries, Traditionalists, and Dictators in Latin America (New York: Cooper Square Publishers, 1973); Charles A. Hale, "Political and Social Ideas, 1870-1930" (unpublished typescript), "The Reconstruction of Nineteenth Century Politics in Spanish America: A Case for the History of Ideas," Latin American Research Review 7:53-73 (Summer 1973); Richard M. Morse, "The Heritage of Latin America" in The Founding of New Societies, ed. by Louis Hartz (New York: Harcourt, Brace and World, 1964), pp. 123-177; Fredrick B. Pike, Hispanismo, 1898-1936 (Notre Dame: University of Notre Dame Press, 1971), Spanish America, 1900-1970: Tradition and Social Innovation (New York: W.W. Norton, 1973), The New Corporatism, Social-Political Structures in the Iberian World (Notre Dame: University of Notre Dame Press, 1974), The United States and the Andean Republics (Cambridge, Mass.: Harvard University Press, 1977); Martin Stabb, In Quest of Identity: Patterns in the Spanish-American Essay of Ideas, 1890-1960 (Chapel Hill: University of North Carolina Press, 1967); Claudio Veliz, ed., Obstacles to Change in Latin America (2nd ed., New York: Oxford University Press, 1970), The Politics of Conformity in Latin America (2nd ed., New York: Oxford University Press, 1970); Leopoldo Zea, The Latin American Mind, trans. by James H. Abbot and Lowell Dunham (Norman, Oklahoma: University of Oklahoma Press, 1963).

4. Gómez served as President of Colombia from 1950 to 1953. Betancur served from 1982 to 1986.

5. Mariano Ospina Rodríguez (1805-1885) was President of Colombia for the period 1857-1861. Miguel Antonio Caro (1843-1909) was President of Colombia for the period 1892-1898.

6. Eduardo Frei Montalva (1911-1984) was president of Chile for the period 1964-1970. Chilean writer and politician Alberto Edwards Vives was born in 1873 and died in 1932.

Diego Portales was born in 1773 and died in 1837.

7. Manuel Gómez Morín was born in 1897 and died in 1981. Lucas Alamán (1792-1853) was a leader of Mexico's Conservative party.

8. Russell Kirk, ed., The Portable Conservative Reader (New York: Penguin Books, 1982), p. xxxiii.

Chapter I

1. Antonio López de Santa Anna (1794-1876) was the dominant figure in Mexican politics from the late 1820s to the mid-1850s. Juan Manuel de Rosas (1793-1877) was dictator of Argentina from 1829 to 1852. José Gaspar Rodríguez de Francia (1766-1840) ruled Paraguay from 1814 to 1840.

2. Rudolf Vierhaus, "Conservatism" in Dictionary of the History of Ideas, I, ed. by Philip P. Wiener (New York: Charles Scribner's Sons, 1968), 477.

3. José Eusebio Caro was born in 1817 and died in 1853.

4. La Civilización, August 9, 1849.

5. Sergio Arboleda's dates are 1822-1888; José Manuel Groot's are 1800-1878.

6. When capitalized, the words "Liberal" and "Conservative" refer to political parties. When uncapitalized they refer to philosophic liberalism and conservatism.

7. Rafael María Carrasquilla was born in 1857 and died in 1928.

8. See: Jaime Jaramillo Uribe, "La esencia teológica de la historia," El pensamiento colombiano en el siglo XIX (Bogotá: Editorial Temis, 1964), pp. 263-268, for a perceptive discussion of Sergio Arboleda's view of history.

9. Rafael Núñez (1825-1894) was president of Colombia for the periods 1880-1882 and 1884-1894.

10. Economic historians argue that the Historical-Nationalist split was based in conflicting economic interests of the two groups. Charles W. Bergquist, for example, in Coffee and Conflict in Colombia, 1886-1910 (Durham: Duke University Press, 1978), pp. 51, 59, finds the Nationalist Conservatives to have been defenders of traditional agricultural interests, and the Historical Conservatives, like the Colombian Liberals, representatives of import-export interests.
    Other students of nineteenth century Colombian history disagree. Helen Delpar, in Red against Blue, the Liberal Party in Colombian Politics, 1863-1899 (University, Alabama: The University of Alabama Press, 1981), pp. 159, 161, finds that "Bergquist's analysis also exaggerates the dissension within the Liberal party in the late 1890s as well as the possibilities for collaboration between the Liberals and the Conservative opposition, whose members continued to regard Liberalism with 'aloofness'. . . ." She concludes that "Bergquist's assertions rest on a tenuous foundation."

11. El Gráfico, June 11, 1932.

12. Ralph Lee Woodward, Jr., ed., Positivism in Latin America, 1850-1900. (Lexington, Mass.: D.C. Heath, 1971), p. ix. The citation is from the fourth volume of Comte's Cours de philosophie positive, published in 1838.

13. It should be noted that they did so during a time in Colombian history when the Liberal party was suffering a long period of powerlessness dating from the 1880s and extending to the year 1930.

14. Miguel Antonio Caro, "Al Director de Libertad y Orden," Obras completas, VI (Bogotá: Imprenta Nacional, 1932), pp. 304, 305.

15. Marco Fidel Suárez, "Lo que significa ser conservador," Antología del pensamiento conservador en Colombia, I, ed. by Roberto

Herrera Soto (Bogotá: Colcultura, 1982), pp. 402-403.

16. M. F. Suárez, "Lo que significa," p. 402.

17. M. A. Caro, "Al Director," p. 305.

18. Júlio César de Morais Carneiro, "Apóstrofes," in Antología do pensamiento social e político no Brasil, ed. by Luís Washington Vita (Sao Paulo: Editorial Grijalbo, 1968), p. 159.

19. J. C. de Morais Carneiro, "Apóstrofes," p. 164.

20. Jackson de Figueiredo, "Algunas reflexoes sobre a filosofía de Farias Brito--Profissao de fé espiritualista," in Antología, ed. by Washington Vita, p. 180.

21. José Enrique Rodó, Ariel, (3rd. ed., Mexico City: Espasa-Calpe, 1963), p. 123.

22. J. E. Rodó, Ariel, p. 123.

23. Manuel Gálvez, "En el solar de la raza," in Latin American Social Thought, ed. by H. E. Davis, p. 425.

24. M. Stabb, In Quest of Identity, p. 25.

25. M. Stabb, In Quest of Identity, p. 19.

26. Laureano Vallenilla Lanz, Cesarismo democrático. Estudios sobre las bases sociológicas de la constitución efectiva de Venezuela (2nd. ed., Caracas: Tipografía Universal, 1929), pp. 296, 307.

27. L. Vallenilla, Cesarismo democrático, pp. 309-310.

28. H. Stuart Hughes, Consciousness and Society, the Reorientation of European Social Thought, 1890-1930 (New York: Alfred A. Knopf, 1958), p. 29.

Chapter II

1. The other key figure in twentieth century
   Colombian history was Liberal party leader
   Alfonso López Pumarejo, counterpart and
   contemporary of Gómez. This writer is tempted
   to place the Liberal populist Jorge Eliécer
   Gaitán alongside Gómez and López. But
   Gaitán's assassination in 1948 ended the
   career of a man whose impact upon Colombian
   society would surely have equalled, and might
   have surpassed, that of either Gómez or López.

2. This is not the place to discuss the mechanism
   by which public opinion is formed in Colombia.
   Suffice it to say that the two most important
   organs of news and opinion in that country are
   the newspapers El Tiempo and El Espectador.
   Both are owned by prominent members of the
   Liberal party. As such they have been exceedingly critical of the historical Gómez. It
   would be no exaggeration to say that there has
   been little change in the tone of their
   comment upon Gómez from the time he assumed
   control of the Conservative party in the early
   1930s.

3. Departments are Colombian political divisions
   roughly equivalent to states in the U.S.A.

4. El Siglo, September 30, 1940.

5. Obras selectas, Part I, ed. by Alberto
   Bermúdez (Medellín: Editorial Bedout, 1981),
   p. 762.

6. El Siglo, January 21, 1962.

7. Los efectos de la Reforma de 1953 (Bogotá:
   Imprenta Nacional, 1953), p. 15.

8. Indalecio Liévano Aguirre, Rafael Núñez
   (Bogotá: Editorial Cromos, 1944), p. 237.

9. Nicolas Berdiaev, El sentido de la creación
   (Buenos Aires: Ediciones Carlos Lohlé, 1978),
   p. 392.

Chapter III

1. Interrogantes sobre el progreso de Colombia
   (Bogotá: Editorial Revista Colombiana, 1970),
   p. 87.

2. Robert V. Farrell, "The Catholic Church in
   Colombian Education, 1886-1930, in Search of
   Tradition" (unpublished doctoral dissertation,
   Columbia University, 1975), pp. 179-180.

3. La Unidad, August 16, 1916.

4. Robert Farrell, "The Catholic Church," p. 195.

5. El Siglo, December 5, 1939.

6. El Siglo, December 5, 1939.

7. El Colombiano, March 14, 1902.

8. El Siglo, December 5, 1939.

9. Manuel Dávila Florez, Catolicismo y protestantismo comparados en forma epistolar (Rome:
   Escuela Tipografía Salesiana, 1924),
   pp. ii-iii.

10. La Unidad, July 12, 1915.

11. La Unidad, July 10, 1915.

12. El Siglo, July 14, 1965.

13. El Siglo, July 14, 1965.

14. Obras selectas, p. 758.

15. See Chapter IV, below, for a discussion of
    some of these intellectual sources.

16. The process through which the Colombian people
    became captives of their political parties is
    explained in the literature of Colombian
    political history. See, for example, Chapter
    III of my volume When Colombia Bled, a History
    of the Violencia in Tolima (University,
    Alabama: The University of Alabama Press,
    1985).

17. Ospinismo denotes the faction of the Conservative party headed by Mariano Ospina Pérez (1891-1968).

18. Comentarios a un régimen (Bogotá: Editorial Minerva, 1934), pp. 266-267, 269-270.

19. Comentarios, pp. 244, 248.

20. Jorge Ferreira Parra, Novena al glorioso senador San Laureano de Chía (El Líbano, Tolima: Tipografía Renovación, November 1932).

21. La Unidad, October 14, 1909.

22. Sábado, September 15, 1956.

23. El País, August 15, 1934.

24. El Siglo, January 14, 1961.

25. Here Gómez referred to the rioting attending Gaitán's assassination. The killing and its immediate consequences are referred to in Colombia simply as the 9 de abril. The rioting of that day in Bogotá, the Colombian capital, is referred to as the bogotazo.

26. Desde el exilio (Bogotá, 1954), p. 16.

27. Obras selectas, p. 630.

28. El Siglo, June 27, 1949.

29. El Siglo, June 21, 1942.

30. Obras selectas, p. 817.

31. El Siglo, June 27, 1949.

32. El Siglo, December 11, 1949.

33. Obras selectas, p. 135.

34. El País, November 2, 1934.

35. Laureano Gómez, Discursos (Bogotá: Editorial Revista Colombiana, 1968), pp. 57, 58-59.

36. La Unidad, August 25, 1910.

37. Comentarios, pp. 267-269.

38. El Siglo, June 27, 1949.

39. El Siglo, September 30, 1938.

40. El Siglo, December 11, 1949.

41. El Siglo, May 31, 1953.

42. Laureano Gómez, obra selecta, 1909-1956 (Bogotá: Imprenta Nacional, 1982), pp. 27-28.

43. Obras selectas, pp. 602, 603.

44. Comentarios, pp. 275-276.

45. Obras selectas, pp. 818-819.

46. El Siglo, October 13, 1949.

47. El Siglo, October 11, 1958.

48. Heinrich A. Rommen, The State in Catholic Thought, a Treatise in Political Philosophy, 2nd. ed. (New York: Greenwood Press, 1969), p. 469.

49. La Unidad, July 9, 1912.

50. El Siglo, October 31, 1951.

51. El Siglo, October 31, 1951.

52. Desde el exilio, p. 88.

53. Los efectos de la reforma de 1953, p. 10.

54. Sábado, September 15, 1956.

55. Obras selectas, p. 759.

Chapter IV

1. Obras selectas, p. 346.

2. La Unidad, December 13, 1915.

3. La Unidad, August 30, 1910.

4. *La Unidad*, October 14, 1909.

5. Vicente Azuero is, with Francisco Paula de Santander, looked on as a founder of the Liberal party of Colombia.

6. *La Unidad*, February 16, 1912.

7. The Battle of Palonegro, fought near Bucaramanga, May 11-25, 1900, was one of the most costly of the War of the Thousand Days.

8. The ostensible cause of the trouble was his occupancy of a Liberal-designated seat, coupled with charges that Gómez's election to the seat was fraudulent.

9. *Vanguardia Liberal*, March 26, 1927.

10. *Laureano Gómez, obra selecta*, pp. 196-198.

11. *El Diario Nacional*, April 29, 1928.

12. *Mundo al Día*, June 6, 1928.

13. *El Tiempo*, June 9, 1928.

14. *Universidad*, June 9, 1928.

15. *El Espectador*, June 6, 1928.

16. *El Gráfico*, June 9, 1928.

17. *El Tiempo*, June 6, 1928.

18. *El Diario Nacional*, June 6, 1928.

19. *El Diario Nacional*, June 7, 1928.

20. *El Tiempo*, June 7, 1928.

21. *El Espectador*, June 8, 1928.

22. *Interrogantes*, p. 26.

23. *Interrogantes*, pp. 47, 49. Here Gómez expressed beliefs widely held in the Western world early in the twentieth century. Not only were such racist sentiments widely held, but they were thought to be scientifically based; thus the editorialist for Liberal *El

Espectador, while basically critical of the
Gómez talk, could write in the June 6, 1928
edition: "Ethnologically we can't be said to
figure among the superior races. Many years,
no doubt, will pass before the excellent
racial type presently forming in the mountains
of Santander and Antioquia, and already quite
abundant in the highlands of Nariño,
Cundinamarca, and Boyacá, will predominate
among our people. There are still zambos,
mulattoes, and degenerate Indians in Colombia,
but . . . [other nations are] even worse
populated."

24. *Interrogantes*, pp. 53, 55.

25. Contained in Charles A. Hale's unpublished
essay "Political and Social Ideas, 1870-1930,"
p. 44.

26. *Interrogantes*, pp. 46-47.

Chapter V

1. *El Tiempo*, March 15, 1936.

2. A.O. Lovejoy, "On the Discrimination of
Romanticisms," *Essays in the History of Ideas*
(Baltimore: Johns Hopkins University Press,
1948), pp. 228-253.

3. Jaime Jaramillo Uribe, *El pensamiento
colombiano en el siglo XIX* (Bogotá: Editorial
Temis, 1964), pp. 174, 36.

4. The best survey of this movement is Isaiah
Berlin, "The Counter Enlightenment," *Against
the Current, Essays in the History of Ideas*
(New York: The Viking Press, 1980), pp. 1-24.

5. Jaime Jaramillo Uribe points out that nineteenth and early twentieth century Colombians
conceptualized their nation's social problems
in an idiosyncratic, highly subjective, and
romantic way. They preferred to employ senti-
mental, paternalistic, and even religious
language in describing "the poor," referring
to their "nobility" and "virtue," and exalting
them. (Jaramillo himself admitted being first
moved to an appreciation of Colombia's social

179

problems through reading Victor Hugo's <u>Les miserables</u>.) He concludes that the romantic inclination of nineteenth and early twentieth century social critics caused discussion of the "social problem" always to seem a bit out of focus in Colombia. "El pensamiento social colombiano del siglo XIX," lecture delivered at the Biblioteca Nacional de Colombia, Bogotá, November 23, 1982.

6. <u>El Siglo</u>, June 25, 1950.

7. <u>El Siglo</u>, August 6, 1950.

8. Felipe Antonio Molina, <u>Laureano Gómez, historia de una rebeldía</u> (Bogotá: Librería Voluntad, 1940), p. 243.

9. The term "new idealism" is that of historian Charles Hale. The present writer is indebted to him for insights contained in his essay "The New Idealism and the Persistence of the Authoritarian Tradition," contained in his unpublished study "Political and Social Ideas," pp. 63-73.

10. In an article written for the Mexican publication <u>Todo</u>, Vasconcelos referred to Gómez as "the Colombian Moses," saying that future generations will praise him for showing the nation through its time of trouble. <u>El Siglo</u>, January 20, 1952.

11. <u>La Unidad</u>, February 24, 1916.

12. <u>La Unidad</u>, December 15, 1915.

13. <u>El Tiempo</u>, January 30, 1921.

14. <u>Obras selectas</u>, p. 544.

15. "El carácter del general Ospina," <u>Universidad</u>, Nos. 68, 70, 75 (February 11, 25; March 10, 31, 1928).

16. <u>El cuadrilátero</u>, 4th ed. (Bogotá: Editorial Centro, 1935), p. 302.

17. "El carácter del general Ospina," <u>Universidad</u>, No. 70 (February 25, 1928), pp. 154-155.

18. Noel K. O'Sullivan, Conservatism (New York: St. Martin's Press, 1976), p. 93.

19. Obras selectas, pp. 346-347.

20. N.K. O'Sullivan, Conservatism, p. 94.

21. El Siglo, October 18, 1937.

22. El Tiempo, January 30, 1921.

23. Felipe Antonio Molina, Laureano Gómez, p. 96.

24. La Unidad, June 17, 1912.

25. La Unidad, November 2, 1912.

26. La Unidad, June 28, 1915.

27. El Tiempo, May 21, 1928.

28. Interrogantes, p. 60.

Chapter VI

1. "Decadencia y grandeza de España," Revista colombiana, Vol. IX, No. 105 (February 1, 1938), 260.

2. Felipe Antonio Molina, Laureano Gómez, pp. 237, 235.

3. Felipe Antonio Molina, Laureano Gómez, pp. 237-238.

4. Colombia, Ministerio de Relaciones Exteriores, Legajo Alemán, 1929-1936, Documento #166-1930.

5. The acts of violence occurred, for the most part, in the departments (states) of Boyacá, Santander, and Santander del Norte. While the acts of violence were ostensibly political, resulting from the sudden passing of political, legal, and police power from the hands of Conservatives to those of their Liberal antagonists, the motives for specific acts were complex. Personal vendetta, rape, robbery, theft of movable property and real estate, and crimes of passion are only a few of the sources of the abuses. Some dynamics

of the anti-Conservative violence of the 1930s, with setting in the department of Tolima, are discussed in my volume When Colombia Bled, pp. 83-88, 165-167.

6. Colombians refer to the period 1930-1946 as that of the "Liberal Republic." Its high point--or low point to Conservative eyes--was that of the Liberal overhaul of the national constitution. Presided over by President Alfonso López Pumarejo, that liberalization is known as the "Reform of 1936."

7. Román Gómez was not a relative of Laureano Gómez.

8. "El debate contra Román Gómez," Laureano Gómez, discursos, p. 51.

9. "Inutilidad de la violencia," Comentarios, pp. 29-36; "La escandalosa impunidad," Comentarios, pp. 63-68; "Un caso de barbarie," Comentarios, pp. 91-97; "No más sangre!," Comentarios, pp. 167-172; "Chaux, o el capitalista bolchevique," Comentarios, pp. 183-187; "Bajo el poder del señor Alfonso López," El Siglo, March 27, 1936; "Derecho de defensa de las colectividades," El Siglo, February 14, 1939; "Catilinaria contra el presidente Santos," Obras selectas, pp. 581-591; "Denuncia de un ministro contratista," Obras selectas, pp. 637-660; "Síntomas de descomposición," El Siglo, July 12, 1942; "Carta al padre del caos," El Siglo, November 30, 1943; "Una patraña miseranda," El Siglo, July 18, 1945.

10. Comentarios, pp. 244-245.

11. The essays, first published in Revista colombiana, appeared along with others on Stalin and Gandhi in El cuadrilátero.

12. "La tradición ante la barbarie," Revista colombiana, Vol. VIII, No. 92 (May 1, 1937), pp. 210-214; "La opresión del mundo moderno," Obras selectas, pp. 808-813; "Síntomas de descomposición," El Siglo, July 12, 1942; "Despersonalización de la vida," El Siglo, June 5, 1943; "La pérdida del hombre," El Siglo, July 7, 1943.

13. "El expresionismo como síntoma de pereza e inhabilidad en el arte," Laureano Gómez, obra selecta, pp. 385-392; "Una maravilla literaria, 'La cuádruple canción' de León de Greiff," Laureano Gómez, obra selecta, pp. 137-140; "Pablo Neruda, un bromista," El Siglo, August 28, 1943.

14. These editorials are collected in Laureano Gómez, obra selecta, pp. 19-44.

15. El mito de Santander, 2 vols. (Bogotá: Editora Colombiana, 1966).

16. Guillermo Camacho Montoya, Santander, el hombre y el mito (Bogotá: Ediciones Revista Colombiana, 1941), p. 11.

17. "La bancarrota del liberalismo," Laureano Gómez, obra selecta, pp. 245-250; "No escapan a la historia," El Siglo, September 17, 1944. Gómez's Senate debates in opposition to the Concordat are found in Obras selectas, pp. 695-767.

18. "El peor enemigo, el moderado," Obras selectas, pp. 826-831; "Como en los días de Panamá," El Siglo, December 5, 1939; "El desprestigio de los poderes," El Siglo, July 16, 1945.

19. "Telón de fondo," El Siglo, June 16, 1945; "Amores reales, un asesinato de estado en tiempos de Quevedo," El Siglo, July 28, 1945.

20. El Siglo, February 12, 1946.

21. Obras selectas, p. 718; Comentarios, p. 58; Obras selectas, p. 762.

22. El Siglo, October 7, 1949.

23. El Tiempo, August 13, 1942.

24. José Francisco Socarrás, Laureano Gómez, psicoanálisis de un resentido (Bogotá: Siglo Veinte, 1942), p. 340.

25. El Espectador, August 20, 1942.

26. The following discussion of ideology owes much to D.J. Manning's treatment of the subject in his book Liberalism (New York: St. Martin's Press, 1976), pp. 28-29, 81-89, 139-157.

27. Manning, Liberalism, p. 83.

28. El Siglo, August 18, 1942.

29. This is the argument used by students of the Civil War of the United States who find the ideologically held beliefs of the abolition- ists explosively antithetical to the equally firm beliefs of proslavery ideologists. As James G. Randall wrote in his essay "A Blundering Generation," Mississippi Valley Historical Review, 27 (June 1940) 13, "When history is distorted it becomes a contributor to those 'dynamic' masses of ideas, or ideologies, which are among the sorriest plagues of the present age." A recent treatment of ideological differences as a cause of the U.S. Civil War is Eric Foner, Politics and Ideology in the Age of the Civil War (New York: Oxford University Press, 1980).

30. "La masonería en su historia," Obras selectas, p. 680.

31. "La masonería," Obras selectas, pp. 680, 681, 690.

32. Senate speech of September 25, 1940, Obras selectas, p. 592.

33. Interrogantes, pp. 24-25.

34. "Decadencia y grandeza de España," Revista colombiana, Vol. IX, No. 105 (February 1, 1938), p. 258.

35. El Siglo, August 14, 1949.

36. "Senate Speech of September 16, 1940," Obras selectas, p. 580.

37. "Senate Speech of October 29, 1942," Obras selectas, p. 757.

38. El Siglo, December 6, 1939.

39. "La salvación viene de Rusia," Laureano Gómez, obra selecta, pp. 227-228.

40. Obras selectas, p. 812.

41. Obras selectas, pp. 808-809.

42. Obras selectas, pp. 808-809.

43. El Siglo, December 6, 1940.

44. Arturo Abella, El florero de Lorente (Medellin: Editorial Bedout, n.d.), p. 8.

45. El Siglo, August 17, 1952.

46. El Siglo, August 17, 1952.

47. Laureano Gómez, obra selecta, p. 59.

48. El Siglo, December 6, 1939.

49. Laureano Gómez, obra selecta, p. 74.

50. Obras selectas, p. 811.

51. El Siglo, May 31, 1953.

52. El Siglo, May 31, 1953.

53. El Siglo, May 31, 1953.

54. Obras selectas, p. 812.

55. El Siglo, May 28, 1950.

56. El Siglo, May 28, 1950.

57. El Siglo, May 28, 1950.

58. El Siglo, May 28, 1950.

59. El Siglo, December 6, 1940.

60. El Siglo, October 5, 1952 (under pseudonym Cornelio Nepote).

61. El Siglo, May 10, May 31, 1953.

62. El Siglo, May 10, 1953.

185

63. El Siglo, May 31, 1953.

64. El Siglo, May 31, 1953.

65. La Unidad, April 23, 1912.

66. El Siglo, August 6, 1936.

67. El Siglo, August 6, 1936.

68. Revista colombiana, Vol. IX, No. 105 (February 1, 1938), p. 260.

69. Revista colombiana, Vol. VII, No. 75 (June 15, 1936), p. 68.

70. Obras selectas, p. 812.

71. Obras selectas, pp. 808, 812.

72. Obras selectas, p. 816.

Chapter VII

1. Anne Freemantle, The Papal Encyclicals in Their Historical Context (New York: G.P. Putnam's Sons, 1956), p. 229.

2. A. Freemantle, The Papal Encyclicals, p. 231.

3. Alberto Edwards Vives, La Fronda aristocrática, historia, política de Chile (7th ed., Santiago de Chile: Editorial del Pacífico, 1972), p. 276.

4. A. Edwards, La Fronda, p. 272.

5. A. Edwards, La Fronda, pp. 274-275.

6. Jorge González von Marées, El mal de Chile (Santiago de Chile: Tallares Gráficos "Portales," 1940), passim.

7. J.L. Romero, El pensamiento, p. 163.

8. Jorge González, El mal de Chile, p. 252.

9. Eduardo Frei Montalva, Aun es tiempo (Santiago de Chile: Gráficas el Chileno, 1942), p. 100.

10. Eduardo Frei, Aun es tiempo, p. 110.

11. Eduardo Frei, Aun es tiempo, p. 98.

12. George W. Grayson, El Partido Demócrata Cristiano chileno (Buenos Aires: Editorial Francisco de Aguirre, 1968), pp. 131132.

13. Jacinto Jijón y Caamaño, Política conservadora, 2 vols. (Riobamba: Tipografía "La Buena Prensa del Chimborazo,"

192 1934). According to F.B. Pike, The United States, p. 212, Christian Democratic ideas were introduced into Ecuador during the early 1920s by Spanish priests.

14. El País, August 8, 1934.

15. El cuadrilátero, p. 147.

16. El cuadrilátero, p. 79.

17. El Siglo, July 12, 1937.

18. El Siglo, June 16, 1938.

19. El Siglo, October 17, 1938.

20. El Tiempo, August 5, 1926.

21. El Siglo, July 1, 1943.

22. El Siglo, October 9, 1941.

23. John Gunther, Inside Latin America (New York: Harper and Brothers, 1941), p. 166.

24. José Vicente Concha (1867-1937) was president of Colombia for the period 1914-1918.

25. El Siglo, December 21, 1943.

26. El Siglo, December 21, 1943.

27. El Siglo, February 2, 1961, El Colombiano, December 14, 1932.

28. Comentarios, pp. 221, 117.

29. El Siglo, March 15, 1936; Revista colombiana, Vol. VII, No. 75 (June 15, 1936), p. 66.

30. El País, November 3, 1934.

31. Revista colombiana, Vol. VI, No. 62 (November 15, 1935), pp. 33, 35.

32. El Siglo, July 6, 1937.

33. El Siglo, July 6, 1937.

34. El Siglo, July 17, 1937.

35. Derechas, June 26, 1936.

36. Revista colombiana, Vol. IX, No. 105 (February 1, 1938), pp. 260, 261, 162.

37. Laureano Gómez, obra selecta, pp. 24, 28-29.

38. Laureano Gómez, obra selecta, p. 24.

39. Laureano Gómez, obra selecta, p. 29.

40. Laureano Gómez, obra selecta, pp. 25-26.

41. Laureano Gómez, obra selecta, p. 27.

42. Laureano Gómez, obra selecta, p. 44.

43. Revista colombiana, Vol. V, No. 53 (June 1, 1935), pp. 133, 134.

44. Obras selectas, pp. 830, 831.

45. La Unidad, July 4, 1911; September 28, 1912.

46. El Siglo, January 19, 1938.

47. Revista colombiana, Vol. VI, No. 63 (December 1, 1935), p. 70.

48. El cuadrilátero, pp. 115-116.

49. La Unidad, October 18, 1912.

50. Laureano Gómez, obra selecta, p. 75.

51. Interrogantes, pp. 62, 58; El Tiempo, May 21, 1928.

52. *El Siglo*, January 21, 1946.

53. These photos appeared sporadically between 1945 and 1948.

54. *Obras selectas*, pp. 677-694.

55. *Obras selectas*, p. 677.

56. *Obras selectas*, pp. 677-678.

57. *Obras selectas*, p. 678.

58. *Obras selectas*, pp. 678, 679.

59. *Obras selectas*, pp. 680, 681.

60. *Obras selectas*, p. 681.

61. *Obras selectas*, p. 682.

62. *Obras selectas*, pp. 682, 683.

63. *Obras selectas*, pp. 682, 683.

64. *Obras selectas*, p. 683.

65. *Obras selectas*, pp. 682, 683.

66. *Obras selectas*, p. 194.

Chapter VIII

1. The literature attending the debate is extensive. A substantial portion of it is annotated in F.B. Pike, *The United States*, p. 422.

2. These broad categories are derived through a three step process. First, all "subject matter" and "value" categories are noted. These terms are from Ole R. Holsti, *Content Analysis for the Social Sciences and Humanities* (Reading, Mass.: Addison-Wesley, 1969), pp. 94-126. Second, all related categories are grouped according to thematic affinity; hence, a demand for greater social justice, a denunciation of special privilege, and a demand for equitable treatment of the poor are all assigned to the common "social justice"

category. Third, thematic categories are examined in effort to determine whether "constellations" of themes can be determined. The present writer subjected some fifty samples of conservative writing to the analytic technique described here. The global sample suggested the "liberal/progressive," "traditionalist," and "religious" grouping employed here.

3. Eduardo Frei Montalva, "The Road to Follow," in Latin American Social Thought, ed. by H.E. Davis (Washington: The University Press of Washington, D.C., 1961), pp. 545, 549.

4. Jorge Iván Hübner Gallo, "Catholics in Politics," in The Conflict between Church and State in Latin America, ed. by Fredrick B. Pike (New York: A.A. Knopf, 1966), pp. 206-207.

5. J. I. Hübner Gallo, "Catholics in Politics," pp. 206-207.

6. J.I. Hübner Gallo, "Catholics in Politics," p. 199.

7. J.I. Hübner Gallo, "Catholics in Politics," p. 207.

8. Eduardo Frei, "The Road," p. 548.

9. The writings subjected to content analysis, excluding the Frei and Hubner pieces cited above, are as follow: Sergio Fernández Larraín, Aspectos de la división del Partido conservador (Santiago de Chile: Partido Conservador Tradicionalista, 1952), pp. 77-125; Laureano Gómez, Ospina y otros discursos (Bogotá: Populibro, 1966), pp. 45-61; Manuel Gómez Morín, "Democrácia en lo social y en lo económico," in El pensamiento de la reacción mexicana, ed. by Gastón García Cantú (Mexico City: Empresas Editoriales, 1965), pp. 978-991; Alceu Amoroso Lima, "Voices of Liberty and Reform in Brazil," in Freedom and Reform in Latin America, ed. by Fredrick B. Pike (South Bend: University of Notre Dame Press, 1959), pp. 281-302; Mariano Ospina Pérez, Obras Selectas, ed. by Francisco Plata Bermúdez (Bogotá: Editorial Bedout, 1982),

pp. 245-295; Carlos José Solórzano, *La ideología que debe sustentar el Partido Conservador de Nicaragua* (Managua, 1947), pp. 5-13.

10. Two histories of this troubled moment in Colombian history are "Conversations among Gentlemen: Oligarchical Democracy in Colombia," by Alexander Wiley Wilde, in Juan J. Linz and Alfred Stepan, *The Breakdown of Democratic Regimes* (Baltimore: Johns Hopkins University Press, 1978), pp. 28-81; and the present writer's *When Colombia Bled*, pp. 127-152, 302-307.

11. The period of the Colombian Violencia is 1946-1965.

12. *El Siglo*, November 16, 1947.

13. There are many theories as to who had Gaitán assassinated by one Juan Roa Sierra. As the assassin was lynched on the spot, responsibility for the act has never been determined.

14. "Caminos de muerte," *El Siglo*, April 29, 1948; "Catástrofe nacional," *El Siglo*, May 5, 1948; "Deshonra de Colombia," *El Siglo*, May 6, 1948; "La encrucijada de Colombia," *El Siglo*, October 17, 1948.

15. *El Siglo*, June 14, 1949.

16. *El Siglo*, August 23, 1949.

17. *La Unidad*, November 28, 1915; *El Siglo*, December 2, 1939; *El Siglo*, January 15, 1962.

18. *Derechas*, June 12, 1928.

19. *El Tiempo*, May 21, 1928.

20. *Derechas*, June 12, 1936.

21. *Obras selectas*, p. 821.

22. *Obras selectas*, p. 822.

23. *Sábado*, February 23, 1946.

24. *El Siglo*, July 16, 1945.

25. Several nineteenth century Colombian constitutions were quite as utopian as that proposed for Colombia in 1953. During the 1930s members of the Liberal party attempted to make Colombia a "Liberal Republic" through the means of constitutional reform. Following the military coup that deposed Gómez, General Rojas Pinilla promised to create a political "Third Force" for Colombia that would govern under "Bolivarian principles." History judges all these efforts as failures.

26. The García Calderón quote is from Rafael Azula Barrera, De la revolución al orden nuevo (Bogotá: Editorial Kelly, 1956), p. 12; Orlando Fals Borda, La subversión en Colombia: Visión del cambio social en la historia (Bogotá: Tercer Mundo, 1967).

27. Arthur O. Lovejoy, The Great Chain of Being: A Study of the History of an Idea (Cambridge, Massachusetts: Harvard University Press, 1933); Alfred North Whitehead, Science and the Modern World (Cambridge, England: Cambridge University Press, 1926).

28. El Siglo, February 1, 1936.

29. "El expresionismo como síntoma de pereza e inhabilidad en el arte," Revista colombiana, Vol. VIII, No. 35 (January 1, 1937), p. 390.

30. Senate debate of October 29, 1942, Obras selectas, p. 761.

31. The following concepts are developed fully in W. David Ross, The Right and the Good (Oxford: The Clarendon Press, 1930); Abraham Edel, "What is Ethical Relativity?" Ethical Judgement (Glenco, Illinois: The Free Press, 1955), pp. 15-36; Abraham Edel, "Right and Good," Dictionary of the History of Ideas, IV (New York: Charles Scribner's Sons, 1973), pp. 173-187.

32. Discursos, pp. 55-56.

33. El Siglo, May 31, 1953.

34. Senate debate of October 29, 1942, Obras selectas, 761.

35. Senate debate of August 20, 1940, Obras selectas, p. 538.

36. "La opresion del mundo moderno," speech of November 24, 1938, Obras selectas, p. 812.

37. El Siglo, June 8, 1947.

38. Senate debate of October 29, 1942, Obras selectas, p. 758.

39. El Siglo, October 31, 1951.

40. El Siglo, May 31, 1953.

41. "El Teatro de Pirandello," Revista colombiana, Vol. VII, No. 78 (August 1, 1936), p. 179.

42. El Siglo, December 5, 1939.

43. Senate debate of October 29, 1942, Obras selectas, p. 759.

44. El Siglo, June 27, 1949.

45. Discursos, p. 56.

46. Cámara debate of October 20, 1925, Obras selectas, p. 403.

47. See especially, Ernst Cassirer's An Essay on Man (New Haven: Yale University Press, 1944).

48. It will be remembered that he went into self-imposed exile following the assassination of Jorge Eliécer Gaitán.

49. Carlos Restrepo Piedrahita, 25 años de evolución políticoconstitucional, 1950-1975 (Bogotá: Universidad Externado de Colombia, 1976), pp. 17, 32.

50. Interrogantes, p. 144.

51. This centralizing authoritarianism runs through the entire document.

52. El Siglo, January 30, 1950.

193

53. Gómez was alluding to the attempt of the Liberal-controlled Congress of 1949 to impeach Conservative President Ospina Pérez. When Gómez wrote this article, Colombia's Senate and Chamber of Representatives were in the second month of suspension imposed by the state of siege declared by Ospina Pérez. This breakdown of Colombian democracy is described on pp. 127-152 of the author's volume When Colombia Bled.

54. El Siglo, October 31, 1951.

55. Los efectos de la reforma de 1953, pp. 19-20.

56. Noel K. O'Sullivan, Conservatism, pp. 128-9; El Siglo, May 15, 1951.

57. Walter Lippmann, The Public Philosophy (New York: Harper and Row, 1956); Revista colombiana, Vol. VII, No. 78 (August 1, 1936), p. 179.

58. O'Sullivan, Conservatism, pp. 130-131.

59. Obras selectas, pp. 543-544.

Chapter IX

1. Universidad, No. 68 (February 11, 1928), pp. 104-105.

2. Obras selectas, p. 821.

3. Los efectos de la reforma de 1953, p. 10.

4. Semana, January 23, 1956.

5. The letters and other documents of interest are collected in Desde el exilio.

6. Approximately 200,000 Colombians died during the nearly twenty years of Violencia.

7. This information is attributed to Alvaro Gómez Hurtado.

8. El Siglo, August 8, 1958.

9. El Siglo, October 22, 1949.

10. *El Siglo*, May 9, 1958.

11. *El Siglo*, March 7, 1960.

12. *La Unidad*, February 14, 1914.

13. *La Unidad*, January 30, 1915.

14. *El Siglo*, September 30, 1940.

15. Alberto Bermúdez, El buen gobierno de Laureano Gómez (Bogotá: Italgraf, 1974); Antonio J. Véliz and Domingo Jaramillo, *El paradigma, pequeña biografía de un grande hombre* (Medellín: Editorial Granamérica, n.d.); Juan Manuel Saldarriaga Betancur, *Laureano Gómez, o la tenacidad al servicio de la justicia y de la patria* (Medellín: Editorial Granamérica, 1950).

16. Alfredo Cock Arango, *Las víctimas del doctor Laureano Gómez*, 1959; José Francisco Socarrás, *Laureano Gómez, psicoanális*; Carlos H. Pareja, *El monstruo* (Buenos Aires: Editorial Nuestra América, 1955). The Pareja volume is a novelistic account of Colombia and the Violencia during the Gómez presidency. El Monstruo, the perpetrator of the vile acts described in the book, is described as "one of those typical people embodying all the vices that keep our nation from being united, just, and happy."

17. Abel Carbonell in prologue of *Comentarios a un régimen*, p. xiv.

18. Guillermo Camacho Montoya in *El País*, January 7, 1935.

19. Pedro Juan Navarro, *El parlamento en pijama* (Bogotá: Mundo al Día, 1935), p. 129.

20. Abelardo Forero Benavides, "Un golpe militar que resultó sainete," *Encuentro Liberal*, July 8, 1967.

21. *El Gráfico*, June 9, 1928; *El Gráfico*, December 15, 1934.

22. Lleras' protest appeared in *Sábado*, August 18, 1956.

23. El Siglo, August 14, 1965.

24. Christopher Abel, "Conservative Party in Colombia, 19301953" (unpublished doctoral dissertation, University of Oxford, 1974), p. 299.

Chapter X

1. John D. Martz, "The Ecuadorian Elections of 1984" (unpublished typescript), p. 12.

2. Belisario Betancur, "De cambio, cambio!" Antología del pensamiento conservador en Colombia, II, ed. by Roberto Herrera Soto (Bogotá: Colcultura, 1982), p. 1018.

3. Partido de Acción Nacional, Nuestros ideales, principios de doctrina (Mexico City: PAN, 1982), p. 5.

4. Rafael Caldera, Ideario, la Democracia Cristiana en América Latina (Barcelona: Ediciones Ariel, 1962), p. 90.

5. PAN, Nuestros ideales, p. 29.

6. Directorio Nacional Conservador de Colombia, "Programa de 1973," Antología del pensamiento conservador, II, p. 1357.

7. A. Freemantle, The Papal Encyclicals, p. 308.

8. James Petras, The Chilean Christian Democratic Party (Stanford, California: Stanford University Press, 1966), p. 16.

9. Manuel Gómez Morín, "El pensamiento," pp. 989-990.

BIBLIOGRAPHY

Secondary Works, Anthologies, Official Documents

Abella, Arturo. El florero de Lorente. Medellín: Editorial Bedout, n.d.

Azula Barrera, Rafael. De la revolución al orden nuevo. Bogotá: Editorial Kelly, 1956.

Berdiaev, Nicolas. El sentido de la creación. Buenos Aires: Ediciones Carlos Lohlé, 1978.

Bermúdez, Alberto. El buen gobierno de Laureano Gómez. Bogotá: Italgraf, 1974.

Caldera, Rafael. Ideario, la Democracia Cristiana en America Latina. Barcelona: Ediciones Ariel, 1962.

Camacho Montoya, Guillermo. Santander, el hombre y el mito. Bogotá: Ediciones Revista Colombiana, 1941.

Caro, Miguel Antonio. Obras completas. Bogotá: Imprenta Nacional, 1928-1934.

Cassirer, Ernst. An Essay on Man. New Haven: Yale University Press, 1944.

Cock Arango, Alfredo. Las víctimas del doctor Laureano Gómez. 1959.

Colombia, Ministerio de Gobierno. Estudios constitucionales. 2 vols. Bogotá: Imprenta Nacional, 1953.

Colombia, Ministerio de Relaciones Exteriores, Legajo Alemán, 1929-1936, Documento #166-1930.

Crawford, William Rex. A Century of Latin American Thought. Cambridge, Mass.: Harvard University Press, 1963.

Dávila Flórez, Manuel. Catolicismo y protestantismo comparados en forma epistolar. Rome: Escuela Tipografía Salesiana, 1924.

Davis, Harold E., ed. Latin American Social Thought, the History of Its Development since Independence, with Selected Readings. Washington: The University Press of Washington, D.C., 1961.

_____. Latin American Thought: A Historical Introduction. Baton Rouge: Louisiana State University Press, 1972.

_____. Revolutionaries, Traditionalists, and Dictators in Latin America. New York: Cooper Square Publishers, 1973.

Edel, Abraham. Ethical Judgement. Glenco, Illinois: The Free Press, 1955.

Edwards Vives, Alberto. La Fronda aristocrática, historia, política de Chile. 7th ed. Santiago de Chile: Editorial del Pacífico, 1972.

Fals Borda, Orlando. La subversión en Colombia: Visión del cambio social en la historia. Bogotá: Tercer Mundo, 1967.

Fernández Larraín, Sergio. Aspectos de la división del Partido conservador. Santiago de Chile: Partido Conservador Tradicionalista, 1952.

Ferreira Parra, Jorge. Novena al glorioso senador San Laureano de Chía. El Líbano, Tolima: Tipografía Renovación, 1932.

Foner, Eric. Politics and Ideology in the Age of the Civil War. New York: Oxford University Press, 1980.

Freemantle, Anne. The Papal Encyclicals in Their Historical Context. New York: G.P. Putnam's Sons, 1956.

Frei Montalva, Eduardo. Aun es tiempo. Santiago de
Chile: Gráficas el Chileno, 1942.

Gómez Castro, Laureano. Comentarios a un régimen.
Bogotá: Editorial Minerva, 1934.

_____. Desde el exilio. Bogotá, 1954.

_____. El cuadrilátero. 4th ed. Bogotá:
Editorial Centro, 1935.

_____. El mito de Santander, 2 vols. Bogotá:
Editora Colombiana, 1966.

_____. Interrogantes sobre el progreso de
Colombia. Bogotá: Editorial Revista
Colombiana, 1970.

_____. Laureano Gómez, discursos. Bogotá:
Colección Populibro, 1968.

_____. Laureano Gómez, obra selecta, 1909-
1956. Edited by Ricardo Ruíz Santos.
Bogotá: Imprenta Nacional, 1982.

_____. Los efectos de la Reforma de 1953.
Bogotá: Imprenta Nacional, 1953.

_____. Obras selectas. Edited by Alberto
Bermúdez. Medellín: Editorial Bedout, 1981.

_____. Ospina y otros discursos. Bogotá:
Editorial Revista Colombiana, 1966.

González von Marées, Jorge. El mal de Chile.
Santiago de Chile: Tallares Gráficos
"Portales," 1940.

Grayson, George W. El Partido Demócrata Cristiano
chileno. Buenos Aires: Editorial Francisco de
Aguirre, 1968.

Gunther, John. Inside Latin America. New York:
Harper and Brothers, 1941.

Hale, Charles A. El liberalismo mexicano en la
época de Mora, 1821-1853. Mexico City: Siglo
Veintiuno Editores, 1972.

199

Herrera Soto, Roberto, ed. Antología del pensamiento conservador en Colombia. I. Bogotá: Colcultura, 1982.

Hughes, H. Stuart. Consciousness and Society, the Reorientation of European Social Thought, 1890-1930. New York: Alfred A. Knopf, 1958.

Jaramillo Uribe, Jaime. El pensamiento colombiano en el siglo XIX. Bogotá: Editorial Temis, 1964.

Jijón y Caamaño, Jacinto. Política conservadora. 2 vols. Riobamba, Ecuador: Tipografía "La Buena Prensa del Chimborazo," 1929-1934.

Kirk, Russell, ed. The Portable Conservative Reader. New York: Penguin Books, 1982.

Liévano Aguirre, Indalecio. Rafael Núñez. Bogotá: Editorial Cromos, 1944.

Lippmann, Walter. The Public Philosophy. New York: Harper and Row, 1956.

Lovejoy, Arthur O. The Great Chain of Being: A Study of the History of an Idea. Cambridge, Mass.: Harvard University Press, 1933.

Manning, D.J. Liberalism. New York: St. Martin's Press, 1976.

Molina, Felipe Antonio. Laureano Gómez, historia de una rebeldía. Bogotá: Librería Voluntad, 1940.

Navarro, Pedro Juan. El parlamento en pijama. Bogotá: Mundo al Día, 1935.

Noriega, Alfonso. Pensamiento conservador y conservadurismo mexicano. Mexico City: Universidad Nacional Autónoma de Mexico, 1972.

Ospina Pérez, Mariano. Obras selectas. Ed. by Francisco Plata Bermúdez. Bogotá: Editorial Bedout, 1982.

O'Sullivan, Noel K. Conservatism. New York: St. Martin's Press, 1976.

Pareja, Carlos H. El Monstruo. Buenos Aires: Editorial Nuestra América, 1955.

Partido de Acción Nacional. Nuestros ideales, principios de doctrina. Mexico City: PAN, 1982.

Petras, James. The Chilean Christian Democratic Party. Stanford California: Stanford University Press, 1966.

Pike, Fredrick B. Hispanismo, 1898-1936. Notre Dame: University of Notre Dame Press, 1971.

_____. Spanish America, 1900-1970: Tradition and Social Innovation. New York: W.W. Norton, 1973.

_____. The New Corporatism, Social-Political Structures in the Iberian World. Notre Dame: University of Notre Dame Press, 1974.

_____. The United States and the Andean Republics. Cambridge, Mass.: Harvard University Press, 1977.

Restrepo Piedrahita, Carlos. 25 años de evolución político-constitucional, 1950-1975. Bogotá: Universidad Externado de Colombia, 1976.

Rodó, José Enrique. Ariel. 3rd. ed. Mexico City: Espasa-Calpe, 1963.

Romero, José Luis. El pensamiento político de la derecha latinoamericana. Buenos Aires: Editorial Paidos, 1970.

_____. ed. Pensamiento conservador, 1815-1898. Caracas: Editorial Arte, 1978.

Rommen, Heinrich A. The State in Catholic Thought, A Treatise in Political Philosophy. 2nd. ed. New York: Greenwood Press, 1969.

Ross, W. David. The Right and the Good. Oxford: The Clarendon Press, 1930.

Saldarriaga Betancur, Juan Manuel. Laureano Gómez, o la tenacidad al servicio de la justicia y de la patria. Medellín: Editorial Granamérica, 1950.

201

Socarrás, José Francisco. Laureano Gómez,
psicoanálisis de un resentido. Bogotá: Siglo
Veinte, 1942.

Solórzano, Carlos José. La ideología que debe
sustentar el Partido Conservador de
Nicaragua. Managua, 1947.

Stabb, Martin. In Quest of Identity: Patterns in
the Spanish-American Essay of Ideas, 1890-
1960. Chapel Hill: University of North
Carolina Press, 1967.

Valderrama Andrade, Carlos. El pensamiento
filosófico de Miguel Antonio Caro. Bogotá:
Instituto Caro y Cuervo, 1961.

Vallenilla Lanz, Laureano. Cesarismo democrático.
Estudios sobre las bases sociológicas de la
constitución efectiva de Venezuela. 2nd. ed.
Caracas: Tipografía Universal, 1929.

Vásquez Cobo Carrizosa, Camilo. El Frente Nacional,
su origen y desarrollo. Cali: Carvajal y
Cía., n.d.

Véliz, Antonio J. and Domingo Jaramillo. El
Paradigma, pequeña biografía de un grande
hombre. Medellín: Editorial Granámerica, n.d.

Veliz, Claudio, ed. Obstacles to Change in Latin
America. 2nd. ed. New York: Oxford
University Press, 1970.

_____. The Politics of Conformity in Latin
America. 2nd. ed. New York: Oxford
University Press, 1970.

Whitehead, Alfred North. Science and the Modern
World. Cambridge, England: Cambridge
University Press, 1926.

Zea, Leopolda. The Latin American Mind. Trans. by
James H. Abbot and Lowell Dunham. Norman,
Oklahoma: University of Oklahoma Press, 1963.

Articles

Amoroso Lima, Alceu. "Voices of Liberty and Reform in Brazil." Freedom and Reform in Latin America. Edited by Fredrick B. Pike. South Bend: University of Notre Dame Press, 1959.

Berlin, Isaiah. "Nationalism: Past Neglect and Present Power." Against the Current, Essays in the History of Ideas. New York: The Viking Press, 1980.

_____. "The Counter Enlightenment." Against the Current, Essays in the History of Ideas. New York: The Viking Press, 1980.

Betancur, Belisario. "De cambio, cambio!" Antología del pensamiento conservador en Colombia. II. Edited by Roberto Herrera Soto. Bogotá: Colcultura, 1982.

Directorio Nacional Conservador de Colombia. "Programa de 1973." Antología del pensamiento conservador en Colombia. II. Edited by Roberto Herrera Soto. Bogotá: Colcultura, 1982.

Edel, Abraham. "Right and Good." Dictionary of the History of Ideas. IV. New York: Charles Scribner's Sons, 1973.

_____. "What is Ethical Relativity?" Ethical Judgement. Glenco, Illinois: The Free Press, 1955.

Figueiredo, Jackson de. "Algunas reflexoes sobre a filosofía de Farias Brito--Profissao de fé espiritualista." Antología do pensamento social e político no Brasil. Edited by Luis Washington Vita. São Paulo: Editorial Grijalbo, 1968.

Forero Benavides, Abelardo. "Un golpe militar que resultó sainete." Encuentro Liberal. July 6, 1967.

Frei Montalva, Eduardo. "The Road to Follow." Latin American Social Thought. Edited by Harold E. Davis. Washington: The University Press of Washington, D.C., 1961.

Gálvez, Manuel. "En el solar de la raza." Latin American Social Thought, the History of its Development since Independence, with Selected Readings. Edited by Harold E. Davis. Washington: The University Presses of Washington, D.C., 1961.

Gómez Castro, Laureano. "El carácter del general Ospina." Universidad. Nos. 68, 70, 72, 75 (February 11, 25; March 10, 31, 1928.

Gómez Morín, Manuel. "Democrácia en lo social y en lo económico." El pensamiento de la reacción mexicana. Edited by Gastón García Cantú. Mexico City: Empresas Editoriales, 1965.

Hale, Charles A. "The Reconstruction of nineteenth Century Politics in Spanish America: A Case for the History of Ideas." Latin American Research Review. 7:53-73 (Summer 1973).

Hübner Gallo, Jorge Iván. "Catholics in Politics." The Conflict between Church and State in Latin America. Edited by Fredrick B. Pike. New York: A.A. Knopf, 1966.

Lovejoy, A.O. "On the Discrimination of Romanticisms." Essays in the History of Ideas. Baltimore: Johns Hopkins University Press, 1948.

Morais Carneiro, Julio César de. "Apóstrofes." Antología do pensamiento social e político no Brasil. Edited by Luís Washington Vita. São Paulo: Editorial Grijalbo, 1968.

Morse, Richard M. "The Heritage of Latin America." The Founding of New Societies. Edited by Louis Hartz. New York: Harcourt, Brace and World, 1964.

Randall, James G. "A Blundering Generation." Mississippi Valley Historical Review. Vol. 27 (June 1940), 3-13.

Rodó, José Enrique. "Democracy and Cultural Aristocracy." Latin American Social Thought. Edited by Harold Eugene Davis. Washington: The University Press of Washington, D.C., 1961.

Suárez, Marco Fidel. "Lo que significa ser conservador." Antología del pensamiento conservador en Colombia. I. Edited by Roberto Herrera Soto. Bogotá: Colcultura, 1982.

Vierhaus, Rudolf. "Conservatism." Dictionary of the History of Ideas. I. Edited by Philip P. Wiener. New York: Charles Scribner's Sons, 1968.

Woodward, Ralph Lee, Jr., ed. "Introduction." Positivism in Latin America, 1850-1900. Lexington, Mass.: D.C. Heath, 1971.

Newspapers, Magazines, and Journals

Derechas. Bogotá.
El Colombiano. Bogotá.
El Colombiano. Medellín.
El Diario Nacional. Bogotá.
El Espectador. Bogotá.
El Gráfico. Bogotá.
El País. Bogotá.
El Siglo. Bogotá.
El Tiempo. Bogotá.
Encuentro Liberal. Bogotá.
La Civilización. Bogotá.
La Unidad. Bogotá.
La Universidad. Bogotá.
Mundo al Día. Bogotá
Revista colombiana. Bogotá.
Sábado. Bogotá.
Semana. Bogotá.
Universidad. Bogotá.
Universitas. Bogotá.
Vanguardia Liberal. Bucaramanga.

Unpublished Sources

Abel, Christopher. "Conservative Party in Colombia, 1930-1953." Unpublished doctoral dissertation, University of Oxford, 1974.

Farrell, Robert V. "The Catholic Church in Colombian Education, 1886-1930, in Search of Tradition." Unpublished doctoral dissertation, Columbia University, 1975.

Hale, Charles A. "Political and Social Ideas, 1870-1930." Unpublished essay.

Jaramillo Uribe, Jaime. "El pensamiento social colombiano del siglo XIX." Lecture delivered at the Biblioteca Nacional de Colombia, Bogotá, November 23, 1982.

Martz, John D. "The Ecuadorian Elections of 1984." Unpublished essay.

Bunge, Carlos O., 66.
Burke, Edmund, 22, 27.

Caldera, Rafael, 165,
    167.
Cano, María, 119.
Capitalism. See Con-
    servative thought,
    Latin America; Gómez,
    Laureano.
Carlyle, Thomas, 22, 73-
    75.
Caro, José Eusebio, 8, 9,
    36, 58, 70-71, 171n.
Caro, Miguel Antonio, 1,
    9, 10, 12-13, 30, 33,
    74, 101, 167.
Carrasquilla, Rafael
    María, 9, 171n.
Cartesian philosophy, 42.
Casas Castañeda, Vicente,
    71.
Cassirer, Ernst, 142.
Catholicism. See Roman
    Catholicism.
Caudillismo, 15-16.
Chile, 1, 5, 6, 107-10,
    125-31.
Chilean National
    Socialist Party, 108.
Christian Democratic
    Party (Chile), 125,
    127-30, 163, 166.
Church in Latin America,
    5-6.
Científicos, 23.
Class, social. See
    Gómez, Laureano.
Class conflict. See
    Conservative thought,
    Latin America.
Cold War, 21, 155-56.
Colombia, 1, 3, 6, 8-11,
    17-103, 105, 109, 130-
    61, 163-64, 165, 174n,
    175n; democracy in,
    36; Concordat of 1887,
    30, 42, 47, 87;
    Constitution of 1863,
    101; Constitution of
    1886, 30, 101-2;

constitutional reform
    of 1936, 182n; eco-
    nomic liberalism in,
    36; education in,
    100; French influence
    in, 70; Frente
    Nacional, 18, 25, 27,
    49, 151, 154-55, 161;
    Gachetá Massacre, 84;
    ideological discourse
    in, 91-92; lack of
    critical tradition
    in, 159-60; liberal-
    ism in, 36; "Liberal
    Republic" in, 182n;
    modernization in,
    132; political
    culture in, 158-59,
    175n, 181n; political
    polimic in, 159;
    populism in, 36-37;
    "Reform of 1953," 40-
    43, 51-52, 75, 91,
    136-37, 142-49;
    romantic movement in,
    70-71, 179n; social-
    ism in, 36-37;
    utopianism in, 137;
    Violencia, 17, 26,
    92, 125, 132, 145,
    153, 181n, 191n,
    195n; War of the
    Thousand Days, 11.
Colombian Conservative
    Party. See Conserva-
    tive Party, Colombia.
Common good, 9, 48, 52,
    106, 145, 164, 165.
See also Conservative
    thought, Latin
    America; Gómez,
    Laureano.
Communism. See Con-
    servative thought,
    Latin America; Gómez,
    Laureano.
Comte, August, 9, 12,
    13, 22. See also
    Positivism.
Concha, José Vicente,
    58, 113, 187n.

Conservative liberal, 23.
Conservative Party of
Chile, 107-110.
Conservative Party of
Colombia: factions in,
8-11, 12-13, 17, 56,
58, 86, 110-13, 131-
32, 151, 172n;
founding of, 8-9, 165.
Conservative Party of
Nicaragua, 166.
Conservative thought,
Anglo America, 3.
Conservative thought,
Latin America:
agrarian reform, 126;
anti-Americanism in,
106; antiauthoritar-
ianism in, 108-9, 126,
127-28; antiimperial-
ism, 126; anti-
majoritarianism in,
105, 126; anti-
Semitism in, 107;
authoritarianism and,
16; capitalism, 126,
147. See also Gómez,
Laureano; censorship,
127; centralism,
political, 127; Chile,
1; class conflict and,
127, 148; code words
and, 164, 165;
Colombia. See Gómez,
Laureano; common good
and, 127; communism
and, 47, 126; content
analysis and, 125-31,
164-65, 189n; corpora-
tism in, 37, 105, 126.
See also Gómez,
Laureano; definition
of, 2; democracy and,
14-16, 50-51, 126.
See also Gómez,
Laureano; determinism
and, 15-16; division
in, 106-10, 167-68;
economic dependence,
126; economics, 106,
126, 127, 165. See

also Gómez, Laureano;
educational reform,
126; egalitarianism,
on, 9, 126; elitism,
107. See also Gómez,
Laureano; empirical
analysis of. See
Conservative thought,
Latin America, con-
tent analysis of;
factions in, 105-10;
fascism and, 105-13,
167. See also Gómez,
Laureano; federalism,
127; flexibility of,
166; freedom and, 37;
hierarchy in, 105,
126. See also Gómez,
Laureano; historicism
and, 127. See also
Gómez, Laureano;
idealism, 127; indi-
vidualism, 47, 127;
justice, distributive
and, 8-9, 126;
liberalism in, 164;
Mexico, 2; national-
ism in, 109, 127;
natural law and, 7,
37, 43, 50; order in,
37-38, 126; organic-
ism and, 41-42, 47,
105, 127, 145, 165.
See also Gómez,
Laureano; Pan-
Americanism and, 106,
108, 112-13;
pessimism and, 15.
See also Gómez,
Laureano; philosophia
perennis in, 21, 25,
31, 88, 93, 102, 105,
129, 148; populism
in, 163-164, 166;
private property and,
126, 165; progress
idea and, 15; pro-
gressivism in, 109-
10, 125-31, 163-168;
racism and, 15, 178n;
Roman Catholicism

and, 7, 126-27, 165;
secularization and,
165; social contract,
50; socialism and,
131; socialism in,
164; social justice,
126, 127-28, 179n-
180n; society, view
of. See Society,
conservative view of
subsidiarity princi-
ple, 166-67; tradi-
tionalism in, 125-36,
163-68; turn-of-the-
century division in,
11-16; virtue, public,
on, 127, 165; writing
on, 1-2.
Conservative thought,
Western: factions in,
38; flexibility of,
165.
Conservatives, Latin
America: fascism and,
103, 105-7; liberalism
and, 103; United
States, on, 14-15.
Conservatism, Latin
America: nineteenth
century origins, 5-7;
twentieth century
division in, 125-31.
Constant, Benjamin, 23.
Content analysis. See
Conservative thought,
Latin America.
Corporatism, social, 37,
105. See also
Colombia, "Reform of
1953;" Conservative
thought, Latin
America; Gómez,
Laureano.
Cosmes, Francisco, 23.
Counter Enlightenment,
30, 70-71.
Crisis in history, 95.
See also Gómez,
Laureano, pessimism
of.
Cromwell, Oliver, 74- 75.

Cuervo, Rufino José, 74.

Dante Alighieri, 140.
Dávila Florez, Manuel,
34.
Delpar, Helen, 172n.
Democracy. See
Conservative thought,
Latin America; Gómez,
Laureano.
Descartes, Renee, 22.
Determinism, 23, 55,
152. See also
Conservative thought,
Latin America;
Gómez, Laureano.
Díaz, Porfirio, 23.
Donoso Cortés, Juan, 38,
71, 76.
Dostoevski, Fedor, 26.
Dozy, Reinhardt, 154.
Dumas, Alexander, 70-71.

Echandía, Darío, 35,
140, 159.
Economic depression of
1930s, 105.
Ecuador, 6, 109, 163,
187n.
Edwards Vives, Alberto,
107, 108, 167.
Egalitariansim. See
Society, conservative
view of.
Einstein, Albert, 23.
El Espectodar
[Colombia], 174n,
178n.
El Tiempo [Colombia],
174n.
Elitism. See
Conservative thought,
Latin America; Gómez,
Laureano.
Enlightenment, the, 6,
12, 16, 26, 29, 30,
41-43, 71, 73, 99-
100, 165.
Erasmus, Desiderius, 98.
Espronceda, José de, 70,
71.

210

63, 99-100, 146, 156-57; egalitarianism, on, 99-100; Enlightenment, on, 99-100; elitism of, 50, 143; exile of, 132-33, 153-154, 156, 193n; falangism, on, 111-12; fascism and, 110-13, 114; French Revolution, on, 47, 93, 98-99, 101, 111, 124; hierarchy, on, 42, 97, 100, 140-41; Hispanism, on, 111-12; historicism of, 73, 152-53; Hitler, on, 110-11, 113; ideological character of, 19-20, 32, 35, 88-103, 121, 148, 158; inconsistencies in thought of, 151-53; Indians, on, 67, 95-96; individualism, 47; inegalitarianism of, 42-43, 50-51, 140; Jesuits and, 29-35, 71; juridical temperament of, 139-40; labor, 147; La Unidad and, 34-35, 55-59; liberalism of, 55-63 passim; liberalism, on, 41, 48, 114-18, 141; Liberal party members, on, 100-1; majoritarianism, on, 44-45, 50-51, 98-99; Masons, on, 58; metaphysical beliefs, 140-42; Mussolini, on, 113; nationalism of, 56, 77-80; neo-scholastic thought of, 35, 52, 141-42; optimism of, 38-39; oratory of, 61-63, 85-86, 158; organicism in thought of, 41-42, 52, 73, 75, 145; Pan-Americanism, on, 112-13; pessimism of, 39-40, 52, 56, 76, 93, 102; philosophy of, 24-27, 35-103 passim; positivism of, 63-67 passim; private property, on, 48-49; progress idea and, 40; Protestantism, on, 98; race mixture, on, 65; racial thought of, 66; relativism of, 52, 152; revolution, on, 58, 95, 133; Roman Catholic thought of, 35-53, 93, 96, 138, 141, 151-52; romanticism of, 69-77; Rousseau, on, 98-99; sectarianism, on, 155; Spain, on, 65, 99; state, on, 45, 50-51; subversion, on, 46-47; Teatro Municipal conference, 63-67, 152; Thomism of, 77, 140; traditional conservatism of, 132; United States, on, 56, 73, 74, 112, 155-56; view of history, 88-103, 114-18, 141, 151-52; Violencia, on, 153-55; virtue, on, 47-48, 141; women, on, 39, 58, 146; workers, on, 49.

Gómez, Román, 85-86, 182n.

Gómez Hurtado, Alvaro, 194n.

Gómez Morín, Manuel, 2, 109, 129, 131, 166-67, 171n.

González, Ramon, 34.

González von Marees, Jorge, 107-8.

213

Latin American Common
Market, 156.
Latin American conserva-
tive thought. See
Conservative thought,
Latin American.
Law, conservatives on,
44, 100.
LeBon, Gustave, 15.
Lenin (Vladimir Ilich
Ulianof), 117.
Leo X, 97-98.
Leo XIII, 22, 30, 48, 49,
50, 51, 106, 124.
Letelier, Valentin, 23.
Liberalism in Latin
America, 3, 6-7;
church, and, 5-6;
conservative criticism
of, 21-24, 30, 31;
nineteenth century, 5.
See also Conservative
thought, Latin
America; Gómez,
Laureano.
Liberal Party of
Colombia, 105, 178n,
191n.
Lima, Alceu Amoroso, 129,
131, 167.
Lincoln, Abraham, 73.
Lippman, Walter, 148.
Lleras Camargo, Alberto,
18, 151, 154-55, 161.
Lleras Restrepo, Carlos,
113, 159, 160.
López de Mesa, Luis, 44,
63.
López Pumarejo, Alfonso,
63, 82, 84, 87, 115,
117, 159-60, 174n,
182n.
Lovejoy, A.O., 70, 137.
Lozano, Carlos, 120.
Lozano Torrijos, Fabio,
65, 80.
Luther, Martin, 98.

Macmillan, Harold, 147.
Maistre, Joseph de, 12,
22, 26, 38, 39, 71,

76, 77.
Majoritarianism. See
Gómez, Laureano.
Mallarino, Manuel M.,
57.
Manning, D.J., 183n.
Mariana, Juan de, 31,
100.
Maritain, Jacques, 26,
76, 102, 103.
Marroquín, Manuel, 33.
Marx, Karl, 20.
Marxism, 22, 23.
Masonry. See Gómez,
Laureano.
Maura, Antonio, 115.
Maurras, Charles, 22,
26, 77, 117, 147.
Mazuera, Fernando, 88.
Mexico, 2, 6, 23, 72,
96, 105, 109, 129,
148, 164-65, 166,
169n, 171n.
Michelet, Jules, 26.
Mill, John Stewart, 22.
Montalembert, Marquis
de, 38.
Morais Carneiro, Julio
César, 13.
Moreno y Escandón,
Fiscal, 100.
Müller, Adam, 26.
Mussolini, Benito, 51,
86, 106, 110, 118.

National Falange Party
[Chile]. See
Christian Democratic
Party [Chile].
National Front
[Colombia]. See
Colombia.
Nationalist Party
[Colombia], 10-11.
National University of
Colombia, 34.
Natural law, 148. See
also Conservative
thought, Latin
America.
Nazism, 107.

214

Neitzsche, Friedrich
Wilheim, 22, 76.
Neo-Thomism, 2. See also
Gómez, Laureano,
Thomism of.
Newton, Sir Isaac, 22.
Nicaragua, 79, 129.
Nieto Caballero, Luis
Eduardo, 11, 90, 160.
Nordau, Max, 122.
Novalis. See Frederick
Leopold, Baron of
Hardenberg.
Núñez, Rafael, 10, 23-
24, 30, 101, 172n.

Olaya Herrera, Enrique,
74, 81, 83, 84, 114.
Order. See Conservative
thought, Latin
America.
Organicism. See
Conservative thought,
Latin America.
Ospina, Pedro Nel, 55,
59, 60, 74-75, 152.
Ospina, Santiago, 11.
Ospina Pérez, Mariano,
36, 88, 91, 125, 130-
33, 151, 153, 193n.
Ospina Rodríguez,
Mariano, 1, 8, 36, 57,
58, 70-71, 170n.

PAN. See: Partido de
Acción Nacional.
Panama, 33, 77-78.
Panama Canal, 33.
Pan-Americanism. See
Conservative thought,
Latin America; Gómez,
Laureano.
Paraguay, 6, 171n.
Parsons, Talcott, 20.
Partido de Accion
Nacional [Mexico], 2,
164-65, 166-67.
Partido Radical [Chile],
23.
Parties, political,
conservative,

formation of, 6-7.
Pena, Luis D., 18.
Peru, 2, 15, 56, 72, 80,
96, 105.
Philosophia perennis.
See Conservative
thought, Latin
America.
Pike, F. B. , 187n.
Piñeros, Insignares, 80.
Pius IX, 22, 30, 47, 51,
106, 166.
Plato, 35, 45, 46.
Political parties, con-
servative. See
Parties, political,
conservative.
Polygenism, 66.
Portales, Diego, 1,
171n.
Portugal, 105.
Positivism, 2, 9, 10,
12-13, 16, 42, 63-67
passim, 89, 100, 167;
law and, 44. See
also Comte, August;
Gómez, Laureano.
PRI [Institutional
Revolutionary Party
of Mexico], 166.
Private property. See
Gómez, Laureano.
PRM [Party of the
Mexican Revolution],
105, 109.
Progress, idea of, 10,
13, 15.
Puentes, Milton, 60.

Quiroga, Cesares, 116.

Ramírez Moreno, Agusto,
91, 160.
Randall, James G., 184n.
Rasch Isla, Miguel, 71,
72.
Ratzel, Frederick, 152.
"Reform of 1953." See
Colombia, "Reform of
1953".
Renan, Ernest, 26.

Restrepo, Carlos E., 36, 56.
Reyes, Rafael, 34, 51, 77-78.
Riva-Agüero, Jose, 76.
Rivera, Diego, 138.
Roa Sierra, Juan, 191n.
Rodó, José Enrique, 2, 14, 72, 167.
Rojas Pinilla, Gustavo, 18, 39, 51, 91, 92, 132, 151, 153-54, 191n.
Roman Catholic Church: "Modernist" movement in, 38; communitarian thought in, 37, 41; corporatism in, 37; hierarchy and, 43; in conservative thought, 7-9, 13, 25, 30, 37-39. See also Conservative thought, Latin America; Gómez, Laureano.
Rosas, Juan Manuel, 6, 171n.
Rousseau, Jean Jacques, 22, 44, 98-99, 135.
Russia. See Soviet Union.

Samper, José María, 70.
Santander, Francisco Paula de, 57, 74, 87, 100, 178n.
Santa Anna, Antonio López de, 6, 171n.
Santos, Eduardo, 64, 84, 120.
Santos, Enrique, 63, 89, 91.
Sierra, Justo, 23.
Silva, Carlos Martínez, 72.
Socarrás, José, 89.
Social Contract. See Conservative thought, Latin America.
Socialism, conservative criticism of, 31.

Society, conservative view of; egalitarianism and, 9, 13, 14. See also Gómez, Laureano, inegalitarianism of; Inegalitarianism; hierarchy and, 13, 14, 41.
Solevief, Vladimir, 76.
Solórzano, Carlos José, 129-31.
Sorel, Jorge, 22, 76, 102.
Soto, Domingo de, 31, 100.
Soviet Union, 49, 102, 116-18, 123.
Spain, 25, 65, 99, 105, 112, 115-16, 122-23, 154; Bourbon monarchs, 99-100; Civil War of 1936-1939, 115-16; Conservative party of, 115; Hapsburg monarchs, 25, 97, 99-100, 102.
Spencer, Herbert, 10, 22, 24.
Spengler, Oswald, 22, 26, 76, 102, 111.
Stalin, Joseph, 82, 106.
State. See Gómez, Laureano.
Strauss, Leo, 148.
Suárez, Francisco, 31, 51-52, 57, 76, 100.
Suárez, Marco Fidel, 12-13, 17, 56, 59, 60, 72, 78.
Subsidiarity principle. See Conservative thought, Latin America.
Sué, Eugene, 70.

Taine, Hipólito, 26.
Teixeira Mendes, Raimundo, 23.

MONOGRAPHS IN INTERNATIONAL STUDIES

Africa Series   ISBN Prefix 0-89680-

25. Kircherr, Eugene C. ABBYSSINIA TO ZIMBABWE: A
    Guide to the Political Units of Africa in the
    Period 1947-1978. 1979. 3rd ed. 80pp.
    100-4   (82-91908) $ 8.00*

27. Fadiman, Jeffrey A. MOUNTAIN WARRIORS: The
    Pre-Colonial Meru of Mt. Kenya. 1976. 82pp.
    060-1   (82-91783) $ 4.75*

36. Fadiman, Jeffrey A. THE MOMENT OF CONQUEST:
    Meru, Kenya, 1907. 1979. 70pp.
    081-4   (82-91874) $ 5.50*

37. Wright, Donald R. ORAL TRADITIONS FROM THE
    GAMBIA: Volume I, Mandinka Griots. 1979.
    176pp.
    083-0   (82-91882) $12.00*

38. Wright, Donald R. ORAL TRADITIONS FROM THE
    GAMBIA: Volume II, Family Elders. 1980.
    200pp.
    084-9   (82-91890) $15.00*

39. Reining, Priscilla. CHALLENGING DESERTIFICA-
    TION IN WEST AFRICA: Insights from Landsat into
    Carrying Capacity, Cultivation and Settlement
    Site Identification in Upper Volta and
    Niger. 1979. 180pp., illus.
    102-0   (82-91916) $12.00*

41. Lindfors, Bernth. MAZUNGUMZO: Interviews with
    East African Writers, Publishers, Editors, and
    Scholars. 1981. 179pp.
    108-X   (82-91932) $13.00*

42. Spear, Thomas J. TRADITIONS OF ORIGIN AND
    THEIR INTERPRETATION: The Mijikenda of Kenya.
    1982. xii, 163pp.
    109-8   (82-91940) $13.50*

43. Harik, Elsa M. and Donald G. Schilling. THE
    POLITICS OF EDUCATION IN COLONIAL ALGERIA AND
    KENYA. 1984. 102pp.
    117-9   (82-91957) $11.50*

44. Smith, Daniel R. THE INFLUENCE OF THE FABIAN
    COLONIAL BUREAU ON THE INDEPENDENCE MOVEMENT IN
    TANGANYIKA. 1985. x, 98pp.
    125-X   (82-91965) $ 9.00*

45. Keto, C. Tsehloane. AMERICAN-SOUTH AFRICAN RELATIONS 1784-1980: Review and Select Bibliography. 1985. 159pp.
128-4   (82-91973) $11.00*

46. Burness, Don, and Mary-Lou Burness, ed. WANASEMA: Conversations with African Writers. 1985. 95pp.
129-2   (82-91981) $ 9.00*

47. Switzer, Les. MEDIA AND DEPENDENCY IN SOUTH AFRICA: A Case Study of the Press and the Ciskei "Homeland". 1985. 80pp.
130-6   (82-91999)   9.00*

48. Heggoy, Alf Andrew. THE FRENCH CONQUEST OF ALGIERS, 1830: An Algerian Oral Tradition. 1986. 101pp.
131-4   (82-92005) $ 9.00*

49. Hart, Ursula Kingsmill. TWO LADIES OF COLONIAL ALGERIA: The Lives and Times of Aurelie Picard and Isabelle Eberhardt. 1987. 156pp.
143-8   (82-92013) $9.00*

Latin America Series

1. Frei, Eduardo M. THE MANDATE OF HISTORY AND CHILE'S FUTURE. Tr. by Miguel d'Escoto. Intro. by Thomas Walker. 1977. 79pp.
066-0   (82-92526) $ 8.00*

4. Martz, Mary Jeanne Reid. THE CENTRAL AMERICAN SOCCER WAR: Historical Patterns and Internal Dynamics of OAS Settlement Procedures. 1979. 118pp.
077-6   (82-92559) $ 8.00*

5. Wiarda, Howard J. CRITICAL ELECTIONS AND CRITICAL COUPS: State, Society, and the Military in the Processes of Latin American Development. 1979. 83pp.
082-2   (82-92567) $ 7.00*

6. Dietz, Henry A., and Richard Moore. POLITICAL PARTICIPATION IN A NON-ELECTORAL SETTING: The Urban Poor in Lima, Peru. 1979. viii, 102pp.
085-7   (82-92575) $ 9.00*

7. Hopgood, James F.   SETTLERS OF BAJAVISTA:
    Social and Economic Adaptation in a Mexican
    Squatter Settlement. 1979. xii, 145pp.
    101-2   (82-92583) $11.00*

8. Clayton, Lawrence A.   CAULKERS AND CARPENTERS
    IN A NEW WORLD: The Shipyards of Colonial
    Guayaquil. 1980. 189pp., illus.
    103-9   (82-92591) $15.00*

9. Tata, Robert J.   STRUCTURAL CHANGES IN PUERTO
    RICO'S ECONOMY: 1947-1976. 1981. xiv, 104pp.
    107-1   (82-92609) $11.75*

10. McCreery, David.   DEVELOPMENT AND THE STATE IN
    REFORMA GUATEMALA, 1871-1885. 1983. viii,
    120pp.
    113-6   (82-92617) $ 8.50*

11. O'Shaughnessy, Laura N., and Louis H. Serra.
    CHURCH AND REVOLUTION IN NICARAGUA. 1986.
    118pp.
    126-8   (82-92625) $11.00*

12. Wallace, Brian.   OWNERSHIP AND DEVELOPMENT: A
    Comparison of Domestic and Foreign Investment
    in Columbian Manufacturing. 1987. 186pp.
    145-4   (82-92633) $12.00*

Southeast Asia Series

31. Nash, Manning.   PEASANT CITIZENS: Politics,
    Religion, and Modernization in Kelantan,
    Malaysia. 1974. 181pp.
    018-0   (82-90322) $12.00*

38. Bailey, Conner.   BROKER, MEDIATOR, PATRON, AND
    KINSMAN: An Historical Analysis of Key Leader-
    ship Roles in a Rural Malaysian District.
    1976. 79pp.
    024-5   (82-90397) $7.00*

40. Van der Veur, Paul W.   FREEMASONRY IN INDONESIA
    FROM RADERMACHER TO SOEKANTO, 1762-1961. 1976.
    37pp.
    026-1   (82-90413) $4.00*

43. Marlay, Ross.   POLLUTION AND POLITICS IN THE
    PHILIPPINES. 1977. 121pp.
    029-6   (82-90447) $7.00*

44. Collier, William L., et al. INCOME, EMPLOYMENT AND FOOD SYSTEMS IN JAVANESE COASTAL VILLAGES. 1977. 160pp.
031-8   (82-90454) $10.00*

45. Chew, Sock Foon and MacDougall, John A. FOREVER PLURAL: The Perception and Practice of Inter-Communal Marriage in Singapore. 1977. 61pp.
030-X   (82-90462) $6.00*

47. Wessing, Robert. COSMOLOGY AND SOCIAL BEHAVIOR IN A WEST JAVANESE SETTLEMENT. 1978. 200pp.
072-5   (82-90488) $12.00*

48. Willer, Thomas F., ed. SOUTHEAST ASIAN REFERENCES IN THE BRITISH PARLIAMENTARY PAPERS, 1801-1972/73: An Index. 1978. 110pp.
033-4   (82-90496) $ 8.50*

49. Durrenberger, E. Paul. AGRICULTURAL PRODUCTION AND HOUSEHOLD BUDGETS IN A SHAN PEASANT VILLAGE IN NORTHWESTERN THAILAND: A Quantitative Description. 1978. 142pp.
071-7   (82-90504) $9.50*

50. Echauz, Robustiano. SKETCHES OF THE ISLAND OF NEGROS. 1978. 174pp.
070-9   (82-90512) $10.00*

51. Krannich, Ronald L. MAYORS AND MANAGERS IN THAILAND: The Struggle for Political Life in Administrative Settings. 1978. 139pp.
073-3   (82-90520) $ 9.00*

54. Ayal, Eliezar B., ed. THE STUDY OF THAILAND: Analyses of Knowledge, Approaches, and Prospects in Anthropology, Art History, Economics, History and Political Science. 1979. 257pp.
079-2   (82-90553) $13.50*

56. Duiker, William J. VIETNAM SINCE THE FALL OF SAIGON. Second edition, revised and enlarged. 1986. 281pp.
133-0   (82-90744) $12.00*

57. Siregar, Susan Rodgers. ADAT, ISLAM, AND CHRISTIANITY IN A BATAK HOMELAND. 1981. 108pp.
110-1   (82-90587) $10.00*

58. Van Esterik, Penny. COGNITION AND DESIGN PRODUCTION IN BAN CHIANG POTTERY. 1981. 90pp.
078-4   (82-90595) $12.00*

59. Foster, Brian L. COMMERCE AND ETHNIC DIFFER-
ENCES: The Case of the Mons in Thailand.
1982. x, 93pp.
112-8   (82-90603) $10.00*

60. Frederick, William H., and John H. McGlynn.
REFLECTIONS ON REBELLION: Stories from the
Indonesian Upheavals of 1948 and 1965. 1983.
vi, 168pp.
111-X   (82-90611) $ 9.00*

61. Cady, John F. CONTACTS WITH BURMA, 1935-1949:
A Personal Account. 1983. x, 117pp.
114-4   (82-90629) $ 9.00*

62. Kipp, Rita Smith, and Richard D. Kipp, eds.
BEYOND SAMOSIR: Recent Studies of the Batak
Peoples of Sumatra. 1983. viii, 155pp.
115-2   (82-90637) $ 9.00*

63. Carstens, Sharon, ed. CULTURAL IDENTITY IN
NORTHERN PENINSULAR MALAYSIA. 1986. 91pp.
116-0   (82-90645) $ 9.00*

64. Dardjowidjojo, Soenjono. VOCABULARY BUILDING
IN INDONESIAN: An Advanced Reader. 1984.
xviii, 256pp.
118-7   (82-90652) $26.00*

65. Errington, J. Joseph. LANGUAGE AND SOCIAL
CHANGE IN JAVA: Linguistic Reflexes of Modernization in a Traditional Royal Polity. 1985.
xiv, 198pp.
120-9   (82-90660) $12.00*

66. Binh, Tran Tu. THE RED EARTH: A Vietnamese
Memoir of Life on a Colonial Rubber Plantation.
Tr. by John Spragens. Ed. by David Marr.
1985. xii, 98pp.
119-5   (82-90678) $ 9.00*

67. Pane, Armijn. SHACKLES. Tr. by John McGlynn.
Intro. by William H. Frederick. 1985. xvi,
108pp.
122-5   (82-90686) $ 9.00*

68. Syukri, Ibrahim. HISTORY OF THE MALAY KINGDOM
OF PATANI. Tr. by Conner Bailey and John N.
Miksic. 1985. xx, 98pp.
123-3   (82-90694) $10.50*

69. Keeler, Ward. JAVANESE: A Cultural Approach.
1984. xxxvi, 523pp.
121-7   (82-90702) $18.00*

70. Wilson, Constance M., and Lucien M. Hanks. BURMA-THAILAND FRONTIER OVERSIXTEEN DECADES: Three Descriptive Documents. 1985. x, 128pp.
124-1   (82-90710) $10.50*

71. Thomas, Lynn L., and Franz von Benda-Beckmann, eds. CHANGE AND CONTINUITY IN MINANGKABAU: Local, Regional, and Historical Perspectives on West Sumatra. 1986. 363pp.
127-6   (82-90728) $14.00*

72. Reid, Anthony, and Oki Akira, eds. THE JAPANESE EXPERIENCE IN INDONESIA: Selected Memoirs of 1942-1945. 1986. 411pp., 20 illus.
132-2   (82-90736) $18.00*

73. Smirenskaia, Ahanna D. PEASANTS IN ASIA: Social Consciousness and Social Struggle. Tr. by Michael J. Buckley. 1987. 248pp.
134-9   (82-90751) $12.50

74. McArthur, M.S.H. REPORT ON BRUNEI IN 1904. Ed. by A.V.M. Horton. 1987. 304pp.
135-7   (82-90769) $13.50

75. Lockard, Craig Alan. FROM KAMPUNG TO CITY. A Social History of Kuching Malaysia 1820-1970. 1987. 311pp.
136-5   (82-90777) $14.00*

78. Chew, Sock Foon. ETHNICITY AND NATIONALITY IN SINGAPORE. 1987. 229pp.
139-X   (82-90801) $12.50*

79. Walton, Susan Pratt. MODE IN JAVANESE MUSIC. 1987. 279pp.
144-6   (82-90819) $12.00*

80. Nguyen Anh Tuan. SOUTH VIETNAM TRIAL AND EXPERIENCE: A Challenge for Development. 1987. 482pp.
141-1   (82-90827) $15.00*

81. Van der Veur, Paul W., ed. TOWARD A GLORIOUS INDONESIA: Reminiscences and Observations of Dr. Soetomo. 1987. 367pp.
142-X   (82-90835) $13.50*

Ordering Information

Orders for titles in the Monographs in International Studies series should be placed through the Ohio University Press/Scott Quadrangle/Athens, Ohio 45701-2979. Individuals must remit pre-payment via check, VISA, Mastercard, CHOICE, or American Express. Individuals ordering from the United Kingdom, Continental Europe, Middle East, and Africa should order through Academic and University Publishers Group, 1 Gower Street, London WC1E 6HA, ENGLAND. Other individuals ordering from outside of the U.S., please remit in U.S. funds by either International Money Order or check drawn on U.S. bank. Residents of Ohio please add sales tax. Postage and handling is $2.00 for the first book and $.50 for each additional book. Price and availability are subject to change without notice.